Acknowledgements

The study of society is itself a product of social activity. The research for this book could not have taken place but for the work of archivists and librarians, nor the book produced without the editorial and productive skills of the Cambridge University Press. I am indebted to them all. Special thanks, however, are due to Linda Randall of Cambridge University Press, and to Janet Parkin for transcribing the interviews.

The study would not have been possible without the contribution of the East Anglian fishing families who so generously allowed me into their homes, gave hospitality and shared their knowledge. I recall our conversations with pleasure and respect. I cannot thank them enough. I have preserved their anonymity in the text but would like to acknowledge them here: Mr W. Balls, Mr W. Bennett, Mr Bessey, Mr and Mrs E. Botwright, Mr G.W. Brown, Mr J.H. Brown, Miss L. Brown, Mr Burrell, Mrs Cator, Mrs Cockerton, Mr H.E. Cook, Mr L.A. Cook, Mr W. Cook, Mr T.W. Crisp, Mr W.E. Dawes, Mr H.H. Death, Mrs Eade, Mr C.V. Eastick, Mr C.R. French, Mr Frost, Mr E. Gager, Mrs L.J. Gardner, Mr and Mrs Garnett, Mr F. Garrod, Mr B.L. Harris, Mr H.A. Harvey, Mrs Hayward, Mr J. Heard, Mr C.W. Hicks, Mrs E.L. Hitter, Mr and Mrs E.T. Hitter, Mr W.C. Hume, Mr G.E. Jacobs, Mr Jarvis, Mrs E.M. Kerr, Mr W.J. Killett, Mr C. Knights, Mr F.G. Knights, Mrs E.M. Lacey, Miss A. Leggat, Mr H. Leggatt, Mr G.A. Manthorpe, Mr Mewse, Mr W.J. Miller, Mr and Mrs W. Mussett, Mr R. Nickerson, Mr J.F. Osborne, Mr Palmer, Mrs Parker, Mrs B.M. Playle, Mr R. Pullen, Mr R. Reade, Mr Rook, Mrs E.M. Rudd, Mrs Rushmore, Mr R. Saunders, Mr and Mrs M.H. Sheales, Mrs M. Smith, Mrs Solomon, Mr R. South, Mr Spencer, Mrs A. Studd, Mr and Mrs Symmonds, Mrs E. Symmonds, Mr A.B. Symonds, Mr A. Tungate, Mrs F.M. Ward, Mr J. Watt, Mr S. Watts, Mr P. Westrup, Mr J. Whicks, Mr S.G. Willder, Mrs Woods, Mrs A. Wright, Mr C.A. Wright, Mrs M.A. Wright. I would like to thank Bridget Yates for supplying me with an interview with Mr Bensley, and Lawrence James for interviewing Mr S. Merry of Newlyn.

Many of those named above helped by giving me the names of friends

and neighbours who might also be interviewed. Among the many others who helped in this respect I would like to mention Senior Superintendent John Hance of Lowestoft Royal National Mission to Deep Sea Fishermen and David Savoury of Yarmouth.

I owe a particular debt of gratitude to Paul Thompson for having introduced me to the practice of oral history, for directing the research on which the book is based and for supervising my doctoral thesis. I value this opportunity to thank him for his support and encouragement over a number of years. Leonore Davidoff has been a valued colleague and her comments on an earlier draft materially improved the final result. Geoff Crossick's comments were trenchant and welcome, as were those of the publisher's anonymous readers. Robert Moore's support came at an opportune time and was much appreciated.

My final acknowledgement is to Sandra. My general indebtedness is profound: here I would like only to note our struggles over punctuation, grammar and style. Such errors and infelicities as remain are due entirely to her exhaustion and my intransigence.

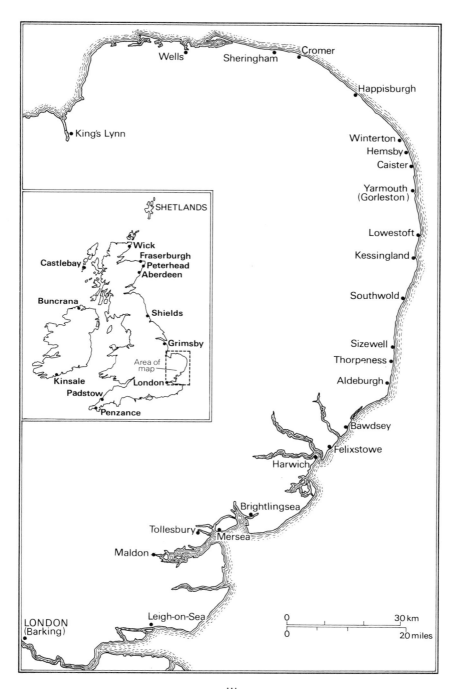

Wells
Sheringham
Cromer
Happisburgh
King's Lynn
Winterton
Hemsby
Caister
Yarmouth
(Gorleston)
Lowestoft
Kessingland
Southwold
Sizewell
Thorpeness
Aldeburgh
Bawdsey
Felixstowe
Harwich
Brightlingsea
Tollesbury
Mersea
Maldon
LONDON
(Barking)
Leigh-on-Sea

SHETLANDS
Wick
Fraserburgh
Peterhead
Aberdeen
Castlebay
Buncrana
Shields
Grimsby
Area of
map
Kinsale
London
Padstow
Penzance

0   30 km
0   20 miles

xiii

Introduction

If social thinkers also possess a sense of *history*,... they know that any pattern of sociostructural relations is actually ongoing transformations and that the real object of sociological thinking is not only 'sociostructures' but also *their historical movement*.

Daniel Bertaux 1981

This book attempts to explain the development of the economic structure of a particular occupational group and to understand the relation of this to individual and collective values and behaviour. It has drawn on the historian's usual range of written sources but the understanding of those sources was greatly enriched by the intervention of another source of evidence, that of life history interviews with people who experienced this particular place, occupation and time.[1] Anyone who has worked with a number of interviews will appreciate just how much the informant's insights contribute to the final analysis. That is not written to avoid responsibility for the interpretation which follows but to acknowledge a debt and to make a methodological point:

The historian should start with the actor's interpretation of his situation, his actions in that situation, and the consequences of those actions for his interpretation in the future. Superimposed on this model, however, is that of the historical observer, who can see both the actor's 'real' situation (not necessarily coincident with the actor's interpretation of his situation) and the intended and unintended consequences of action in that situation.[2]

My informants' accounts of their situation revealed the importance of historical experience in their response to contemporary 'real' situations. The participant's memories were not an inert archive of what had happened but a web of sequential experience which influenced contemporary activity. I started this study with the assumption that occupational identity would determine social being, and this remains the fundamental thrust of the argument, but I have been convinced that the material conditions of the industry cannot account for industrial and

1

social attitudes to the degree that I had assumed. Fishing was an intensely competitive occupation and economic individualism a central value of the workforce so it was not a very convincing location for their community practices and values. Perhaps occupational history and sociology has too often been written as if individuals, particularly males, enter the workforce *table rasa* to be moulded by their occupation, or from the assumption that the link between occupation and communal values is unproblematic.

A family's class position may depend on the father's occupation in most cases but it is equally evident that individuals' first experience and knowledge of class comes long before they enter the workforce. It is absorbed in domestic life, at school and in the way other people treat them and their parents: also the way in which their parents react to others. In other words our first *class* experiences are largely mediated through domestic life, our mothers and local community, however much they may be determined by occupation, our fathers and wider class divisions. The values and expectations formed during this pre-work experience are the basis upon which subsequent experience is evaluated.

The problematic nature of the link between occupation and community and class practice is connected to the separation of home and work. It is not self-evident how the solidarity values of the workplace, whether it be coalface, shopfloor or ship's deck, are transferred back into the domestic and residential community. It is, after all, the female network of mutual aid which sustains a community and the individual female network of aid does not necessarily reflect the male network of the particular gang or shift. Certain work situations promote sectionalism and intra-class conflicts, or, as with the fishermen studied here, individualism, and do not provide the appropriate values for a unified community. But, whatever the divisions at the workplace, the experience of the families living on a given income in a particular milieu is a class experience: it is a direct experience of women and children and nowhere is this more apparent than in this occupation where men were away from home so much of their time.

Behaviour is shaped by memories of the past, as well as by present social forces; the importance of both is responsible for the scope of this text. The contents of its three parts are outlined below.

Part one divides the fishermen into three sections: inshore, trawling and drifting.[3] Each section had a distinctive capital structure, degree of crew autonomy, level of earnings and so forth; each experienced the peak of prosperity, technical and commercial changes at different

points in time. This variation in the timing and causes of potential and actual conflicts provides the advantages of comparative analysis while being contained within a common socio-economic, cultural and historical framework. As fishermen tended to work exclusively in one or other of the sections they are 'real' categories and ones which include social and family life through the very different pattern of interaction permitted by the work pattern in each case. Nevertheless, the study is not entirely self-referring and draws on studies of the Humber trawling industry (Tunstall 1962), of the Scottish drifter industry, which developed parallel to the East Anglian one (Gray 1978), and of Scandinavia (Wadel 1972), where the modern herring industry demonstrates similar industrial and social practices from a similar mode of production.

The drifting and trawling sectors experienced the greatest technical change and capital investment and, therefore, the greatest potential for industrial and social dynamic. They are the main focus of the study.

The timing of strikes and points of conflict within these two sections highlight relations of production as the major element in shaping industrial attitudes. The drifting section had a record of strikes during the 1850s and 1860s prior to the introduction of new technology but none later. The early record in trawling is obscure but 1887 saw a major strike accompanied by the formation of a union and that was a direct result of the employers' decision to change the method of payment. After this early conflict and unionisation of previously unorganised workers (which anticipated the great upswing in other industries and areas by two years) industrial conflict and militancy virtually disappear. Although the union survived in the region until the turn of the century there was no response to the 1901 Grimsby strike/lockout nor to the unrest between 1911 and 1914 which saw the formation of unions in the drifter section in Scotland. Trade unions sent organisers to Yarmouth and Lowestoft in 1904 and again in 1911 but the response of the fishermen was minimal. The phenomenon to be explained, then, is the decline of conflict.

The detailed analysis is strengthened through the comparison of the markedly different economic development in the two sections and of different methods of rewards within sections. Trawling did not adopt steam propulsion and modern nets and became less profitable and increasingly anachronistic as existing capital was worked out. By contrast, in the drifting section technical change increased productivity by some 200 per cent in a decade, much of it requiring a similar increase in the intensity of labour: a situation where industrial conflict might have been anticipated. From the employers' point of view their

capital costs increased some threefold and yet the proportion of the product going to labour remained constant, which raises the question if labour was acquiescent, why did the employers not try to change the wage bargain to compensate for their higher capital input? Or, to put the issue another way, how did labour with no formal organisations manage to maintain its share of the increased productivity?

Part one, then, is concerned with a detailed examination of the economic structure of the industry and the record of industrial conflict. It is also essential to establish the industrial context in detail as a basis for Parts two and three. The pattern of work and of income level place obvious constrictions on the pattern of relations with families and community ashore as well as determining their social location.

Part two considers the social structure of the fishermen through the concept of community, the distribution of ownership within the industry and its links with local commerce as well as the social and political perceptions of the fishermen themselves. Fishermen are central to the debate on community in so far as they have been considered to be the epitome of two different concepts of community, the first of which was destroyed by the second. Late nineteenth- and early twentieth-century observers (Jenkins 1920, Johnstone 1905) considered that the traditional forms of fishing, namely the inshore and drifting sections, produced communities which the development of steam trawling and the subsequent concentration of ownership and centralisation into large ports was destroying. Later sociological studies (Tunstall 1962, Horobin 1957), however, identify trawling as a fully developed occupational community. This contradiction is partially explained in terms of the historical formation of new communities but there has also been a shift of emphasis from social to occupational factors in the concept of community.

As with the earlier examination of the fishermen's industrial consciousness their perceptions on community, social structure and relations are integrated with the economic reality of their position. For this reason the detailed analysis of ownership within the industry and the sources of capital which might well have been presented earlier has been reserved for this section. In categorising and analysing class images particular care has been placed in trying to establish the real boundaries of the diverse terms used by informants to stratify their social experience. The result of this categorisation is then related to the typification of traditional workers (Lockwood 1966), images of class (Bulmer 1975) and occupational community (Allcorn and Marsh 1975). One of the more suggestive results of this approach is the

implication that perception of the shape of the class structure may be more germane to conflictual views of class than the number of classes perceived. One advantage of the life history evidence is that it reveals how the shift from agricultural work to fishing released the men from the social control exercised by local landowners: this change of circumstances itself contributing to the fishermen's weak sense of class conflict.

The difference between their class views as fishermen compared to the account of their class views as rural workers is amply demonstrated by their accounts of political behaviour. The fishermen were largely willing to follow the wishes of their employer and might be classified as deferential voters. As they considered themselves the social equals of their employers, however, they are not so in the usual sense of deferring to class superiors (Newby 1977). Their fathers and relatives in agriculture, by contrast, were forced to show outward deference but exercised their political right against the wishes of their employers, perhaps the only right they could exercise in secrecy. The value of oral evidence in distinguishing between action and meaning is particularly apparent in this section.

Part three looks briefly at the work of women in the fishing community, at domestic life, leisure and belief. These themes are chosen because they integrate with and elaborate earlier points.

Fishermen and miners have been identified as members of extreme occupations, the particular conditions of which, it is alleged, result in a devaluation of domestic life. The evidence here totally refutes this image of the fishermen and the more widely held view (Young and Willmott 1957) that the working-class male before the First World War was a mean and violent husband and a brutal father. The chapter on leisure shows that the level of drinking was modest and that neither the men nor their wives carried the image of fishing as being a tough hard-drinking occupation. Similarly domestic labour was assumed to be a fit and natural task for men and boys. Within the context of wider gender conditioning and occupational opportunity they made a larger than expected contribution to domestic labour. The evidence shows that most marriages were caring partnerships and mutually supportive.

Religion is the final topic and is found both in the chapter on domestic practice and the chapter on belief where it is compared with the practice of superstition. Contrary to the popular historical image (and actuality in many regions) East Anglian fishermen were not religious. The fact that religion is, or can be, practised privately in the home or publicly at an institution means that one can perceive where

observance is being made for reasons of conformity, social control or from commitment to its values.

Actual belief is more difficult to establish with any certainty but it is apparent that the evidence on superstition contrasts sharply with that of religion. It entered into the daily practice of the fishermen in a way which religion did not; even more significantly, it was practised to different degrees in the three different sections of the industry. That it had least hold in the small inshore locations demonstrates that it was not a survivor of 'traditional' practice, and economic anxiety emerges as the clear motive for its greatest prevalence in the most modern section of the industry. This returns attention to the importance of occupation as a source of values and belief.

The final chapter serves as a summary conclusion. It also provides the opportunity for a rather more speculative consideration of the role of domestic and neighbourhood practice in forming basic social attitudes through which industrial life will be experienced; and, indeed, whether this configuration of social practices can usefully be termed 'community'.

I am only too aware that many of the areas of experience covered in this book by one brief chapter are specialised fields which really demand more space than I can give them. Indeed, many could have been the subject of monographs even within the limitations of my own knowledge and research. My reason for including them is that occupational, social and family life is a unified experience; more than that, those experiences are all facets of a unified socio-economic structure which shapes the relationship between those parts. I trust that the weakness of particular sections is compensated for by the advantages of a comprehensive approach. To take a different approach would be to lose one of the major advantages of life histories. They enable us to perceive the real conjuncture of particular phenomena where much other evidence allows only inferences. The relationships which are apparent between different spheres of experience in an open-ended interview *are real and known to coexist because they are simply facets of the one individual experience*, they are not the result of empirico-positivistic inductions nor of specific 'data' collected to inform some preconception or theory. Analysis through grounded-theory from oral evidence has been called 'thick description', by which is meant a strategy of approaching a historical situation neither with preconceived theories nor with the assumption that empirical fact gathering will provide one in favour of 'a strategy of perception that is open-minded and concrete'.[4] In placing weight on life histories I do not want to establish a false distinction between oral and other forms of evidence; the

essence of what follows is an attempt to provide maximum triangulation for the description and interpretation of events. I only hope that my informants might still recognise themselves and their experiences in my analysis of their lives.

Occupational structure

Introduction

A study of the economics of the fisheries is indeed baffling and it is most difficult, having regard to the variety and complication of the symptoms presented, to accurately diagnose the case of the British fisheries as a whole.

Annual Report of the Inspector of Sea Fisheries for the year 1913:
1914, Vol. XXX Cd 7449

Introductions to local studies are customarily used to provide a brief outline of national developments as a context. This procedure is not followed here because where national developments are relevant to the aims of this study, they are embedded in the text. Our limited purpose is to show the number of fishermen in the three sections and why even simple regional comparisons are 'indeed baffling'.

Figure 1 graphs the number of fishermen. It shows my figures for the number of men employed by section, the census figures and the figures published by Customs Officers responsible for supervising much of the legislation applicable to fishing vessels. 'Active' is the total number of driftermen, inshoremen and trawlermen.

The most noticeable feature is the inutility of the census data as a guide to the numbers employed. The census not only failed to record numbers of fishermen but actually distorts regional totals by recording fishermen in the ports they happened to be working from on census day. As between 1,000 to 2,000 East Anglian fishermen could be working from West Country ports in the spring, this meant that, if recorded at all, they merely inflate the county totals for Devon and Cornwall. My own figures have been established from the number of boats active.[1] These come quite close to the estimate of resident fishermen provided annually by Customs Officers and confirm those as the most reliable published figures: on the basis of these, East Anglia contained about a quarter of all the fishermen in England and Wales.

Regional comparisons could be made along a number of different dimensions such as the weight or value of fish landed, the amount of

11

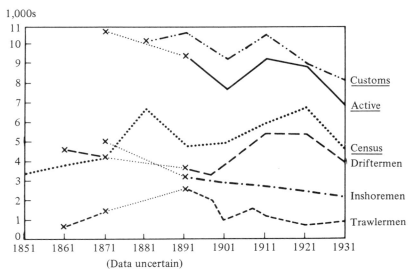

Figure 1 Number of East Anglian fishermen 1851–1931

ancillary work generated and so forth, but all present the same problem of allowing for the migratory nature of many fishing vessels. For example, in 1900 Lowestoft and Yarmouth were third and fifth in terms of the value of fish handled, but much of that fish was caught by Scottish drifters working the autumn herring fishing, just as much of the tonnage recorded in other regions was landed from East Anglian boats. Taking the number of full-time fishermen employed, however, shows that only the Humber ports are on a scale with East Anglia's two main centres with only one other port of the period having over 1,000 men. The great dynamism of East Anglia in the decade and a half before the First World War is apparent in table 1. The labour force of full-time fishermen increased by about a third. The change from sail to steam, with all that implies in terms of capital investment and productivity, saw a 160 per cent increase compared with less than 9 per cent on the Humber, which confirms the late development of steam technology in East Anglia. Figure 1 shows that the peak was short-lived before declining in the interwar period. Our period from the 1880s covers a high point, decline and recovery in trawling, a steady decline followed by a steep rise in drifting set against the unremitting decline of the inshore section.

Our most detailed consideration of the economics of the industry will concentrate on the most advanced sectors and the inshore sector is used mainly as a 'traditional' framework to the new developments.

Table 1 *Number of vessels and men at the four leading ports of England and Wales 1903 and 1912*[2]

		Grimsby	Hull	Lowestoft	Yarmouth
Steam	1903	484	423	101	101
	1912	582	403	329	198
Sail	1903	39	13	387	88
	1912	27	20	264	10
Regular fishermen	1903	4,939	4,272	4,100	2,780
	1912	5,969	4,720	5,400	2,710
Occasional fishermen	1903	–	150	50	650
	1912	–	168	950	440

1

Inshore

We were faced at the outset with a difficulty in arriving at any definition of the term 'Inshore Fisheries', ... We have therefore approached the subject from the point of view of the 'inshore fisherman'. He as a rule goes out either for a day or a night's fishing; he usually fishes from his own boat, which is of limited dimensions and without steam power, fishing within sight of land, although not necessarily of home; and he also carries on all those fisheries which do not in all cases require the use of a boat, such as fishing with stake nets and the gathering of shellfish by hand.

Report of the Departmental Committee on Inshore Fisheries 1914, Vol. XXX Cd 7373

The difficulty of distinguishing inshore from traditional trawling and drifting was one of the few conclusions to emerge from the above report. Both of the latter could be defined in so far as they used one type of gear, and this was not possible with the inshore section. Apart from a few specialised cockle and shrimp fishermen they used a mixture of equipment according to season.

Distinguishing inshore regionally for this study is easier for it is virtually a residual category. Deepsea trawling and drifting were located solely at Lowestoft and Yarmouth and were distinguished by the higher capital cost of each unit and a pattern of work which took them away from home and out of sight of land.

Undoubtedly natural geography made a large contribution to the original location of inshore fishing with some level of activity wherever there was a settlement with access to the sea. In the late nineteenth and early twentieth centuries there were some forty fishing stations in the region with the actual number of men involved steadily declining.

The reasons for this were as varied as the locations. In some areas, notably the Thames, commercial and urban development polluted fishing grounds. Urbanisation took land which had previously been used by fishermen for their nets and gear; at King's Lynn, for example, much of the

harbour was developed for commerce to the inconvenience of fishermen. There was some decline in fish stocks but according to the oral evidence lack of fish was not a problem until after 1918; informants are agreed that they could always catch more fish than they could sell. Their evidence confirms the conclusions of the 1914 Committee cited above, in identifying market access as the most crucial element in the survival or decline of inshore fisheries.

Access to market was not a simple matter of being near a railway: to place fish on the national market in good condition called for a number of ancillary services. Because inshore fishermen worked local grounds they had to wait until the seasonal movements brought fish within their range; catches, therefore, were irregular and unpredictable. In a small location having occasional seasonal surpluses it was not worthwhile to arrange the necessary supplies of ice, boxes and labour to place it on the national market. Small consignments of fish were not popular with railways because they could easily pollute general passenger goods traffic, so rail charges were heavy. Specialised fish trains from major centres meant that it was often cheaper to send fish from Grimsby to London than from a location in Suffolk or Essex. The economic efforts of inshoremen tended, then, to be limited by their local market.

National outlets were only developed for particular specialisations. One Leigh-on-Sea informant[1] who worked exclusively at cockling with his boat-owning father stated that they used to send their catch direct to customers at seaside places as far away as Wales. London provided a regular winter market for them and for the shrimpers from the port. In both of these cases the fish was cooked by the fishermen which preserved it long enough to be transported without ice, so fishermen were less dependant on auxilary services. The oyster trade enjoyed a similar advantage in that they were marketed alive.

Although in the specialised shellfish industries of Essex work could follow a fairly regular pattern, the intensity of work varied for most inshoremen and was pre-industrial in its rhythms. No one experience is typical but many locations in Norfolk and Suffolk shared the experience of seasonal fishing from exposed beaches so the pattern from Thorpeness might be used as an illustration. In March fishing would start with crabs and lobsters; from mid-May trawling for plaice and soles; shrimps would come in the summer. Fishermen would work one or more of these according to their commercial judgement. Herring would arrive in October followed by sprats which would be fished until December. After this, bad weather and lack of fish meant that little fishing was done until March and this period was used to overhaul boats and gear. Given fair weather and the

availability of fish most men would work six days a week. On the whole the occupation is remembered with satisfaction but with no illusions about the degree of labour: 'Oh they were long days they were, long days. Been fishing all night, then got to walk to Leiston, that's three miles, six miles there and back – or Aldeburgh's two mile – to take your fish. There wasn't much sport about that' (3003:13).

All the fishermen were remunerated by a share of the catch. Not all the fishermen, however, shared in ownership. As a rough generalisation there were probably as many owners as crew along the Norfolk and Suffolk coasts with a ratio of two or three crew to each owner with the larger boats of Essex. These owners were invariably working skippers. The usual earnings' division was for one share to go to each man and one to the boat and gear. The varied nature of the fishing meant, however, that the system altered to accommodate different circumstances. At Thorpeness, for example, two owners would join together in one boat at the beginning of the year until they felt that there was fish in sufficient quantity to merit each operating a boat with a crew member. While they worked together they simply split the catch fifty-fifty. The short sprat season needed a third man and once again each of the three men received equal shares with one for the boat.

The seasonal variation in the share system and the differing prices received for their catches meant that inshore fishermen were unable to give an estimate of their earnings. Informants (3048 and 3057) who did volunteer an average put it at between £1 and 25s. a week. One more general guide to earnings is the solid agreement that they were much better off than the farm labourers who were their most common point of reference. Farm workers' wages in East Anglia in 1911 were between 11s. to 13s.[2]

In addition to fishing, men, particularly from Essex, worked as crew on the large luxury yachts of the period. These men seem to have been something of an elite and although the work is remembered as very exacting they did earn more than men who stayed fishing all year. Wages varied according to crew position but before 1914 ranged from £1 to 25s. a week. On top of their weekly money they were paid a bonus for each race their yacht entered and larger bonuses for being placed. One man recalled gaining an extra £35 racing money in one season. The yachting season ran for about twenty weeks between April to October so even much less competitive boats would earn their crewmen the equivalent of the annual wage of a farm labourer during the season. Some men were even paid a retainer during the rest of the year, but in any case, anything they earned at fishing for the rest of the year would lift them above the standard of the unskilled ashore. There was less unanimity as to whether they were better

off than a skilled man in a regular job ashore, and it might be that the owners were a little above that level and non-owners a little below. But it was a risky occupation: the inshore fisherman had his independence, his chance of good seasons and modest working-class comfort, but that was all; an adverse season could mean experiencing the hardship and poverty common to many workers.

That nearly half of the inshore fishermen owned their own means of production led some commentators to regret the change from sail to steam because 'It means that the fishing community as a whole will be divided into "employers" and "employees"' (Jenkins 1920:191). Self-employed fishermen were seen as a socially independent yet conservative class which exemplified the virtues of individualism, hard work and thrift. Parliamentary Committees met in an effort to preserve them as a desirable sector of the population as well as a valuable nursery for the Royal Navy and the basis of an efficient and comprehensive lifeboat service. It is slightly ironical that the Departmental Committee of 1914 placed no small blame on the problems of the inshore fisheries on the psychology of the fisherman, finding him 'reticent, conservative, independent and distrustful of his neighbours. He is an indifferent man of business.'[3] There can be no doubt that the fishermen were very individualistic. The explanation for this lies in direct experience of market relations. Their sense of self-interest did not come from competition on the fishing grounds however much they would enjoy outfishing their rivals. This is illustrated in an account from Harwich (3037) which described how they felt no resentment against the forty or so Leigh-on-Sea bawleys which would move to Harwich for three months in the year to fish the same grounds as the Harwich men, but how they did resent the occasional visits of only three or four Tollesbury smacks. The explanation was that the Leigh-on-Sea men were working to supply their own (distant) customers whereas the Tollesbury men placed their catch on the local market.

That there was nothing inherently non-cooperative about the fishermen is revealed in the accounts of the shrimpers who would borrow and loan shrimps with other fishermen so as to be able to fulfil orders to regular customers. If, in general, the fisherman was in competition with his fellows it was through competition in marketing the product, not the process of production itself.

2

Trawling

Method, location and development

The real rise of the trawl industry at Lowestoft commenced about the year 1860. At that period there would be about a dozen to twenty vessels, with a tonnage averaging from twenty-five to thirty tons. At that time ice was scarcely introduced into the fishing industry, and the vessels worked more at home on what is known as the Lowestoft Flats, where they caught a large quantity of soles. Shortly after 1860 some of the men who had migrated from Brixham to Ramsgate, commenced coming to Lowestoft with their fish, and eventually made Lowestoft their home, and this laid the foundation of the enormous trawling business now carried on at Lowestoft.

Mr Hame, witness to the Select Committee on Sea Fisheries
1893–4, Vol. XI

Historically the method of trawling was very little used; until the early part of the nineteenth century it was found only in the Thames and at Brixham. The beam trawl consisted of a stout wooden beam which was attached to the top front edge of a long roughly triangular net. On each end of the beam there was a trawl-head, a thick iron hoop which kept the beam clear of the seabed while sliding along like a sledge: in this manner the top of the net was held open and over the seabed. The bottom lip of the net was heavily weighted with rope and dragged on the seabed in an ellipse behind the top of the net so that as fish feeding on the bottom – plaice, turbot, soles and so on – were disturbed they already had the net over and around them. The rest of the net trailed behind and became stocking shaped at the end where the fish were retained. The beam was attached to a warp, lowered to the bottom and towed by the fishing vessel for a number of hours before being hauled to the surface and the net emptied.

The size of the net varied with the size of the vessel and East Anglian sailing smacks used trawls with beams 35 to 40 feet long. Subsequent improvements in trawling-gear such as the otter trawl doubled the width of the net and enabled fishing to continue in rougher weather than hitherto possible but they required the constant power and speed of a steam vessel to

operate them. Steam trawlers were so rare in East Anglia prior to 1914 that they do not merit separate consideration.[1]

The only notable technical change in the region was the adoption of steam capstans for hauling the trawl which increased capital and running costs but increased efficiency.

The location, growth and decline of major fishing centres emerge from the combination of the following factors: suitable harbours, the location of fish stocks, the technology of fish preservation and transport facilities to a mass market. From the eighteenth century attempts were made to supply London with fresh whitefish through the use of welled smacks. These had a section of the hull full of seawater and fish were caught by hook and line and placed in the well and landed alive. Not all species would survive this treatment and the main catch was cod. The method was expensive and productivity low so fish remained a luxury food. Fishermen using conventional boats would sometimes attempt to take their catches to London but the long sail upstream often meant that the catch spoiled before arrival. In any case such intermittent supplies could not establish demand or sustain regular retail outlets so most of the catch was sold cheaply to hawkers.

Trawl fishing was the most productive method of catching whitefish but until a method was devised of getting such a highly perishable product from the fishing grounds to the mass market the potential of trawling could not be realised. The accepted explanation is that the growth of the railway network provided the means and that was the case in most regions. But from the 1840s much of London's fish was seaborne and even in 1900 seaborne fish still made London the fourth largest fishing port with landings in excess of Milford Haven and Fleetwood combined. Transport by rail and transport by water created two very distinctive methods of fishing which had repercussions on the structure of ownership, industrial relations and a whole range of occupational matters. From the mid-1860s trawling in the region centred at Yarmouth and Lowestoft, the former as a base for waterborne fish to London and the latter as a centre of railway transport. Figure 2 demonstrates the development of trawling in the two ports. Yarmouth had a mushroom growth to the 1880s only to experience a total collapse of the industry around 1900 whereas Lowestoft had growth to 1908 and then steady decline into the interwar period. The distinction between the two communities is apparent in many ways and here we consider only the broad origins of the difference.

Barking, now part of London's urban sprawl, was the pioneer fishing village of commercial fleeting. Fleeting was the system by which trawlers fished together and the daily catch was loaded into a fish-carrier at sea so that fish was only one day old when it started for market. This proved vastly

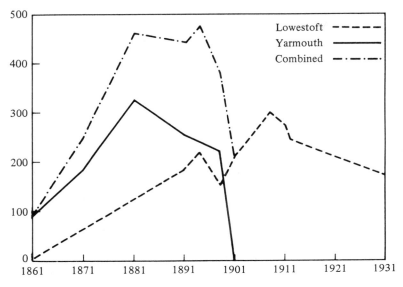

Figure 2 Number of trawlers 1861–1931

more effective than the old system of each vessel fishing individually for a few days until it had a large enough catch to be worth returning to port, by which time much of the catch was less than fresh. Two Barking companies started the system in 1847, introduced the use of ice in 1852 and in the 1860s were using specially designed fast steam fish-carriers to run fish daily to Billingsgate. The main fishing grounds were about eighty miles from Yarmouth so once it was no longer necessary for each trawler to make the long sail back to London it made commercial sense to base them at Yarmouth. Yarmouth was chosen only for its port facilities, as good market or rail facilities ashore were not essential. The system of fleeting did not depend upon the railways but upon the existence of at least one large capitalist company to provide the necessary infrastructure of carriers, ice and boxes. Of necessity these companies were trawler owners on a large scale as they needed direct working control of sufficient boats to ensure a fleet large enough to finance the operations of the carriers.[2] Once a fleet was in operation small owners could join the fleet at will and solve their own marketing problems. All smacks paid the carrier a fixed charge for each box of fish so it was in the companies' interest to allow independent owners to compete with their own smacks. Indeed, given enough business for the carrier operation the company could be profitable while ostensibly its own smacks were showing a loss, for the handling charges were a convenient point at which to exploit their workforce as well as independent fishermen.

Figure 2 shows that trawling collapsed completely after only thirty years at Yarmouth. This was due mainly to the financial difficulties of the largest company: without the large capitalist the small independent could not operate.

Lowestoft, some twelve miles down the coast, was a trawling centre with a totally different pattern of development. Here the railway company owned the port facilities (Yarmouth's were municipal) and developed special fish docks with direct rail links in order to generate goods traffic for themselves. These facilities allowed the small fishermen to operate independently of large-scale fishing capital. The results can be seen in the capital structure of the industry as well as industrial relations. As rail transport, complete with supplies of ice and all the auxiliary services, was available the smacks sailed individually icing their catch for four or five days before returning. Although still exploitable through the handling charges the fishermen were left with greater autonomy on their fishing operations. The slow growth of Lowestoft to 1908 and the slow interwar decline was due to national factors, and these are briefly mentioned before considering the region in more detail.

East Anglia declined as a centre for trawling because of regional disadvantages. One underlying factor was the exploitation of more prolific fishing grounds further north which advantaged the ports nearest to them. These grounds were worked by steam trawler, using the vastly more efficient otter trawl to catch enormous quantities of fish. By the 1890s one steam trawler caught as much fish as five or six sailing trawlers. East Anglia could not compete in this development because the local grounds were not prolific enough to sustain such intense exploitation and because they lacked cheap coal. The cost advantages accruing to those fishing ports near to coalfields was a dual one, for not only did steam trawling consume large quantities of coal but so did the manufacture of ice. It was, then, the location of raw materials, coal and fish which led to the growth of the Humber at the expense of East Anglia, just as the growth of Milford Haven at the expense of the older West Country ports was due to its position near the Welsh coalfield.

That trawling survived at all in Lowestoft was due to the following factors: the low operating costs of sail, which meant that existing capital could continue to be worked at a low profit; the availability of high-priced fish such as soles and turbot which gave good returns for low bulk; and the fact that sailing trawlers and the beam trawl were actually more efficient in catching these species than the newer methods.

With these broad features in mind we can now look at the work routines specific to the two systems of trawling operated in East Anglia.

Work and income: fleeting

During the tedious dreary winter the smackman's life is one prolonged battle with the raging elements, and there is little time, amid the strife, for aught but a hastily snatched meal, or a few brief hours of uneasy slumber – broken by the cry of the watch on deck to 'Rouse out! rouse out, there!'

E.J. Mather 1889

Trawling fleets fished continuously twenty-four hours a day, fifty-two weeks a year in the North Sea. A hundred or more sailing smacks fished in one location; each vessel would sail from Yarmouth and join the fleet for a period of eight weeks and then return to port for a week or two before sailing for another spell of eight weeks; on the average each smack made five trips a year. The fleet was in continuous operation because a few vessels would leave and new ones join every day. The vessels worked under command of one of the smack skippers who was designated 'Admiral'; he would decide where to fish, when to shoot the trawls and on what tack to sail; this discipline was essential to avoid collisions and to keep the fleet together. At night signals were made by coloured rockets. Every morning a fish-carrier from Billingsgate would find the fleet and take aboard that day's catch and steam for market, a relay of carriers ensuring daily landings.

This system was disliked and feared by the fishermen. Disliked because of the loss of working autonomy and judgement which subjected them to a routine discipline similar to factory production. It took them from their homes for two months of unrelieved toil in harsh conditions. In winter men never removed more than their oilskins and boots for the entire period, water was available only for drinking, even the cooking being done in seawater. The system became a byword for brutalising the men who endured it. The system was feared for its dangers. Apart from the need to stand at sea throughout all the winter gales, the need to transfer one's catch to the carrier every day meant that at eleven o'clock the ship's dinghy would be launched, loaded with trunks of fish weighing seventy lb. each and rowed to the carrier where they had to be thrown up on its deck, fresh boxes obtained and the dinghy regain its smack.[3] Crushed limbs and drownings were the regular result of placing men into small boats in the open sea.

A skipper could decide that the weather was too rough to risk his crew but anyone who failed to work his smack as intensively as others was likely to lose his employment. Market forces, too, intensified the pressure to take risks for if a number of smacks did not board fish it was certain that the fish which did reach market would command high prices. Breakfast was taken after boarding fish, the trawl was then shot and the crew would sleep from midday to five o'clock (save for the helmsman) when they had their evening

Occupation and Society

Figures and tables

Contents

*To Derek Gray and
Newbattle Abbey College of
Adult Education*

Published by the Press Syndicate of the University of Cambridge
The Pitt Building, Trumpington Street, Cambridge CB2 1RP
32 East 57th Street, New York, NY 10022, USA
10 Stamford Road, Oakleigh, Melbourne 3166, Australia

First published 1985

Printed in Great Britain at the University Press, Cambridge

Library of Congress catalogue card number: 84 – 17068

British Library cataloguing in publication data

Lummis, Trevor
Occcupation and society: the East Anglian
fishermen 1880-1914.
1. Fishermen – England – East Anglia – History
2. East Anglia (England) – Social life and customs
I. Title
942.6081   HD8039.F66G7

ISBN 0 521 26602 5

Occupation and Society

The East Anglian Fishermen
1880–1914

TREVOR LUMMIS

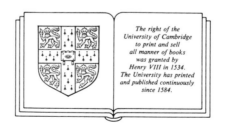

The right of the
University of Cambridge
to print and sell
all manner of books
was granted by
Henry VIII in 1534.
The University has printed
and published continuously
since 1584.

CAMBRIDGE UNIVERSITY PRESS

Cambridge

London   New York   New Rochelle
Melbourne   Sydney

meal. The trawl was then hauled and shot again and the fish packed. The next haul would be about five in the morning prior to boarding fish again. This was the daily routine for eight weeks.

The only change in this routine between the 1860s and 1900 was the introduction of the steam winch.[4] Hauling in the trawl by hand had entailed up to three hours of exhausting toil; two hauls a day was the normal workload, although if fishing in the extra deep water only one haul a day would be possible. The steam winch enabled the trawl to be hauled in twenty minutes or so. This obviously eliminated a great deal of drudgery, on the other hand it meant that the normal workload was increased to three hauls daily; consequently rest periods became shorter. The degree to which the winch intensified work is difficult to decide: on the whole fishermen welcomed it and the evidence for this is presented in the context of single-boating. It must be remembered that this was the routine only when there was enough wind to trawl. Smacks were literally powerless without the wind, preferably a stiff breeze, and during calms there were simply hundreds of smacks floating around unable to work. If this provided a welcome respite from work it carried the penalty of reduced earnings.

The exploitation of pauper children, bound as apprentices from the age of fourteen to twenty-one, in providing cheap legally controlled labour for the Humber fishing fleets at a time of intense capital accumulation is well known. The ill-treatment of these apprentices was the subject of a parliamentary enquiry and is still part of the folk-lore of the industry. This use of tied labour simply did not exist in East Anglia. Table 2 gives the data on apprentices for several traditional fishing ports, with Grimsby as a contrast.[5] Yarmouth, the only centre of fleeting apart from Grimsby, is in fact notable for its lack of apprentices. There are a number of reasons for this difference in development of the labour force, including the existence of numerous centres of fishing and seafaring along the coast from which labour could be recruited. But Norfolk and Suffolk contained a great reservoir of labour with few other industrial developments to absorb the rural surplus. In such a low-paid area the rewards of being a fisherman were sufficient to recruit all the labour needed. Colchester contained the highest number of apprentices in East Anglia and this was due to other factors. The right to share membership of certain oyster fisheries was invested in the fishermen from certain villages. Indentures were a convenient proof of rights and boys were usually bound to neighbours or kin but effectively treated as free labour. Throughout the period the fishermen were under no particular restrictions nor was their bargaining position on wages and conditions weakened by the presence of tied labour.

Table 2 *Sea-fishing apprentices 1889–93 at selected ports*

	Anulled or cancelled	Absconded	Died	To prison	Total number of apprentices
Colchester	6	–	–	–	121
Harwich	11	1	2	–	24
Lowestoft	16	10	2	1	41
Yarmouth	–	–	–	–	5
Brixham	60	12	4	7	245
Ramsgate	50	18	5	1	194
Grimsby	486	43	92	14	1,420

Earnings in fleeting were a mixture of a fixed weekly wage plus a poundage on the value of the catch. Wage rates appear to have been static from 1884[6] to 1900 when the system came to an end. Most vessels carried six men, with wages from the skipper downwards of 14s., 14s., 14s., 11s., 9s., 9s., and where a seventh hand was carried 8s. Similarly the poundage payment ranged downwards in status 1s., 6d., 4d., 3d., and the three most junior 1d. in the pound sterling earned by the smack. It can be seen that productivity was the major element for giving the senior crew members earnings substantially higher than the junior members. The incentive was sharpened in most agreements by increasing the skipper's poundage to 1s. 5d. if the vessel earned more than £150 in an eight week trip. In which case the mate and third hand also gained an extra penny on their poundage. My estimate for crew earnings is skipper £81, mate £50 and an average of £30 for the other four crew positions. Because the vessels fished together under orders it is doubtful whether there was a large fluctuation round this average and a range from £65 to £90 would include most skippers. With less income from the poundage lower crew earnings would fluctuate even less.

These were high wages in local terms and there was a substantial differential between the two senior positions and the rest. This does not indicate the existence of a distinction similar to the one between skilled and unskilled labour or any such structured difference in entry to the occupation, nor is it even distinction between adult and boy labour. Wages were paid by crew

Table 3 *Age profile of trawler crews 1884*

	Skipper	Mate	Third	Fourth	Fifth	Sixth	Seventh
Average age	34.8	29.3	26.2	23.0	20.5	22.8	22.0
Min./max. range	28/50	22/40	21/38	18/40	15/40	16/51	13/57

position and not by age or years of experience; in fishing there was a confusion of reward across the age range that is absent from most employments. This flexibility up and down the status ladder was a contributory factor to the individualism of the East Anglian fisherman which is elaborated in the context of the drifting industry. Nevertheless, table 3 gives the details for the first class trawlers at Yarmouth and Lowestoft.[7] There is an age gradient for the lowest age at which men move up the status ladder but the age range shows the degree to which ages were mixed at all positions. There are few occupations where a thirteen-year-old and a fifty-seven-year-old receive the same wage even if they are doing the same job. The thirteen-year-old is an exception, the next lowest age is fifteen. He appears on his first signing as a cook and then on resigning as an apprentice, but as his wage remained the same with the same allotment payed to his mother one might assume that his apprenticeship was a legal fiction. Indeed, out of the 262 signings checked only six were recorded as apprentices which confirms the general use of unbound labour by the 1894 enquiry. The number of older men in junior positions reflects something of physical demands of the job with elderly men moving down to lighter duties where, for example, they would avoid the onerous work of boarding fish.

Work and income: single-boating

We'll go to the Knoll or Tea Kettle Hole,
And anywhere else in the sea.
We'll mind the trawl-net
While the owners a-bed,
But none of your fleeting for me.

3014

That piece of folk-memory from a Lowestoft smacksman typifies what is recalled of the attitudes to fleeting. There are scattered references to Lowestoft smacks working with the Yarmouth fleets, as indeed did smacks from Ramsgate and beyond, but these always occurred in the summer. There was one attempt to run a fleet from Lowestoft in 1885 but it lasted only a year.[8] The reasons for its collapse are obscure but as it had to rely on the voluntary cooperation of dozens of small owners it may simply be that it could not keep a fleet in being. Up until about 1900 the routine of work was to sail for trips which lasted from four to six days on fishing grounds within an eighty to ninety miles radius from port. Once in port the crew had to unload the fish, load ice, coal for the capstan and their other stores. If they docked before 4 p.m. they were expected to sail next day, if they arrived after that they would have a second night in and sail on the morning tide. Four times a year the smack would have a week or two in port for necessary maintenance. The decline of fish stocks so close to port gradually changed this routine. The seasonal movement of the fish meant that from the end of March to the end of June there were few fish to be found so close to Lowestoft. Some would then work closer to the Dutch coast but this presented problems in sailing the catch back and they occasionally landed their catch in Dutch ports. But from around 1900 they began to sail to the West Country in this slack period and fish out of Padstow and Milford Haven. A report of 1911 states that although few had done the voyage ten years earlier about half the entire number then went.[9]

Normal working practice was to shoot and haul three times between about five in the evening and eight in the morning and then spend the daylight hours sailing back over the ground they had covered in order to be in a position to trawl again. The situation aboard these smacks with their five man crew is so different from the modern steam trawler that the distinction must be made explicit. The fact that there was only one cabin meant that the skipper could not keep any artificial distance from the crew, nor did a smack possess a bridge or wheelhouse where he is elevated above the crew. The skipper was about at all times and snatched sleep when he could. He was there at night every time the trawl was shot or hauled and he was on deck all day while the mate and third hand slept. The third hand and mate did six hours of the night watch each, changing at midnight. The skipper also iced and packed the catch:

Did the fish keep alright when you were away six days?
Oh the fish was kept absolutely perfect, a hundred per cent better than what it is at the present time. Now the skipper used to do all the icing up on the smack. The prime – which was soles, turbot and things like that, they'd got to be laid out absolutely perfect in pairs, so every part of it was covered in fine ice, not thick heavy ice, it had all got to be crushed so fine that didn't mark 'em. The fish at that time of day was – well, you'd think it was gold dust the way the old skipper used to look after it.

He'd actually pack it himself would he?
He'd pack it himself. He done all the packing when he was at sea and he used to pack the fish when they were landed on shore for sale. Yes, oh yes, the skipper did his amount of work. (3012:41)

The care of the catch by the skipper is a startling contrast to the pictures of steam trawler crews gutting and hurling heaps of fish around the deck. According to information taken from Tunstall (1962) the average daily catch of Hull and Grimsby steam trawlers between 1951 and 1958 was 800 st. There were twelve men in the deck hierarchy (excluding the skipper who did not handle fish), an average of 8 cwt per man to be hauled, gutted and iced. The national average daily catch of a sailing smack around 1909 was just 3 cwt.[10] Lowestoft smacks were slightly above the national average and table 4 shows the average per trip rising from about 12 to 19 cwt in a ten year period: that is from about 0.5 cwt in 1883 to 0.75 cwt in 1892 for each man per day.[11] It is difficult to assess whether this actually meant that work intensity was increasing because that is the decade during which the steam winch was introduced. The labour saved in hand hauling was probably greater than the effort of an extra haul a day. The increasing reliance on offal (i.e. cheap fish, anything not classed as 'prime') reveals the decline in prime fish stocks upon which the smacks really relied for their survival.

If there is a possibility that the physical workload decreased from the 1880s to 1914 the responsibility carried by skippers of these smacks grew more intense; they had to work their vessel and gear without mechanical power; they were doing this in the even busier and constricted water of the southern North Sea and they often had to work close to coasts and shoals in order to find fish. The Lowestoft single-boater undoubtedly stood at the pinnacle of skilled boat-handlers and fishermen.

As at Yarmouth labour in Lowestoft was not significantly affected by apprenticeships. London County Council did open a boys' home in Lowestoft in 1902 as an extension of their Feltham Industrial School but they were only few in number and did not materially affect industrial relations or bargaining power.

The Lowestoft single-boaters had a fundamentally different method of payment from the fleeters of Yarmouth. Here the earnings of the boat were divided into eight shares after necessary running expenses had been deducted. Of these the skipper received 1⅜ and the mate 1⅛, the owner had the remaining 5½ from which he paid the other three crewmen.[12] Between 1884 and 1911 crew wages did not alter; they varied for any individual between 19s. to 20s. for the third hand, 13s. to 16s. for the decky and 9s. to 12s. for the cook. They received no incentive payment or poundage at all.

Table 4 *Average catch of Lowestoft smacks 1883 and 1892*

	Prime fish (cwts)	Offal fish (cwts)
1883	128	380
1892	100	684

Their food on board was free. The main extra they gained was stockerbait (colloquially 'stocky'). This was species of fish which were not considered to be the object of the voyage. What counted as stocky varied from region to region, at Lowestoft the main saleable species were gurnard and weavers. This was placed on the market and sold by the salesman in the usual way but the cash was given to the skipper who divided it with the crew. This perquisite probably added about £4 to the annual wage of each crewman. Another perk was the shellfish found in the trawl which were not put on the market but simply shared between the crew. Finally, there was the custom of taking fish home at the end of the voyage for their own use. With smacks in port once a week this was an obvious help in feeding a family. The scale on which this was done seems remarkably free by today's standards and owners claimed that smacksmen supplied all their neighbours as well as themselves. Certainly the informants mentioned exchanging fish for meat at the butchers, supplying fish and chip shops in return for fried fish and chips and one with a large garden in a rural area used to get it ploughed in return for gifts of fish. But as the worth of this would vary with the attitude of the man involved no attempt to value this has been made. The earnings of the skipper and mate from the share system has been estimated from a combination of documentary and oral sources: this data is internally consistent and yields a convincing hierarchy of earnings shown in table 5. This put the mates on par with the earnings of skilled men in the area and the skippers some way ahead. This range of earnings applies to about half the smacks. Those that did not go to the West Country in the spring could be laid up or earning low money for a few months. Also from 1908 the number of smacks was diminishing and the industry entered a decline; so just before 1914 some smacksmen were beginning to experience difficult times and reduced earnings. But the weight of evidence indicates that there was no general distress among the Lowestoft trawlermen before the First World War.[13]

Table 5 *Average crew earnings: Lowestoft smacks circa 1900*

	£
Skipper*	75–90
Mate*	59–73
Third	40–4
Decky	30–6
Cook	21–7

* The skipper and mate had to pay for their own victuals at sea. This charge has been deducted and earnings are directly comparable.

Industrial relations

Notice. On and after the 1st March the following rates will be paid to the crews of trawling smacks sailing from Yarmouth and Gorleston, all nets used for the voyage will be deducted from the earnings, and a third of the remainder will be paid to the crews in place of wages and poundage in the following proportions:

1st Hand	8 Shares
2nd Hand	5 Shares
3rd Hand	4 Shares
4th Hand	3¼ Shares
5th Hand	2¾ Shares
6th Hand	2 Shares
	25 Shares

Hewett & Company, (Limited), Great Yarmouth Steam Carrying Co., (Limited), North Sea Trawling Company, (Limited), F. & J. Leleu, G. Saville King, Thos. J. Dore, J.L. Allen, W.H. Willis, E.A. Durrant, Morgan Bros., J.G.Bass, A. Farringdon, W. Soards, J. Allen, Senior, J. Brown (March 1st, 1887)

Eastern Daily Press, 5 March 1887

The above notice caused the one major strike; it took place only in Yarmouth and was directed solely at the capitalist trawling companies engaged in fleeting. The owners were trying to change the relations of production from a system of weekly wages and poundage already described to one where all earnings were a matter of chance and the cost of nets became an expense borne jointly by owner and crew instead of an expense to the owner.

There is no doubt that these firms were in financial difficulties as there had been a considerable over-investment in the industry as a result of the interest in fishing aroused by the International Exhibition of 1883.[14] Their claim that the new scheme would increase earnings rings hollow in the circumstances. Certainly their offer of one third share to a crew of six compared very badly with the local 'Lowestoft' share system for trawlers, under which the skipper and mate alone received almost a third of the net product (a ratio of fifteen to the owners' thirty-three) while the owner had to pay the fixed wages of the rest of the crew and the cost of nets.

The fishermen formed a union subsequent to their refusal to work the new conditions – the Fishermen's Society – although membership was open only to skippers, mates and, after some debate, third hands. The owners should have been in a powerful position with the majority of smacks at sea for eight weeks, but those at sea returned 'to harbour to vociferous cheering'[15] and joined the strikers. The strike was absolutely solid but at no time affected the small owners who continued to operate as single-boaters under the local share system:

> It seemed that the *Speedwell* was going to sea, when a number of the lock-out men boarded her under the impression that she was going out under the new rules. With this idea they hauled down the sails and prevented her starting; but it was afterwards understood that the arrangements were that she should sail under the old agreement.[16]

Quite clearly the strikers were prepared to use force to maintain a complete stoppage while at the same time making no attempt to prevent fishing by those who worked the customary agreement. In spite of this underlying element of physical control by the strikers they quickly gained public sympathy and the regional press covered the situation as a 'lock-out'. Part of the reason is that the strikers drew attention to their cause by presenting themselves to the eyes of the townspeople and traditional authorities in a quiet and orderly manner. On the two Sundays of the strike they processed through the town and attended church 'many of them, no doubt, going to the Parish Church for the first time, and many others probably not having been in a church before'. A thousand attended on the second Sunday but the press reported that the Chief-Constable took no precautions against disorder whatsoever and none were needed.[17]

The men won a partial victory in so far as they retained the old system of payment but they were obliged to allow for the cost of nets to be charged to the gross. It is clear that some level of union activity was maintained for there was trouble again in October 1891 when two skippers were victimised for leading a move for an increase in poundage payments.[18] This demonstrates that there was nothing 'inherent' or 'traditional' about the East

Anglian[19] worker which inhibited trade union activity and overt conflict: faced with large-scale capitalist companies they responded in the usual manner. Owing, however, to the growth of steam trawling and the natural advantages gained by other ports, the operation of sailing fleets from East Anglia was being superseded. Early in 1899 Hewett was laying up smacks and over the next two years fleeting operations collapsed with widespread distress and the dispersion of Yarmouth fishermen to ports all over Great Britain. The disappearance of large-scale capitalism took with it effective trade unionism.

The 1887 Yarmouth strike found no response in Lowestoft. The Yarmouth Fishermen's Society disappeared after the strike, presumably absorbed or replaced by the National Federation of Fishermen formed in 1890. According to the union journal, from March to November 1891 membership at Yarmouth fluctuated between 142 and 309. In spite of direct editorial appeals there was no response from Lowestoft for four of the nine issues. One rather ambiguously worded report implies a membership of about forty and states that they were with the fleet. But the virtual absence of formal organisation should not, as is frequently the case, be taken to indicate a weak workforce.

There is evidence for two conflicts in Lowestoft, one between the fishermen and owners, the other between small owners and larger commercial interests. The fishermen won the first conflict and the small owners the second. Taken together they illuminate the relationships between capital and labour and something of the balance of power in the industry.

The steam winch was introduced to the sailing smacks in the 1880s. As this increased capital and running costs as well as increasing productivity it was an obvious point at which there could be a need to adjust the existing share system. Steam winches had apparently been accepted in the Yarmouth fleeters without conflict and an article in the trade union journal states that the steam winch had been introduced by the owners as a means of enticing and then of holding good skippers.[20] The reasons are quite clear: steam power increased the number of hauls from two to three thus giving a potential 50 per cent increase in share earnings. Nevertheless, the introduction of these winches a few years later did cause friction at Lowestoft. A letter in the local press in 1889 signed 'A Skipper' claims that the owners were altering the traditional eight shares to eight and a half or even nine and retaining the extra portion to compensate for the cost of installing steam. It stated that they 'welcome the winch' as a great advantage and indicated a willingness to pay 5 per cent of the gross for it. This issue is not followed up in the press. The outcome, however, can be deduced from the share agreements in the Public Record Office. In 1884 before the general use of the winch they are all at eight shares. The agreements for 1889 have a number at eight and a half thus confirming the accuracy of the letter. A later sample of 1911 agreements shows them all back at eight shares with 5 per cent of the gross for the capstan.

Neither the evidence for the dispute nor the actual activity appears in the dramatic events of a strike but it is quite evident that there was a dispute, that the owners did attempt to alter the relations of production as the large capitalist owners had done by altering the existing share agreement. It is equally clear that they failed to do so and that the issue was settled without overt conflict on the basis suggested by labour.[21]

The difference in how industrial relations were handled is instructive and there can be little doubt of the crucial importance of the structure of ownership. For, whereas, at Yarmouth some 160 crews had the same employer and needed unity to resist exploitation, in Lowestoft there were few owners with more than two or three vessels and so the power of capital was as dispersed as the power of labour. Both employees and employers saw industrial relations in personal terms. It was almost as difficult for the owners to organise themselves as it was for the men and in such a situation traditional practices cannot easily be altered. When capital is widely dispersed it is not only less easily perceived to be a *system* it is less easily *managed* as a system.

Within the usual cycle of booms and slumps the Lowestoft trawling industry was quite profitable up to its peak (in terms of number of vessels working) in 1908. After that the industry was undoubtedly working on low profits. The response of a dispersed ownership, however, could not parallel that of a unified one as in the case of the Yarmouth fleeters. The response of small owners to economic difficulties was to manage more tightly, cut expenses, attack perks and generally push the workforce. Their ability to do this at the personal level undoubtedly enabled Lowestoft trawling to survive the difficult period which provoked the attack on the fleeters' wages. At Lowestoft this period did not bottom-out until 1894. It even brought a collective front of sorts:

They [smack owners] have had a special meeting, and notice has been given to skippers and crews that no fish must be given to or taken away by anyone. There is no desire to stop the crew from having fish to take home, and there is no wish to interfere with their stocker-bait: but no member of the crew must take fish from the smacks between six in the evening and nine the following morning.[22]

How effective that warning would be was to a great extent dependent on the relationship between owner and employees and the personal attitude of the individual concerned. It appears from information in the local press that fish had been given away in a very free manner. The docks were open to the public and it was the custom for the fishing boats to give a pair of soles or similar valuable fish to visitors. There is no public record of this issue again until 1909. That was the first year of the reduction in the number of boats and the return of bankruptcies to the industry. A skipper was taken to court for taking fish valued at 10s. This was after the owner had specifically warned him not to take any prime fish on that occasion as it was a particularly small catch. The evidence is interesting in that as the owner gave a special warning it indicates that he must have been aware that the skipper usually took such fish and that was tolerated while catches were good. Also the value of the fish, over half the weekly wage of a third hand, was quite a considerable sum and if taken on most trips represented a substantial fiddle.

The oral evidence gives the most detailed accounts of industrial relationships and it is quite apparent that the trawlermen were conscious of being squeezed and cheated by their employers. The following extract, from a later period, is presented at length (although edited) to establish both attitudes and practices:

Do you think that any of these companies used to fiddle your settling sheet, put in heavy expenses?

Well – fiddling? Oh yes, yes. Now I'll give you this example. You ordered a half a dozen new fish baskets and perhaps there was one or two trips when you didn't want anything, so the horse and cart wasn't needed for you. But when you settled up you used to pay for them baskets and you'd only had 'em once. There was cartage. Perhaps those two or three trips when you didn't want cartage. And the commission, and all the other expenses, your coal, your food, your ice. And then another bit of swindle was – perhaps you was in a smack what only runned on eight and nine hundredweight of coal a trip, occasionally half a ton. In your settling trip would be every trip ten and eleven. You couldn't swear to it. Oh no. You couldn't swear to how much coal you're burning. But you knew. I don't care who you talk to, the present day and in them days – fishing – there's one of the biggest swindles under the sun. By the shore staff. That *is* a real swindle. That's one of the biggest swindles out, fish. You pay for things over and over again that you haven't had. And we used to sometimes speak of it. But that wouldn't do to speak of it in them days, you'd be out.

With so much fiddling going on why didn't fishermen have a trade union or something to try and stop that sort of thing?

No. No, the situation in them days was that you were afraid to speak out. Because if you came out of a ship and spoke to the owner about overcharging they would turn round to you and say to you, look, sign off, clear out of it. Well, you never knew when you was going to get a ship no more, and one owner would pass the information to another owner, and tell him what happened and such and such and perhaps you'd be months before you got another ship. Oh my word you were afraid to speak. You see I was robbed of hundreds of pounds: pounds and pounds and pounds I was robbed. I was skipper in that firm for about thirteen years, but I couldn't say anything. I'd got a family of children. And if you said anything you were out. You see that owner, he was buyer and all, and he used to come on the market in the morning about half past seven. There was your trip of fish in the kits, and he was the fish buyer. Now he used to take his tallies out and put on them kits of fish, tell you you'll get market price. He used to leave all the rough stuff, whitings, dabs, rooker and the like of that. Well supposing the markets were going up as they were coming through the market, supposing the prices were going up. You only got the lowest. (3035:32–5)

This account actually relates to the interwar period when the number of smacks were declining annually and there were few opportunities of alternative employment, so it reflects relationships when the bargaining position of the skippers was much weaker than pre-1914. Nevertheless, it is instructive in the actual points of conflict and how they were handled:

One trip there was four or five of us in, landed our fish, and none of the skippers was satisfied. I wasn't satisfied but I dare not say anything because I'd a family of children. And yet I'd been doing all right. So they kicked up a stink with the owner. Well a clerk said he won't be here for another hour yet. Well we're going to wait for him. And I waited with them. Away came the owner. What's up, what's wrong? They're all dissatisfied said the clerk, with what they have made. Well eventually he had to call us all in the office, and eventually he put five pound on every trip. (3035:34)

These confrontations are the obvious points at which the particularistic relationship can be dissolved by either party using the opportunity presented by overt confrontation. The informant presents himself in the above account as being an almost reluctant supporter of his fellow skippers and it might be noted that he worked for the same firm for at least thirteen years and became a tenant in one of his employer's houses at the earliest opportunity. His employer was about the largest in the trawling industry of Lowestoft and had other commercial interests, but even here it is noticeable that he handled the dispute directly. Much more typically only one or two skippers would be employed by any one man and relationships would be on a very much more individual level for both parties: no employer, however, would be over-hasty in dismissing, or provoking into leaving, a skipper who was careful, reliable and reasonably successful. After all the small owner saw all his capital sail out of the harbour and although two-thirds of the value of the vessel was insurable the gear was not.

The most serious fiddle in the above account is that his employer, in his role as fish dealer, used to pre-empt the best of his catch at the lowest market price of the day. The market price of their product was a matter of very keen interest for all fishermen whether they were owners or sharemen for both wanted high prices. It was the operation of a market system which concealed the actual price from the fishermen and was open to corruption which led to the second conflict at Lowestoft in 1891.

The nature of the dispute was concisely expressed in the local press:

The fishers, and a section of the owners, have struck against the system of disposing fish at the market. It is known as Dutch auction, and it is a complicated system of 'lowers' by which the seller offers the produce of his boat's work at an estimated value, and, not finding a buyer, reduces the price by five shillings a time until it is purchased. After this had to be deducted four five shilling 'bids', in some cases more, before the actual price could be ascertained. To small buyers, owners and fishermen this has been unfair, and they desire to adopt ordinary English, not Dutch auction. A start was made on Monday last [January 5th]. How the change will act yet remains to be seen, as large owners and large buyers are standing out against it.[23]

Fishing continued as normal but those taking action simply refused to have their catch auctioned under the old system, thus hoping to force fish buyers to purchase under the new system of open auction. The large buyers and some of the large owners continued to operate the old system.

It was most obviously a conflict between small owners and dealers against the larger business interests. It is an interesting example of unity of interests, however, for the local union branch supported the end of Dutch Auction. The dual system did not last very long and victory went to the fishermen and small owners. It was not until nine months later that organised labour through the Trades Union Congress passed a resolution that all fish should be sold on fixed commission and Dutch Auction ended. That unorganised Lowestoft could take successful action to eradicate an abuse and swindle that the better organised ports of Hull and Grimsby could not raises a number of important points.[24]

It shows that militancy, in the sense of taking action, and power, in the sense of being strong enough to enforce the desired conditions, can be carried by groups lacking formal organisation. It also points to an identity of interest between the numerous small owners and their sharemen (two in a crew of five) who were aware that they shared an interest in the open working of the market. This is so unlike the situation in most industries where the marketing of the product is considered to be part of the concern of management not of workers, and the workers fight for their remuneration on the grounds of productivity, differentials, cost of living and similar factors. Whatever factors brought the sharemen and their employers into conflict, the most basic one, that of the value of their product, brought them together and gave them a collective interest. The fisherman's constant awareness of prices and market forces served to displace his discontents from his employer to the market and those who manipulated it. This issue will be further considered in the context of drifting where the market was even more important because all crewmen's income depended on the share system.

3

Drifting

Method, location and development

In value and renown the herring takes an unassailable position as lord of the fishes.
                                                                  Walter Wood 1911

Various forms of driftnet have been used for centuries. They hang stationary in the water like a curtain; fish are captured because as they swim along they strike the net, the mesh of which is wide enough to admit their heads but too narrow to permit their whole bodies to pass through; they cannot back out because the string of the mesh closes behind their gills and traps them. The net is suspended from a series of buoys and has corks along its upper edge and can be adjusted to float a given distance below the surface.

The net itself was traditionally made of hemp twine and the introduction, first in Scotland, of a machine-made net of fine cotton mesh had a dramatic impact on the efficiency of the drifters:

The substitution of cotton for hemp nets may be said to have revolutionised the fishery. A boat that used to carry 960 yards of netting, now carries 3,300 yards. The nets used to be 6 or 7 yards, they are now 10 yards deep. They used to present a catching surface of 3,300 square yards, they now present a catching surface of 33,000 square yards; without increasing the weight of nets to be worked each boat has increased its catching power fivefold.[1]

In the 1890s the English adopted this 'Scotch net' as superior to their old twine 'English net' (although the latter continued to be used by the Dutch). The Scottish net was more efficient too because of the way in which it was rigged. The old English method was to attach the nets to the main warp at their top end and to leave the bottom edge hanging free, but in strong tides the force of the water tended to push the bottom of the net out of the vertical towards the horizontal so presenting a smaller catching surface to the shoal of fish. Because it was so light the Scottish net had a solerope along its bottom edge to stop it from tearing and the mainwarp was attached to this rope; with this weighting the bottom edge, the nets remained more vertical and so presented a more efficient surface to the shoals. By the turn of the century nets had standardised at 35 yards long and 15 yards deep. Each steam drifter would shoot up to 100 nets, some one and three-quarter miles long, with over 10 acres of surface.

The essential point to grasp is the passive nature of driftnet fishing. Once the nets had been streamed the drifter and nets lay motionless in the water simply being carried backwards and forwards with the tide until it was time to haul.

The greater productivity of cotton nets did nothing to change the method of fishing neither did the introduction of the steam capstan in the 1880s or steam propulsion at the end of the 1890s. Their importance lies in their effect on crew wages and work intensity.

The location of the major drifting ports was determined above all by the migrations of the herring shoals. Those off the coast of Norfolk between September and December were the largest of the year and of herring in perfect condition for curing. The market urgency with herring came from the moment it was caught to the moment it was cured; drifters fished at night and returned their night's catch to port in the morning for processing that day. As the bulk of this catch went for export the location of domestic markets, transport networks and so forth were less important than with trawling.

The development of the industry can be seen in figure 3. Development at Lowestoft and Yarmouth was much more parallel than in the case of trawling. This was due to a greater similarity in working practice and capital structure. Nevertheless, there are differences between the two communities which are crucial. Yarmouth's nineteenth-century peak is higher than its twentieth-century one whereas although Lowestoft suffers the same mid-period slump its general trend is up to overshadow Yarmouth. As in the case of trawling the superior port facilities offered at Lowestoft fostered the growth of drifting. By 1914 one quarter of the East Anglian catch was going on the home market in fresh or lightly cured herrings, and most of that went through Lowestoft. Both the late nineteenth-century decline and that of the interwar years were due to external factors affecting the export market rather than any internal factor. Herring shoals appeared inexhaustible and fishing capital expanded to meet the demand.

It should be emphasised that the actual capital investment is far more intense than is apparent from the graph. Until 1897 all drifters were sailing craft but by 1914 virtually all were steam, so the doubling of the number of Lowestoft drifters in that seventeen years represents a capital increase of around 800 per cent. The development of the drifting industry is complex

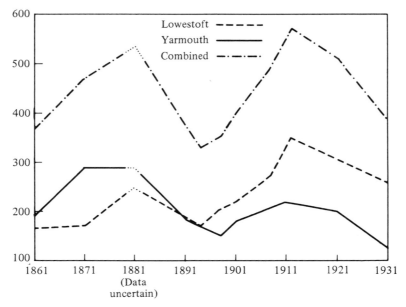

Figure 3 Number of drifters 1861–1931

but as it is so relevant to subsequent sections on work practice and industrial identity the main features must be delineated.

From the medieval period Yarmouth was the main herring port of East Anglia. Indeed, it continued to be so in terms of the amount of herring cured although most of the herring catching was done by Scottish fishing vessels. In the early and mid-nineteenth century the Yarmouth drifters were threemasted luggers which were usually owned by commercial interests rather than by fishermen. These boats would stay at sea for a week or more salting the daily catch and returning to port only when loaded.[2] This was an acceptable system as it started the long process of salting and smoking necessary to produce red herrings. Because of the movement of herring, September to December was the main season. Indeed, some of these boats were then laid up for the rest of the year. All were idle until April when some would fit out for cod fishing, a few would try for mackerel from May onwards. The practice of drifting virtually all the year was introduced from the 1840s by fishermen-owners using smaller and cheaper vessels. They fished for herring and mackerel through the early spring and summer as well as the big autumn season. This development was centred at Lowestoft and in 1866 60 per cent of their drifters were working the spring fishing compared with only 5 per cent of the Yarmouth boats. By 1882 Lowestoft drifters were working for all but the first six weeks of the year.

This development is interesting because it runs counter to the generally accepted tendency for the most capital intensive section of an industry to avoid idle time: 'With the increasingly capital-intensive character of the fisheries there is a strong tendency to eliminate the seasonal laying up of vessels. Basically, this can be achieved either by greater mobility, or by seasonal conversions of vessels to another fishery which is locally available.'[3] In East Anglia it was the least capital intensive sector of small fishermen-owners which eliminated long idle seasons, and that seasonal idleness was to return again with the greatly increased capitalisation of the steam drifters. The evidence of Mr Bloomfield, manager of the largest steam drifter company in Yarmouth, is unequivocal; by 1908 their drifters were idle for four months of the year:

The bulk of the East coast (Yarmouth and Lowestoft) boats are laid up during the months of January, February, March and April. About the 1st May they usually fit out for the East Coast of Scotland and the Shetlands, some going to Castlebay in the Island of Barra, on the West Coast, ... Leaving the Shetlands, the boats usually prosecute the fishing right down the East Coast, some working Grimsby in the month of September, but the bulk of the boats come on to Yarmouth and Lowestoft. There is little spring herring fishing from Yarmouth and Lowestoft during the months of May and June, but the number of boats following it is very small indeed.[4]

Other sources suggest that he underestimated the number of Lowestoft boats which worked more intensively. Newspaper reports indicate that 75 per cent of the Lowestoft boats and 20 per cent of Yarmouth boats were in the West Country for the spring fishing of 1899, and that appears to be a typical example. The local press makes clear that Lowestoft drifters would sail at any time of the year on receiving reports of the herring shoals. Alward reinforces this point: 'One of the particular features of the Lowestoft fishermen is that they frequent almost every fishing port round the British Isles during the drift-net season, reaching even into Irish ports, both for mackerel and herring' (1911:38). It was always the small owner and the fisherman-owner who worked most intensively: it was the larger capitalist who laid idle four months of the year.

This clear regional exception to the general tendency is not presented in order to discount the theory of more intensive use of large capital units but as an opportunity to consider why it did not apply in this place and period. Up to the 1880s when the smaller Lowestoft boats had extended the length of the season compared with the larger Yarmouth boats there is no doubt that the key feature limiting longer use was not the level of capital employed but the relation of capital to labour. The extension was due to the Lowestoft boats adopting the system of paying the crew solely by a share of the product, which placed part of the risk for unprofitable seasons on the shoulders of labour: if the enterprise did not make a profit they received no remuneration. This system and what it meant in terms of income is developed in the following section, but it provides a crucial example of the importance of the attitudes of labour and the relations of production, rather than the levels of capital and technology, in determining industrial development. This system of payment became general in both ports on the steam drifters and so will not serve to explain why the commercial companies worked their capital less intensively than the small owners.

One common feature of the voyages undertaken in the four months that many laid idle was that they were ones of high financial risk, particularly for the owners. As will be seen later the crew could often make quite a substantial reward through their perks. One owner (3055) claimed that these voyages were undertaken more to satisfy the crew and to keep good men together than in any expectation of profits. Such pressures working through the community on a fisherman-owner cannot be discounted although one can be sure that such thoughts would not influence a large company. The main force, however, was undoubtedly the market. These voyages were for the fresh fish market which was soon glutted and sales uncertain; if too many boats decided to engage in the venture it was certain that few would show a decent return. From the point of view of a company it can make better sense to save expense by letting a boat idle for four months than to send it on voyages where it might make a loss.

It was the capacity of the market which dominated the development and employment of drifters. Thus the major part of driftnet fishing, in Scotland as well as England, came to rely more and more on the summer season in Scotland and the autumn one in England as those two seasons could handle virtually any quantity of herring caught and sales were assured. Certainty of a market for the product rather than the level of capital investment seemed to be the crucial element in the laying-up of drifters. The increased capital investment and the greater reliance on the export market of pickled herrings did affect the driftermen's pattern of work so further changes are now considered in the context of the work and income of the fishermen.

Work and income

In the second half of the eighteenth century, the most successful of these fishermen were the Swedes, ... It has been shown that during the three-months season workers frequently earned as much as three to five times as much as Swedish agricultural labourers earned in a year.

J.R. Coull 1972

The basic rhythm of herring fishing was imposed by the movements of the fish. The herring shoals came to the surface at night, therefore the drifter-men would shoot their nets at dusk and then simply drift with the tide until morning, when the nets would be hauled and the boat return to port for the morning market. The boat would then sail again to shoot its nets at dusk and so would continue the daily routine. Fishing for paleagic species, however, was highly seasonal and the seasons worked changed in response to market opportunities.[5]

At the beginning of the nineteenth century many of the large Yarmouth herring luggers would drift for herring for only three to four months of the year, so much of the labour was casual. The autumn fishing followed the peak demand for agricultural labour and agricultural workers were the source of recruitment. The capstanmen, who provided the power to haul the miles of net by tramping round pushing capstan bars, were recruited from field labourers and were not even considered to be fishermen by the rest of the crew. The skipper, mate and some of the crew would be full-time fishermen who would go with the ship when it changed fisheries or would work as seamen on the coastal trade if the vessel laid up. Additional crewmen were recruited from smallholders, dairymen and market gardeners who would occasionally be part-owners. There were no apprentices in the East Anglian drifter industry because 'in the intervals of the season fishing, the lads would be a burden rather than an advantage to their masters'.[6] One can see the logic of their reasoning but as will become apparent the intensity of work was so severe at times that only self-motivated labour could produce the required effort. The labour force was attracted and rewarded without tied labour.

The adoption of the cotton net, steam capstans and motive power undoubtedly increased the intensity of the driftermen's work. They would catch more herring, return to port, discharge and return to the grounds more swiftly. Crew size standardised at ten men on the steam drifter and this had been a common crew size for the sailing drifters; a potential reduction in crew numbers as a result of the introduction of the labour-saving steam capstan being largely balanced by the addition of an engineer and a fireman with the change to steam propulsion. Although the fishermen lost the labour of working the vessels by sail and sweep this was more than out-weighed by the amount of fish handled. Between 1854 and 1863 the average catch for the autumn season was 242 crans, between 1904 and 1913 over 500 crans. Even more important were the variations in the intensity of the work. The top earning vessels would average 40 tons of fish for each crew member and that would be landed in very uneven bouts of labour. Thus the modern drifter industry needed to recruit extremely high-quality labour and keep it highly motivated through the potential levels of reward.

It is argued that this was achieved through the system of payment which developed from mid-century.

Under the traditional system the owner of the vessel contracted to pay the crew a fixed sum for each last of herring they caught. These owners were often curers and were essentially ensuring their own supply; only the surplus was placed on the market. They took all the risks and all the profit. From the crew's point of view it was a system of piecework not dissimilar to those found in other industries save that the unpredictability of herring fishing made the final earnings a complete gamble. It was a poor system in terms of industrial relations. When landings were high, crew wages were high but market prices were depressed and the owners could be making losses; if catches were low, crew earnings were low and this contrasted with the high market price. It was difficult for either to strike a just price which would anticipate the season's catches and prices. Thus, fishing was mainly restricted to the one season as this was the most predictable market.

This system was replaced by 'co-venturing': a system by which labour shared the market risks with capital. This was an extremely efficient method for stimulating productivity while minimising conflict. Both owners and crew were united in wanting the maximum output and minimum running costs. There was no objection to the introduction of new methods as both took their fixed share of the increase in productivity. They both relied on market prices and that gave them a shared interest and sense of unity.

The potential point of conflict in these circumstances lay in adjusting the share system to allow for the increasing level of capital investment. As such, one would expect changes to occur when new technology was introduced and yet the proportion going to capital and to labour did not change by a jump either with the introduction of steam or with increasing boat size. The proportions 61:39 which became standard practice on the steam drifters were used as early as 1866. Table 6 is a summary of share agreements.[7] In the light of this evidence labour seems to have been extraordinarily successful in maintaining its share of the product at a time when the capital investment required increased by 300 per cent from the largest vessel of 1866 to the standard vessel of 1911.

Each crewman's earnings were proportionate to his status: this ranged from a one and three-quarters share for the skipper, around seven-eighths of a share for crewmen down to half a share for the cook. The wide variability of earnings between vessels and from season to season made average earnings difficult to estimate. Indeed, the average may not be an appropriate measure, for the range of earnings was one of the real incentives. The oral evidence shows how high earnings could be: the hawseman (one share) who earned 'half a crown under the hundred pounds in seven weeks of the Home Season of 1912' (3005), the sixteen-year-old cook whose annual earnings in

Table 6 *Yarmouth herring fishing shares: capital and labour*

	Proportions	
Date	Owners	Crew
1860	50	50
1866	56	44
1866	61	39
1876	59	41
1881	56	44
1901	60	40
1911	61	39
1930s	61	39

1907 came to £78 (3013), which would mean that his skipper must have earned over £200, a three-quarter shareman on one of the early steam drifters in 1900 who earned £93 from mid-August to near Christmas (3028), about ten times the local agricultural wage. On the other hand there was one man with long experience who said that he never earned more than £30 in one season (3024), and at least one man had the experience of paying off in debt (3015). Reviewing the Home Season of 1913 the *Fish Trades Gazette* reported that 'several' Lowestoft boats earned more than £3,000 and specified the *Rob Roy* as earning £3,200. If one assumes that the vessel had enjoyed an average Scottish season and to have been laid up for four months the earnings of the skipper would have been about £250. Many Lowestoft boats worked three seasons and would earn more. This superiority of earnings is a feature of the herring industry both historically and geographically.

It should be remembered that in the above case from 1913 the owner would have cleared around £2,500 for the year's work, enough to pay the capital costs of a drifter in one year.[8] Those are, however, the exceptions. The fishery report for the bad Home Season of 1908 gave *average net* earnings of around £500 to £600; for the good season of 1909 it was around £900. The level of crew reward can be read off the graph of figure 4. On the average earnings shown in the figure a skipper's share would range

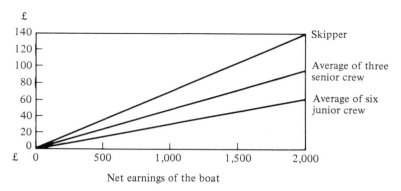

Figure 4 Drifter crew earnings on the Yarmouth share system

from nearly £50 in a poor season to about £60 for a good one. Those, however, are estimated averages, the actual range of earnings for the 1912 Home Season was £500 to £2,000. If one allows for expenses this gives a net range of about £200 to £1,000, thus giving actual earnings from less than £20 to over £100 for ten or twelve weeks' work. It is worth noting, too, that this meant that the lowest status crewmen on a successful boat earned more than the skipper of an unsuccessful one. Indeed, if a boat earned less than its expenses the men had no wages to draw and the owner may have experienced a net outflow of capital. Theoretically, as co-venturers, the men were liable to pay their proportion of the losses, but in practice the owners alone were responsible for the bills to suppliers.

The difficulty of giving an average to such disparate fortunes is exacerbated by the fact that the oral evidence revealed other sources of income. The owners and crew were supposed to share the small quantities of stockerbait sold for cash fifty-fifty, but as the owner was not present when the boat was away from East Anglia the crew took the lion's share of this for themselves. Stockerbait was not important during the Home Season (the shoals were virtually pure herring) but one useful perk was the custom of sending a batch of herrings to a curer who would keep half as payment for curing the other half for the crew. These would be collected by the men at the end of the season where they made a useful contribution to the family larder. Another common practice on the Scotch voyage was that of men fishing for themselves:

Oh yes, we used to pick up a nice bit of money. And of course you worked the line there when you were down at the Shetlands. You had a line over the side and caught cod and blackjack. I once got fifty blackjacks, I know I didn't make a lot of money, about sixpence each you know. But that was money. I had the watch that night and the kit was right full.

And that would be just for you?
Yes. I bought my own line, four bob, don't you see, four hooks on it. Yes, yes. You worked a line, everybody worked a line, everybody worked a line. (3007:48)

Not all of these cod were sold on the spot:

And I'll tell you what we used to do and all, at Lerwick we used to get cod on the lines after we had shot [the nets]. Well then you'd split them open and throw them in the salt locker. Well they'd be like boards when they came out. Well perhaps you'd have sixty or seventy in there when you came home. Well they'd keep them until after Christmas, and then you'd bring them home and hang them up in your shed, anywhere, they wouldn't hurt, and then you would have salt cod and spuds for dinner. Cut a bit off, lay that in fresh water all night, and then your mother would boil it next morning for dinner. Lovely. (3015:13)

The West Country voyage to the mackerel fishing in the spring was, as indicated earlier, a financially risky voyage undertaken mainly by the small owners of Lowestoft. The owner had a more favourable share system for this voyage in that the crew was reduced to nine men and the owner took the missing man's share. Even so boats often did little more than break even and it was difficult to understand why men undertook it. The common oral accounts, however, reveal that men expected to earn more from these marginal sources than they did from the principal. Earnings from stocker-bait were exceptionally high and they had more than the customary amount of time to line for ling, skate, cod and conger to their own individual advantage. It is these largely undocumented earnings which explain why the voyage was attractive.

The skipper had some perks not available to the rest of the crew. There were small cash sums, for example the coaling companies usually gave the skipper a cash discount on the coal taken, although the skipper might put this in the general pool of crew money it was his to keep. The North Sea Coaling Company also used to send every skipper who dealt with them during the summer season a sheepskin rug as a Christmas present, and one woman (3051) related that all her sisters and herself had their own in turn according to their ages. She also related receiving three turkeys one Christmas from various suppliers. It appears to have been normal routine for the baker who supplied the vessel in home waters to send the skipper a large tin of biscuits at Christmas, the butcher to contribute pieces of beef. In other words local tradesmen valued the custom of a drifter and recognised this through annual gifts. The greengrocer always sent a large sack of fruit and nuts in the same way. It was customary also for crews joining a drifter to be allowed to go along to an outfitters to purchase on credit necessary clothing for sea such as oilskins and boots. The owner of the vessel shared with the outfitter the risk of a man absconding with the clothes and not joining the

Table 7 *Average crew earnings: Yarmouth steam drifters circa 1911*

	£
Skipper	115
Three senior crewmen	77
Six junior crewmen	52

ship. The skipper was usually given a guernsey for taking the crew to be so outfitted. These, however, were little more than pleasant additions to earnings and do not fundamentally alter the calculations to be made of skippers' earnings any more than those of the crew.

The foregoing should have demonstrated the difficulty in assessing average earnings: apart from the variability of the principal it is clear that some of the ostensibly less profitable voyages gave the crew sources of income which did not appear in the documentary evidence. A tentative average is given in table 7. This is for two voyages with total earnings of £2,000 less £500 expenses. Incidentals have been added £10, £7 and £5 to the three groups. It should be noted that the Lowestoft men who more often worked a third (low-earning) season would have averaged a little more.[9] The driftermen clearly earned more than the smacksmen and this is supported by the social and industrial perceptions of the fishermen themselves. But more significant than the average was the range of earnings and the chance it presented to manual workers of making a really large sum of money.

Industrial relations

Oh yes, everybody had to pull their weight. Yes, there was no place for a lazy man, you couldn't be a lazy man aboard a drifter. Everybody had to work.

3017

The evidence on drifting confirms that it was the relations of production, mainly the market and the share system rather than technical or capital changes, which dominated industrial relations. As the 'co-venturing' share system replaced the older system of payment by the last so driftermen shared the risks (and advantages) of the market as well as the uncertainties of the catch, so one would expect a difference in industrial relations resulting from the two systems of payment: evidence is scanty, but conforms to the general thesis.

The system of fixed payment by the last was bound to need periodic review and adjustment as developments in the industry affected the general trend of market prices. Evidence given to the Caird Commission at Yarmouth (1863) revealed that this matter had caused conflict. It was stated that 'ten or twelve years earlier' the price paid to the crew per last had been reduced by 15 per cent and that the reduction continued in force for three years 'and then the men made a stand' and had the old rate restored. 'Last season' they again 'agreed' to a 15 per cent reduction. Unfortunately these events took place before the existence of trade journals or of an informative local press so there are few details on the form or intensity of this conflict. But the essence of the trouble was that the reward for labour was fixed at the beginning of the season on estimates of the likely level of the catch and the final market price, both of which were beyond rational prediction.

Two items in the Yarmouth press January 1861 confirm that relations were troubled. One was a letter from De Caux (a prominent auctioneer and boat owner) noting that 1860 had been an unprofitable season and complaining that this was due to fishermen deserting the boats. The accounts suggest that there had been an attempt to make the old fixed payment system more flexible to market conditions by using short engagements. But it is claimed that men would agree to work for 5s. a night and then demand 7s. and finally refuse to sail unless they got half the catch as well. The unreliability of the men was ascribed to the ruling that magistrates had no jurisdiction over fishermen's contracts. Two weeks later the owners formed an association to lobby for a change in the law. Their reasoning does not explain, however, why the men on the share system worked without trouble.

This system of fixed payments was replaced in the 1860s and the 1870s by the flexible share system. By the early 1880s the 'customary' system of payment by the last was followed by only a few exceptions. There is no doubt that the owner's and crew's need to negotiate the level of remuneration before either could know how successful the season would be was a poor one. There can be little doubt that with the complete revolution in catching power resulting from the introduction of the more efficient Scotch net in the 1890s and steam propulsion at the turn of the century industrial relations would have grown considerably worse.

It is argued that the general adoption of the share system, originally as a risk-sharing process necessary to exploit unpredictable seasons, had the effect of neutralising the issue of the proportion of the product which should go to capital or to labour. This is not presented as a necessary function of such a share system but as a contingency in the particular historical circumstances. It must be assumed that if, for example, the men's earnings had been too low it simply would not have been worthwhile to work on the share division as it stood and that there would have had to have been some rearrangement; the same would be true if the share going to capital had not been an attractive investment. It might be argued with some cogency that the rapid pre-1914 expansion provided the boom conditions which enabled the expectations of both capital and labour to be fulfilled for a brief time, but the nature of the disputes reveal an uncommon identity of aspiration between the two. The only trace of a strike in the East Anglian drifting was April 1894 when boats engaged in the spring herring voyage protested against the low prices they received:

[The] ... lining boat owners of Shields and other northern ports have formed themselves into a combination, or 'ring', to use the modern slang term, with the object of getting the Spring herrings, which, as we have said, are principally used for bait, at as low a rate as possible. In order that this might be accomplished various buyers were invited to tender for the supply of herrings for bait, the contract being secured by Messrs. T. Brown and Sons of Lowestoft.[10]

The strike, then, was against a monopoly in the market which eliminated competitive bidding. The matter was settled after three days with the Shields Bait Association agreeing to a minimum price for herrings bought for bait. The structure of the dispute is similar to the effort of the trawlermen to break the monopoly of a few big buyers in the fish market: it was a joint defence by owners and crews of the market arrangements for their joint product. The industrial relations of the fishermen clearly reflect the material reality of their situation.

There were attempts to bring trade unionism to the fishermen. In late October 1904 the National Union of Smacksmen, Deckhands, Lumpers and Unskilled Labour sent down an organiser.[11] He was supported by two local businessmen. His initial meeting was chaired by Mr A. Adams (businessman, smack owner and leader of the Liberals) and Mr John Chambers (who had risen from workman to become a partner in the shipbuilding firm of Chambers and Colby) who stated that he would stand with Mr Picard, the trade union organiser, when he went to Lowestoft market because the Aberdeen fishermen had threatened to throw any union organiser in the dock. This effort disappears without trace and must be judged to have failed. There is no subsequent reference until February 1913 when a letter to the press stated categorically that there was not a seamen's union in Lowestoft.[12] The main content of the letter concerned the implementation of the insurance act which applied only to wage-earning fishermen. There was another attempt to unionise the area in November 1913 with meetings organised by the National Sailors' and Firemen's Union at Lowestoft and Yarmouth. The fact that they took place in the middle of November and that the speeches attacked the share system suggests that they were aimed at recruiting the herring fishermen in particular. This attempt at unionisation is reflected in the oral evidence:

Do you remember any strikes or stoppages before the First World War?
Strikes? No. But there was a union set up in Yarmouth. Yes. That was about – 1912 I think – they formed the union for the fishermen. And – I know there was one man, he was shipped to go in one vessel called the *Snowdrop*, and when he went down to work the skipper didn't want him, said that he'd shipped someone else. He went to the union and they told him to go down and report every day, he went down every day, and when the vessel made up he got his share. Mm, that was 1912 I think.
Did they sack him because they didn't want a union man?
No. I think they had got one too many [i.e. they signed one man too many]. (3013:27)

He goes on to say that he joined the union although he did not do anything active and that the union's main concern was about charges on the share system.

How effective this attempt at union might have been if sustained is impossible to assess because before the next Home Season arrived war had been declared and the East Coast fishing was in disarray. My own assessment is that it would have been no more successful than the 1904 attempt.[13] This view is based on the identity of interests being stronger than the points of conflict. The idea that outside organisers could generate militancy is to ignore the material conditions. Outside organisers with their experience and perspectives as well as their local immunity to victimisation could prove a crucial factor where discontent existed, but given the lack of conflict within the industry from the time the share system became general and the level of prosperity in 1913 it is difficult to see where the split between owners and crew was going to be opened. Local men had proved that they could organise and strike effectively when they felt a sense of grievance. But unless the material conditions were actually perceived as exploitative there would be little effective action. The arguments for non-conflictual relations within the industry are not, however, entirely based on an identity of interest, the share system or the superior level of income enjoyed by the fishermen; there are other aspects to be considered and it is to the next of those, relations at work, that we now turn.

4

Working relationships

Introduction

Physically and morally, it may be said that we all tread out our lives in the dust of past generations. But of none is this more true than of the working man. Owing to various causes, – frequent revolutions in mechanical processes, displacement of certain forms of industry, changes of domicile and position, emigration, etc., – oral tradition is with them at present singularly short-lived, and the leaders of today will often be ignorant of the labours of his immediate predecessors, even when following in their very footprints.

J.M. Ludlow and L. Jones 1867

So far the consideration of working relationships has not proceeded beyond examining the record of conflict. Only in one sub-section did this take the classic form of a union-backed strike against the employers. It is not sufficient, however, to let the analysis rest there. Explaining the absence of conflict is essentially a negative argument in so far as it tends to imply passivity through lack of any stimulus great enough to engender protest. But the interviews reveal that this generation of fishermen were a workforce with an immense amount of industrial pride and a deep identification with their work. Whether this was true of the Yarmouth strikers of 1887 is beyond recall. What is clear is that men who joined the industry only fifteen or twenty years after that strike were unaware that they were treading in the dust of effective union action. Indeed, the general tone of the interviews is either anti-union or dismissive of their relevance to the conditions in the industry. It might be recalled that the fleeters moved from Barking to Yarmouth and in the 1880s a proportion of the workforce were immigrants to East Anglia. One person interviewed was even born in Barking before her father moved, another had relatives there and the origins of many of the fishing families was very much a live tradition. It could be that they carried with them different industrial and social attitudes from the native East Anglians. My own view is that this may have affected activity in 1887 to some degree but that the crucial factor was the existence of a large employer and an identifiable exploiter. The accounts of the fishermen from the turn of the century demonstrate a set of industrial values which cannot be satisfactorily explained in terms of lack of traditions, of organisation, political awareness or any form of 'false consciousness': they shared the aims of their employers to an unusual degree.

This consciousness cannot be explained in terms of immediate employment alone. Entrants to the fishing industry had usually had a previous employment and in any case had been socialised for fifteen or sixteen years in a particular community. Relations at work are not shaped simply by industrial factors in a vacuum, the workforce enters it with many attitudes and expectations already shaped. Furthermore, relations at work are not simply between capital and labour, employer and employee, but between worker and worker, and this is particularly relevant where fellow workers are one's sole social contacts for much of the time and the workplace is also the place of residence. To deepen the understanding of the relations in the fishing industry two further aspects need consideration; first, the regional background as the standard of comparison for those in this particular industry and secondly, the actual relations at the workplace.

Regional context

It will be remembered that some ten years ago there was a serious difference of opinion between Lowestoft and Cornish fishermen ... Gunboats appeared on the scene, police were drafted in, but nothing disturbed the stolid East Anglians; they meant to have their six days a week, and rioting and disturbance could not stop them. This is the keynote of their character, a purposeful determination to carry out the end in view in face of all difficulties, and to this end, of all vessels afloat the Lowestoft man is the first to go to sea if the weather gives the least chance, and the last to leave off.

Joseph R. Bagshawe 1933

The East Anglian fishermen boast of their capacity to work harder than other fishermen and that fundamental orientation to work emerges from a specific regional identity. Norfolk and Suffolk were two of the English counties least changed by demographic growth. Between 1851 and 1911 Norfolk's population increased by 4 per cent, Suffolk's by 14 per cent, while the national increase was about 100 per cent. This stability was due to a lack of employment which forced a constant outflow of population. The two counties also had some of the lowest county percentages for incomers so the experience and identity of the population up to 1914 was unusually homogenous and, if not unique, at least of a particular kind.[1]

The working class of East Anglia was obliged to live and work for decades with a surplus of labour. Writing of a slightly earlier period the Hammonds remind us that it was not just a simple population loss but that 'Village society was constantly losing its best and bravest blood' (J.L. and B. Hammond 1948: 40). Certainly the demographic conditions placed the owners of land and capital in a particularly strong economic and social position: protesters and dissidents of whatever stamp could readily be dispensed with: those who found the power of the employers too irksome were obliged to move as were those who simply wished to improve their economic lot. It would be a mistake, however, to assume from the lack of formal organisation that the worker was entirely isolated, anomic and at the disposal of his masters. The East Anglian character, shaped by the above conditions, was close and underground, tenacious and obstinate; the rural worker would touch his cap with one hand and mulct his employer with the other. In an area of stable population people have a collective experience. There are shared norms about what is a fair day's work, the level of 'legitimate' perks and fiddles: these understandings provide a bedrock of resistance to exploitation while avoiding the victimisation of overt unionism. This type of consciousness, however, is one rooted in earlier and existing standards, it provides a poor basis from which to develop a struggle for improved conditions or a change in the system. Most employment in East Anglia was in small-scale concerns where the employer was a known and recognisable figure and this tended to personalise industrial issues. Employers were comparatively good or bad; the way to improve one's situation was to find a good employer. In other words dissatisfaction was expressed by changing one's employer rather than by attempting to change the system. As there was a large number of small employers the system was less visible than in an industrial area where the employment of thousands might be in the hands of one or two firms.

This structural aspect of their employment introduced a strong element of competitive individualism as a contradictory thread in the collective norms. Given a labour surplus and a great deal of direct supervision work had to be held through the employer's satisfaction in a face to face relationship. One need not resort to the protestant work ethic, internalised middle-class values or false consciousness to account for their work values. They came not from ideology but from a simple struggle to remain at home with family and friends as part of a known community. In the material conditions of the region a reputation as a poor workman could lead to a lack of employment with the consequent need to move or to decline into the semi-employed rural poor. To stay in one's community of origin one had either to be an exceptional worker or to establish a particularistic relationship with an employer based on deference. The worker who wished to remain at home and stay *independent* had to establish a reputation as a *worker* to secure employment on merit in the open market.

Both of these contradictory levels of consciousness can be seen in the consciousness and practices of the fishermen. The local trawlermen working the single-boating tended to establish their security through long-term particularistic relationships with one employer, and it has been shown that their workload was far lower than that of the driftermen and that the whole atmosphere of work was the conscientious care of fish, regularity and application. The driftermen were much more conscious of the need for sheer endurance of hard work. They relied on their reputation as *workers*, had no loyalty to an employer other than to seek the greatest reward. By working in the drifting they were enabled not simply to continue to reside in their own village but to do so at double the income of the local labourers and with four months' 'leisure' in the year. The acceptance of the competitive work ethic, plus the fortunate ability to endure exceptional labour, brought them very real psychological as well as material rewards.[2]

The comparative superiority of the fishermen's earnings can be fully appreciated only in context because local earnings were well below the national average. These local rates can be established with accuracy because just before the First World War there was a building boom in Yarmouth and Lowestoft and the unions became active and engaged on a number of strikes. In 1899 the Lowestoft plumbers called a meeting to urge carpenters and joiners to organise themselves because 'no one else can get higher wages until their rates move up'[3] and the carpenters, so unquestionably top of the wages hierarchy of skilled trades, were being paid 6½d. an hour. This, just to glance at the national context, a decade after the casuals at the London Docks had won their 6d. an hour. The Operative Bricklayers Union reported its members earning 5½d. an hour in 1897, building labourers 4d. These were *urban* rates. One informant (3005) from rural Norfolk claimed that around 1900 bricklayers in his village earned only 3d. an hour and if that seems unbelievably low his ability to recall other wages of the period with accuracy and the fact that he was an apprenticed bricklayer for eighteen months before breaking indentures to go to sea enhances his credibility. In Yarmouth wages were similar to Lowestoft although a strike in 1901 on one site won the carpenters a rise to 7½d. an hour. The boom appears to have been brief, for in 1904 the Yarmouth employers announced their intention of reducing carpenters' rates to 6½d. The best-paid men in Lowestoft were the shipbuilding workers. One informant (3020) stated that labourers were paid 18s. and craftsmen 26s. a week around 1900, another[4] stated that his father earned 21s. before 1914 as a machine operator, and together the two interviews give convincing skill differentials. The yard was fully unionised and a closed shop. If a court case from 1910 is at all typical men employed outside the arduous work of the shipyards earned even less, for it reported a ship's smith as earning 22s. a week.[5] Labourers' rates can be assumed from the 4d. to 5d. in the building trade. Lowestoft councillors heard a proposal in 1913 to raise their employees' wages by 1s. a week; rates were then 13s. to 15s. and the proposal was rejected. It had come as the result of the local Farmers' Federation's intention to raise farm workers pay from 12s. to 14s. a week.[6]

for regional urban work might even be generous: unskilled £34 to £39, semi-skilled £40 to £43 and skilled £57 to £67 a year. These are substantially lower than rates in the fishing industry, even though the averages in drifting include a great deal of teenage labour and the shore rates are for adult males only. As one informant said 'You were *very* lucky if you earned a pound a week before the war' – an experience that echoes Tressell's character Easton who '... knew that, taking good times with bad, his wages did not average a pound a week' (1965:48). The workforce in the seaside towns of East Anglia would have been quite at home in Mugsborough.

The fishermen had reason to view their own earnings with some satisfaction particularly as many of the driftermen who comprised the majority of the workforce were drawn from rural areas. The conditions of employment in the drifting section in particular linked work input with level of reward so justifying the local work ethic. This point will be elaborated in discussing crew relationships below.

It would take further research to generalise beyond the experience of the fishermen, but their evident satisfaction with their position compared to that of the mass of rural workers suggests an explanation for the paradox of a low level of unionism amongst most occupations in the area coexisting with the dogged unionism of rural Norfolk. Bitter experience had taught the agricultural worker that the rewards of hard work and loyal service brought little in terms of material reward, and where the level of exploitation was too blatant no amount of particularistic relations could mask it. Whereas those who moved into better paying occupations were only too conscious both of their relative good fortune and the numbers waiting to replace them if they jeopardised their job through protest.

Certainly as far as the fishing industry is concerned the work ethic not only brought results but with the rapid expansion of the industry it provided a ladder of achievement through to skipper and ownership.

Drifting

1912, 1913 was extraordinary good herring fishing. Germany and Russia was buying all the herring we caught, forced the price up. There was plenty in the sea and, the fishing chaps – we had about twenty-nine in our little village of a population of only about two hundred and ninety – they came home at Christmas with a little bag of golden sovereigns ... I could see that there was more money to be earned on the sea than on the land.

3011

As the routine of a drifter precluded spells at home during the voyage fishermen did not have to live near the port: many driftermen were recruited from the villages in the hinterland of Suffolk and Norfolk within a big oval arc from Southwold through Halesworth, Bungay, Norwich, Aylsham to Cromer. There is no doubt that money was the recruiting sergeant and informants relate how the high earnings of village fishermen attracted others. A large number of the driftermen were, therefore, resident in agricultural villages and started their working lives on the local farms. Their fathers were frequently farm workers although a number of them had also been fishermen at some period of their lives. This background has a bearing on the general perceptions and reactions of these men as 'fishermen'. They were used to outdoor work in conditions of endemic labour surplus when satisfying the employer was the only means of preserving employment; they made good recruits, therefore, to an occupation which was much harder than the worst of farm work: 'But you worked a lot of hours. When I first went I worked out what hours I was working – 'cos I'd been working sixty hours on the farm – and I suddenly found I was working a hundred. It's well – all you thought of was sleep' (3007:2). The incentive was the chance to earn in eight months twice as much as a farm worker would earn in a year, plus the added attractions of escape from the supervision and control of a small village. Those men who went into drifting then were something of a self-selecting group of exceptionally hard workers. Moreover, they found themselves in an industry which placed no artificial limits on their earning capacity nor on their opportunity to improve their status in the industry. As will be shown in the discussion on social class it was possible to rise to ownership, but here we are more narrowly concerned with the crew hierarchy, which was an open one.

- Most industries had entrenched skill and status barriers which served to exclude part of the workforce. The most common of these was the distinction between skilled and unskilled labour. There was no such simple division in the crew of a drifter, for there were no less than six gradations of earnings in the ten man crew. But if one rather arbitrarily decided that the skipper, mate and engineer were substantially better paid than the rest and could be considered an elite, the industry remained an open one. To become a skipper one had to pass a test controlled by the Board of Trade and that opportunity was open to anyone in the industry who had served the requisite number of years at sea. The oral evidence confirms that this was the fundamental situation. Of the owners' sons who went to sea 58 per cent became skippers or owners, of skippers' sons who went to sea 31 per cent and sons of crewmen 37 per cent.[7] Clearly the career prospects of crewmen's and skippers' sons was much the same. There is a substantial difference in the case of owners' sons but part of that increased percentage is caused by men who did not go to sea but approached ownership through their work in ancillary occupations such as ransackers or salesmen. Owners did have an advantage in that they could push their sons along and, providing they passed the Board of Trade examinations, give them the opportunity to act as skippers. Although it should be said that the East Anglian fishermen were almost unanimous in the view that kinship conferred few advantages. Individual career histories also confirm that sons normally did not sail with their fathers and the low proportion of joint ownership reveals that kinship was not a decisive factor.

The degree of flexibility between deck and engineroom was exceptional even by the standards of the fishing industry. Anyone entering the industry in East Anglia could become the engineer for engineroom positions were not the prerogative of men with engineering experience or craft training ashore. The lack of previous or formal engineering skills on the part of those men should be emphasised if only to distinguish local practice from that of the trawling industry of the Humber where the engineers were usually men who had served an engineering apprenticeship ashore. Perhaps as a mark of this distinction the engineer on a drifter was known as the 'driver' which rather nicely refused the skill/status label which that position did not hold. It might be added that even in the interwar period when there were steam trawlers operating from the East Anglian ports the same rather casual attitude to the skills of the 'chief engineer' is observable in the career of one of the fishermen interviewed (3024). He went to sea in 1907 as a lad on the drifters, changed to the sailing smacks and worked as a third hand from 1918 to 1931 in the same vessel before joining a steam trawler. At an unspecified date between 1931 and 1939 he became what was known as the 'deckie-engineer' as these small Lowestoft trawlers did not carry a full-time second engineer and then chief engineer. Had there been a labour force of skilled engineers available in the region doubtless a different pattern of recruitment, hierarchy and flexibility would have developed. This lack of initial specialisation mitigated intra-crew conflict as reported for the trawler industry of the Humber thus emphasising the importance of the regional context in occupational practice.

The owner had little effect on crew relationships unless he was an owner-skipper who worked the boat himself. Indeed, simply as an owner he would be in East Anglia while his boat was away for four months in the summer season. He selected the skipper, but the skipper selected the crew and worked the boat. The owner's main power was his right to terminate the voyage: this gave him the opportunity to end a season which was proving a financial loss, although I have found only one reference to this happening. The owner was under the same compulsion as the crew to continue working through bad spells in the hope that the final few weeks of the season would retrieve the situation.

The potential point of conflict between the owner and crew came at pay-off. The amount of conflict, or even the existence of a sense of grievance, is variously reported. Some informants when asked if the owners fiddled the expenses claim that they could not as the crew knew what they were, and anyway the owners were honest; others said that the owners were twisters and of course they fiddled and overcharged. This total lack of agreement is in itself instructive. For given the number of different employers and the differing levels of personal integrity and/or pressures resulting from personal finances actual practice probably did vary widely from case to case.

The timing of this point of potential overt conflict between owners and men served to defuse the clash of interest. The end of a long season of intensive work away from home, the prospect of receiving a large sum of money, the relief from effort and the prospect of a few weeks of relaxation and leisure invests any seaman's pay-off day with a festive air. This was symbolically acknowledged by the bottle of rum on the pay-off table and the tot that each man drank with, or at least on, the owner. Men were anxious to collect their money, have a few drinks together and to go home. The atmosphere was against the sort of sustained collective effort that would be needed to have enforced any reform or demand that might have been desirable. After the autumn fishing which ended in December most drifters from Yarmouth did not work again until May, by which time most men were anxious to get a 'berth' and had neither the inclination nor the funds to sustain industrial action.

Where there were over 300 employers in one area alone comparisons between the quality of employers were bound to be a matter of comment, and discontent personalised into good and bad employers. The self-evident response was to change employers rather than to attack the system: faults in the system were simply less visible anyway if some employers were believed to be working it fairly. That there are good and bad in all walks of life was a widespread piece of folk wisdom, the structure of the working conditions in the fishing industry did nothing to alter that perception to one of a conflict of class interests.

The relationship between owners and skippers was a matter of personal negotiation and depended upon the skipper's record, successful men being granted the choice of new vessels and being powerful enough to ignore direct orders:

> We came out of the *Ocean Searcher*, we had her new and went down to the Shetlands, when we came home we waited for a fortnight for the *Ocean Plough* to be finished. Well we went to sea, we ran the trial. And so of course – they always had plenty of whisky and beer aboard when they ran the trial so we were all half drunk. So old Bloomfield [managing-owner] he came down to the quay and he said to Old Wee 'You won't go to sea tonight will you William. That's no use going now tonight.' He hadn't left the quay five minutes when Old Wee said 'Put the lights up! We'll go!'[8]

The owner's reluctance to allow a brand new ship to be taken to sea by a drunken crew long after the favourable time for fishing had passed can be understood. Apart from the unusual drunkenness the incident is typical of the oral evidence in that stories about owners usually refer to them urging caution on the skipper and crew such as pressing them to have a night in if the weather was threatening. Boats worked close to port and could usually run for harbour if gales became too fierce; but such weather and action often meant that nets were damaged or lost. The loss of hundreds of pounds worth of nets fell on the owner, whereas fishing in bad weather held the attraction of abnormally high prices for the crew which was willing to take a risk. It was the skipper not the employer who exercised authority over the crew, indeed it was the skippers who commanded the loyalty of crews and it was they who were responsible for hiring and firing men. Recruitment took place through an informal network. At the end of the season the skipper would ask those men he wanted if they were willing to sail again the next season and received assent from those that were. This would then leave several weeks for skippers to fill the gaps in their crews and for crewmen who wanted a change to find a new skipper. It was here that a fisherman's reputation as a worker was important to him, although friendship links were also relevant where men lived together for long periods.

Relations at work were particularly intense because earnings were collective, therefore everyone had to pull their weight and feel that others did the same. These workmates were also domestic partners in cramped quarters. In such a situation personal conflicts could totally destroy the working morale of a crew. The interview evidence indicates that there was rarely conflict on a drifter and this was doubtless due in no small part to the mechanism of self-selectivity by the men themselves which would serve to exclude unsuitable temperaments.

In his study of trawling Tunstall (1962) identified two scapegoats in the crew, the cook and the deckboy. On the drifters these two positions were combined, and yet the overwhelming evidence from personal experience is that boys were not scapegoats and that crews did work as a unity from top to bottom:

Did they tease the boys when you first went to sea?
No. A lot of rubbish whoever told you that. They might have a laugh and joke with you but they were all willing to help you. In fact one old hand, the hawseman, used to turn out early Sunday morning, make two big dumplings and help me fry the eggs and bacon for breakfast, watched me all the Sunday making us food. He'd … make rice pudding for dinner and a cake. I don't say they are all like that, 'cos they weren't. But the crowd I had they'd always be round you. Well, they knew my father and that, like you see. (3008:35)

In most accounts it is apparent that the boys came from the same communities as the men and often sailed with family friends, and this was an important factor in their treatment. In one account where the informant did feel ill-used the mechanism was quite blatant:

They were quite rough on boys were they?
Oh, one or two was. One of the crew was always getting at me. Always. Until – as I learned afterwards – the skipper said to him 'Do you know who that boy's father is?' After that that man treated me the best. Because they didn't like to hear of John. Because my father – he'd murder you with one hand behind him. He was a tough hand my father. So, after a few weeks things began to get a bit brighter along of me. (3065:61)

Even so, it is noticeable that the skipper intervened with the deliberate intention of preventing what he felt to be excessive bullying.

Unlike the response of the cooks the food seems to have been very standardised. While fishing, herring were the stable breakfast – six to nine a man being normal amounts – and the main meal at midday was almost invariably stewed beef with root vegetables, potatoes and Norfolk dumplings. Tea was a scratch meal of the remains of the midday meat with bread and cheese or jam. Tea seems to have been drunk more or less *ad lib*. There were small differences, for example, in Scotland where boats could not fish at weekends some skippers would limit expenses by putting aside salt herrings for Sunday breakfast, others would treat the crew to bacon and eggs. Tunstall[9] has pointed out that very marginal differences could make a large difference in perception and this was undoubtedly true:

But he was the best man to feed the crew that ever I was with. There was ten of you and you used to get an eleven pound boiling of beef a day, so that's just over a pound say.

Was the food more up to the skipper than the company then?
The skipper'd get what he liked. You had to pay for it, they didn't care what you had
you see, 'cos that all came out of expenses. The better you lived the less money you
had to take. (3005:14)

Food was plain and plentiful and the fishermen ate on a scale which would
be envied by many working-class people of the period. There was a tempta-
tion for the skipper-owner to be mean because it did increase his share of the
gross as owner. But there was always the effect of group pressure and
expected norms:

Now there were three brothers, they all had boats each. Well, I was along with one
he wouldn't hardly let you have any grub at all. He was properly mingy. Now, the
other two brothers were just the opposite, you could have what you liked. I went on
the Home Fishing with him and we never had enough food hardly to work with.
Herring. We used to eat them. And I remember he said to me after we paid off – *and
we done well* – all right for next year? I said, *no*, I don't want no more of you mate! Oh
no, no. Well there were a lot of people done that to him, they wouldn't go with him.
Well that's alright isn't it? I don't care how you live aboard the boat – I've heard it
before when you go to the pay quay – your expenses are hardly no more than one
that lived well. (3015:40)

It might be assumed that a skipper's willingness to run up expenses would
depend to some extent on his reputation with the owner. In theory, at least,
a mean skipper could find a crew that would be happy to sail with him
provided that they all perceived the economising on food bills as making a
worthwhile contribution to the final pay-off. But in the above case even a
successful voyage could not compensate for unfulfilled expectations on
victualling.

Actual spacial conditions on board the vessel never arose in the interviews as
a matter of complaint. Conditions were cramped and primitive – the only
washing and toilet facilities were ordinary buckets – but they were an
improvement on the old sailing vessels, and each generation of steam vessels
tended to have slightly better accommodation than the previous one. In any
case conditions were seen as being limited by the size and function of the
vessel and not as the fault of the owners. Having only two cabins, drifters are
too small perhaps to be analysed in terms of allocation of accommodation
according to status and crew specialisation. It may be that on larger ships
space was allocated according to status but this was not so on a drifter. The
smaller forward cabin was occupied by four junior deckmen while the rest,
including the cook, slept in the after cabin. But this cabin was also used as
the space where all the crew ate their meals, thus retaining crew unity. In fact
the allocation of space on any ship might be governed more by common

sense than by sociological reasoning, with space being used to separate watch from watch and daymen from watchmen.[10] This was not possible with only two cabins but it is noticeable that the four men in the forward cabin were the one group which would normally share the same working and sleeping periods.

Within the crew the skipper's formal authority was always balanced by his need to live and work with the same crew for a long period. A man who was abusive and unpleasant, or who was not very successful, faced the problem of finding good men to sail with him. The balance of power between skipper and crew would, to some extent, depend on the wider labour market. There are indications in the interviews that in the interwar years when the industry was contracting skippers did become more overbearing and tyrannical, just as those informants who were still working as skippers in the post Second World War period state that good men became so scarce that they dare not complain about crew behaviour. This suggests that it is not the formal contractual situation that determines power in these situations, but the actual labour market. The skipper did not have to drive the men to work. They worked hard because they were their own paymasters and were united in their pecuniary motivation. In their accounts 'work' and 'money' become virtually interchangeable terms:

Oh yes, well among the crew they all seemed competitive – you understand what I mean – they all wanted to be up the top. In regards catching and earning the money. Everybody was all out for that before the First World War. See, we have been running ten nights on the run – right straight off without having a rest – landing hundred cran, eighty cran, all the weights, every day. Away again. Shooting. (3013:30)

The work could be very severe and most of the interviews contain at least one epic account of work, of which we will give but one example (it has been considerably shortened and as such lacks much of the sense of achievement and genuine drama of the original):

Saturday ... we went and we shot over the Knoll, we got 108 cran of herring, we came in the Sunday noon time and they were sold for £100 – which was a decent run you see. We went to sea again that day and were in on the Monday with 60 cran. And we came in every day that week with herring. All the week, hardly any sleep you know. And the Friday, I remember, the boy he was then going to cook the dinner, he was clearing up the breakfast and he sat and cried. He was only sixteen year old. The skipper came along and said, the boy's done in can you manage on bread and cheese for dinner? We said yes, and he told the boy to turn in. The Saturday morning we again hauled 130 crans, there was a glut at Yarmouth, we made £60 – for 130 crans! We finished at eleven o'clock at night and went down to have our dinner and the mate flopped out like this. He was a man of fifty years old. The ambulance came down and took him – we took a new mate, a young chap, and went off to sea the Sunday morning and we hauled 70 cran. And then when we had hauled the skipper said, salt them, I'm not going in, all the Scotchmen will be coming out and there'll be a crush ... any rate that was about midnight when we got squared up. The skipper [said] go down I'll keep watch. So we turned in. Four o'clock he called us out and we went to work. We hauled 70 cran out of those nets ... (3007:36–7)

The story covers about ten days in which they often had four hours or less sleep a day. But while the 'luck' was in a crew would not ease up. A season's earnings could be made in a single brief spell if only the crew could stand the pace: it was at those times that a total commitment to work was essential. Only self-exploitation can extract work at that pace. In the season of 1913 one Yarmouth drifter was grounded and lost on the Scroby Sands because the two men on deck had fallen asleep at their work and the skipper had fallen asleep at the wheel.[11] The wreck of the 'Sleeping Drifter' was a visible reminder of the pressures of herring fishing.

The collective commitment is reflected in the urgency with which the crew would push the skipper on:

That's right, yes. We were keen for the job. If somebody got more herring than we did, we would want – aboard our boat anyhow – Go! Move skipper! Go! Yes. And very often sit there getting your dinner and [mimes falling asleep]. Oh, that was a laborious job you know, hauling and – and shaking like that – now you'd got to have a *team* for that. (3013:31)

You'd got to be very hard working. I was big work anywhere I went, I had no rest in me. I must be a-doing ...
But say a bloke is a bit lazy or doesn't want to turn out?
You chuck 'em out. Sack 'em. *Move.* That's only one thing you can do. I believe that every time, a man ain't no use, don't carry him, don't carry him. (3007:51)

That last man also related how this pressure to keep working acted directly on the skippers: 'I left this boat through the skipper stopping ashore a couple of nights, he went on the booze, we was laid in, five of us left the crew, we didn't like losing the nights you see' (3007:35). Given this work/money orientation of the crew and the cooperative social identity which was necessary to operate successfully, the crew member who complained of conditions during the course of a voyage was liable to get scant solidarity or sympathy from the rest. Given the circumstances of drifting the militant was easily perceived as a 'moaner' as the social identity superseded the industrial one. This was no doubt doubly true where the skipper was also owner or part-owner. There was no way of attacking the system, either in particular or general, without denigrating the achievements and status of the group leader who was part of the social collective. It was not a case of a militant worker attacking 'them' because 'they' were sharing the same work, risks and conditions. Issues which could be voiced within the social network of the crew were very limited indeed.

Trawling

They got so they walked out and wouldn't go to sea. But they didn't used to call 'em strikes, 'cos it was no unions, nothing of that. Every man had to fight for himself. And if they [owners] had a man who they wanted to go to sea, they'd push out another man, give that man the sack.

> 3018:29

The pattern of work in trawling, with vessels home for a night every week, meant that recruitment was centred on Lowestoft. Some were recruited as lads from the villages close by but they tended to be drawn into Lowestoft on marriage:

They used to go for a week, but if they came in – let us say they came in on a Wednesday night, they had to go to sea next morning. And I lived then at Oulton Broad, and my husband – there was no buses, no nothing running those days – my husband had to walk from Lowestoft trawl market to Oulton Broad. Emily Cottages. He just used to get home, have a good wash, have a meal, get to bed, he'd get up the next morning and walk back. I never saw my husband no more. (3018:5–6)

We left Borough St Peter when I was seven years old. Because at that time of day fishermen were scattered all over the countryside – my father happened to live right out in the country which meant a six mile walk there and back. (3012:1)

Clearly there were advantages in living as near to the fish dock as possible and the life histories show a tendency for trawlermen to move into Lowestoft, whereas driftermen, with their different employment pattern, tended to stay in their village of origin.

In Lowestoft the harbour was unenclosed and was a great playground for local boys and fishing was a highly visible occupation. The informants who spent their boyhood in the port claimed that they knew every smack in the harbour by name and number and the skipper and mate of it, if not all the crew. They could earn a penny 'running up a smack' which consisted of being the first one to run to the fisherman's home address to tell his wife that her husband was approaching the harbour and would be home that day. In many ways the industry was its own source of recruitment. Also there were few other industries:

See, you could either go errand boy for about eighteen pence a week or go to sea. 'Course that was a big job at that time of day, old dear, two or three hundred smacks. And the job was, the men what were skippers and had children, well they used to –

practically all of 'em used to go to sea for a week when they had their summer holidays see. And that's how it came about, when they got old enough. 'Course into the fishing industry they went. (3020:15)

This custom of taking boys to sea was widespread and other members of the crew would do it as well as the skipper, although it had to be with his consent. This was done for a mixture of reasons and not always with the unalloyed enthusiasm of the boy concerned. It was at times a disciplinary measure to keep an older boy who was a trouble to his mother under his father's thumb and out of trouble for a while. Recruitment, then, seems to have been very much due to socialisation within the fishing community rather than the more clearly defined pecuniary reasons which attracted youths from non-fishing backgrounds into the drifting industry. There was, too, a certain pride in being a smacksman. Even in the period before 1914 the large trawling smack was becoming something of an anachronism and the men were not unaware that they were part of an occupation which was viewed with admiration by holiday visitors and even within the fishing fraternity:

Were fishermen's clothes very distinctive in those days?
Well, you wouldn't know. Only Lowestoft men. You'd know a Lowestoft man because he used to have a long tan jumper on and a pair of high heeled boots. Used to think a bit more of themselves than the Yarmouth men did, we used to take away a best suit with us, but they never did. It's very rare you'd see them dressed up – they were clean, and they nearly always had earrings. (3008:35)

The smacksmen became more of a romantic anachronism during the 1920s and 1930s and part of their self-image stems from their memories of that period, but even the other fishermen recognised the smacksman as the fisherman with *real* skills.

On the whole sailing the smacks was seen as a positive pleasure. Accounts given fifty or more years after the event are open to the charge that retrospection has added a charm which did not exist at the time and that the informants' view of their past events has been distorted by the general nostalgia for the romance of sail.[12] To reject the idea that there was a positive satisfaction derived from this aspect of the work would be to ignore one dimension of their work simply to avoid the charge of romanticism:

And then I moved into the *Nil Desperandum*. She was a ship to sail she was. When we used to get out [of harbour] clear of the buoys it was the deckie's job to look out 'til dinner time, that might be one or two o'clock. I used to go through the fleet with her. I used to say to the skipper I'm going to catch that one there, he'd say, you won't catch him. 'Course I used to niggle it up to the wind so we come to the wind of 'em – and when I got through to pass one of 'em [the other skipper would wave his fist]. Oh you bugger, you took the wind out of our sails. But – she would sail, and I *loved sailing*. I really used to enjoy it. She had a big iron tiller and when she was trimmed that would swing like that – and you didn't need hardly touch it. She was perfectly balanced. (3014:12)

Accounts like this placed in the very specific context of a particular ship and crew position carry the stamp of an accurate recollection. Many of the men who sailed the smacks recount at least one particular incident, such as a fast passage, which suggests that the skill needed and exercised in handling these craft imparted a very real sense of achievement at the time.

Not that one has to rely on this rather abstract satisfaction to account for recruitment: the section on shares established that the smacksmen were well paid by local standards and a lad could be a deckie on 15s. a week plus stocker and his keep from about the age of sixteen. For young, unmarried men that gave them a wage above that of an adult labourer and far more than they could have earned as a youth in other occupations.

In trawling the owner was a much more prominent and visible figure who would come down to the docks when the smack berthed to supervise its speedy return to sea:

Would you call the boat-owners middle or upper class?
Well – no, no, that was just the middle class, they had to work. They'd work with you, they'd come and pack your fish and everything. There was no swanking. Once they'd seen you – then they wanted to get rid of you again, be catching some more. *They were quite hard?*
They were hard, yes. Yes, you'd have to go to sea.
Would they sack you easy enough?
Oh yes. Had to do as they told you or – out. Or get out. (3036:44–5)

The general atmosphere is one of hard-driving by the owners. The low profit margin of the smacks meant that most owners helped with the manual work and got the smack back to sea as quickly as possible. That they were always present meant that they exercised their formal power over the skipper and his crew. Men seeking employment would approach them directly. This undoubtedly meant that there was less cohesion and sense of unity in a trawler crew than in the drifters. They had neither work autonomy nor even a common aim. The three junior crewmen were on fixed wages and indifferent to the financial outcome of the voyage save in so far as owners would sometimes stop a smack working for a period if it did not earn enough money. The skipper and mate as sharemen had a common purpose and it is noticeable that these two often formed a stable partnership, but they were looked upon as chargehands by the rest of the crew.

Living accommodation on the smacks was as crude or cruder than on the drifters and all lived together in one cabin aft. Once again the boy was the cook, and smacks took five or six joints of beef and the vegetables for the main meal; small fish were cooked for breakfast and tea was a cold meal, the victualling being similar to the drifting. The actual conditions aboard the smacks are difficult to establish and the data does not allow any simple generalisation:

They used to eat like elephants old fellow. See there used to be the skipper, mate and third hand at the first sitting, they'd go and eat first and what was left the poor bloody cook and deckie had – if there was any. You didn't get a bloody lot. You didn't carry above five or six loaves of bread, well that was gone in a couple of days when you used to revert back to the hard tack, bloody great biscuits. There was weevils used to run out as big as your finger. And bugs. Dear oh dear. They used to eat you up alive. Bloody straight, 'cor dear, were there bugs! There was millions of the sods. Bloody rats. 'Cor there was hundreds of the buggers. And these old boys used to chew tobacco – spit over everywhere. (3020:23–4)

That is one extreme description, and about the only one to rate the food as bad or inadequate, but even the next informant, who experienced a very different standard, agreed that the smacks all had fleas and bugs aboard even though they were fumigated once a year:

But – as I say, it was hard work. I know every time the ship was coming home you had to make the ship spick and span. The deckhand used to have to go all the way round the inside of the bulwarks, which was painted green mostly, with whelk spawn and fine cinder ash to take all the muck, grime and stuff off to make them look fresh and clean. The third hand and the mate had their job, that was to clean the boiler. Of course we couldn't afford Brasso or things like that, so they used to clean the black part with engine oil and soot – and fine powder, like bathbrick powder to clean all the brasswork. That was their job. The cook, he had to go round every panel, and scrub the floors, the cabin and the lockers – all before he got into harbour, perhaps that's six or seven hours to do. That was done every trip so that ship was spick and span for the owner to see when they came in the harbour. (3012:42–3)

The amount of effort expended on keeping a vessel clean and the amount of pride taken in keeping the living space comfortable obviously varied.

As was described in chapter 2 the trawlermen had a regular work rhythm and handled comparatively light catches. Men could be sacked or leave every five days and although crews appear to have been more stable than trawlermen of the Humber[13] the interviews do reveal that there was less crew unity. They were not 'co-venturers' as were the driftermen but workers in a steady job which was quite well paid by local standards in an area with few alternatives. These issues are pursued in the context of the general conclusion to this chapter.

Conclusion

To the people involved relations of work thus appear as the relations of
production.

G.M. Sider 1976

The foregoing analysis of the work situation shows that fishermen were
subject to a particularly intense set of work relations. That it was this which
accounts for the low incidence of industrial conflict receives crucial support
from a comparison with the Scottish drifter industry. Before presenting
this, however, it is worth considering the conditions of employment as they
relate to Tunstall's classic study and to wider issues in labour history. Part of
Tunstall's explanation for the weak trade unionism, insecurity and lack of
solidarity of the fishermen lies in their being casual labour. In this he follows
a widely held objection to casual labour, the reasons for which are typified in
the historical consciousness by the example of dock labour. By Tunstall's
criteria the East Anglian fishermen were even more casual than those of
Hull, for they could be dismissed in forty- eight hours and as they were at sea
only five days that was the effective length of their tenure.

In my view it is far too simplistic to accept that all systems of casualisation
are against the employees' interests. Until recent times few manual workers
have had the right to more than a few hours' notice, even salaried workers
often had only a month's notice; indeed outside of university walls permanence of employment was rare. But the actual security enjoyed by different
occupations at different points in time has varied widely according to
industrial and social assumptions and practices.

It is noticeable that many employers have set a high value on continuity of
service and rewarded it with everything from gold watches to extra holidays.
In many situations labour turnover is counterproductive. That employers
have valued long service should lead labour historians to view it with some
caution. The important issue is not the actual contractual position of the
workforce but how the system worked in practice. It is noticeable that in fact
Tunstall does not establish that the system in Hull worked to the advantage
of the employers. Indeed, he states that the opposition of the men prevented
a system of decasualisation and he always discusses the coming and going of
labour in terms of the men exercising their choice to miss a trip rather than as
the employers dismissing men, except in the case of skippers. They were
quickly demoted if they had poor catches although they would usually be
given another command when someone else failed to have good catches.
But it should be emphasised that 'by annual incomes at the time of their
highest earnings most skippers come in the top one percent of incomes in
Britain' (Tunstall 1962:216) and that this was not only big money in

absolute terms but gave them tremendous differential over the rest of the crew. The one justification for this accepted by the fishermen was that a good skipper ensured their own earnings, and it was not only the owners who wanted to get rid of unsuccessful skippers. The fact that such a plum job was not held as a 'regular' appointment might have been viewed as less than an unmitigated disaster by those fishermen waiting for the opportunity to become skippers.

One might agree with Tunstall that in most cases casualisation was bad for solidarity but once again the interesting thing is that the men wanted to work under a system of casual employment. In the case of the fishermen one cannot overlook the importance of the social element of their work. Personal disagreements can be unpleasant in most work circumstances: aboard a small vessel they could be psychologically insupportable for a long period. Men who did not get on together or who felt physically threatened solved these pressures by leaving. Any system of long-term contracts and a bureaucratic allocation of jobs would have caused much greater personal conflict at sea. Troubles were dealt with through the mechanism of 'casualisation' and we have shown that this pressure was not always from the top down. Fishing earnings were collective and there was a set amount of labour to be performed by the crew collectively; if a man was slow at gutting fish it did not affect his employer at all, it simply meant that the other members would have to gut that many more before they could all go below for food and rest. The 'work-shy', 'moaners' and similar identities as perceived by the crew were ejected by group pressures not employer exploitation.

It is noticeable that the worst brutality had been towards apprentices. They were a permanent workforce and the trouble was that the process of self-selection that such a severe occupation requires could not take place. Boys who found the life intolerable were obliged to continue with it: the skipper and crew allocated an unsuitable boy would, after spending hours of cold and exhausting labour, go below expecting a hot meal and warm cabin to find neither because the boy was seasick or incompetent: a situation bound to lead to frayed tempers. That the violence was not the result of the general hardships of fleeting is established by the lack of cases of brutality from the East Anglian fleets which had no apprentices. Unsuitable boys would not be taken on a second trip and only those who could adapt to the life would continue in it: the Grimsby apprentices would have found casualisation a positive boon. It would have undoubtedly given them a bargaining power which permanence could not.

The lack of militancy and the weak trade unionism of the fishermen can be more convincingly ascribed to their direct experience of the workplace. An important part of that was the mixture of autonomy and of powerlessness. This was particularly so on the drifters away from their home port for several weeks. Within the conventions of the industry they exercised control of where and when they fished, there was no employer to supervise their activities. Whether they had a successful voyage did not depend in any way on the actions of their employer, what they earned was due to their own skills and effort; and, of course, due to their luck in being struck by the shoals of herring. If they were not successful and did not earn much money they did not perceive the remedy to be in the hands of their employer; after all, if they failed to catch fish he also suffered. One of the essential elements of militancy is the ability to perceive precisely who is responsible for the conditions that one would change. But 'to the people involved relations of work thus appear as the relations of production' and through their relations they perceived their direct employer as a fellow victim of circumstances rather than the author of them. If they perceived a cause of their hardships it was in the impersonal workings of the market and they accepted as self-evident that fish could be caught only if they were there and could be sold only at the prices people would pay. Within their direct perceptions of industrial realities no one was responsible and it would have taken a change in wider social and political perspectives to have changed these industrial attitudes.

Within East Anglia the only system of employment to give rise to trade unionism was fleeting where one employer was identifiable as setting the terms and conditions of employment. There were strikes too in drifting when employers and employees bargained over the price to be fixed per last of fish caught: there is no record of conflict once this was changed to both sharing the market price. I have argued that this was due to the subsequent inability of the fishermen to perceive their employers as responsible for those market conditions and feeling powerless in the face of them. Comparison with the Scottish East Coast drifting industry which, although broadly similar to the East Anglian one, had different industrial relations supports this supposition.

The similarities lay in their working the same fishing grounds, with identical gear and earning about the same income. The crucial differences lay in the fact that fisherman-ownership was more widespread in Scotland with up to six owners for each vessel and with that multiple-ownership more frequently organised around kinship links. Yet it was in this context that the intense activity of the Hired Men's Union of 1913 took place. It is interesting that militancy was created among the family-owned boats of Scotland rather than the more commercial and individual ownership of East Anglia. Clearly any assumption that small ownership is the key to good relations between master and man is by no means a safe one. The reason why there was a high level of kinship in ownership in one area and not the other is, perhaps, a separate issue, but one worth brief speculation. It would seem that the material difference in resources between the two areas was the main cause. In East Anglia most of the drifters laid up between December and May. A single-owner would pay off the crew and have no more 'out-goings' save his own until the start of the next season. If the season had been a poor one the crew would be obliged to resort to the Parish rather than to capital assets for support. The inability to 'sack' kin from a joint enterprise could, in these circumstances, be a disadvantage to the accumulation of capital.

In Scotland there was a season of line fishing during the period when there was no herring fishing. This required a smaller crew, six instead of ten, but it did create employment for kin throughout the year. Indeed, if a boat was not to risk being left shorthanded during this arduous winter fishing, capital needed to be certain of the services of men committed to working. In this situation collective ownership provided an industrial solution to the labour supply problem while kinship links reduced the fragmentation and diffusion of capital. The extra men needed for the herring seasons were recruited from the West of Scotland; that they were from a different community made it easier to discharge them at the end of the season without social conflict. This system meant that it was difficult, if not impossible, for an outsider to aspire to positions of authority and through them to ownership. The long-term prospects of about a third of the work-force did not extend beyond seasonal employment in the lower crew positions. The unity of expectations, opportunities and values was split, the family-owners were perceptibly the cause of, and gainers from, this system. As such they were the focus of militant action.

Quite clearly, the wider distribution of capital in Scotland did not succeed in diffusing conflict in the same manner as the East Anglian system of commercial and individual owners. This indicates the importance of the distribution of ownership and the social images associated with it, and Part two addresses itself to these issues.

The social structure

5

The concept of community

In no section of our population is heredity of occupation so rigidly preserved as amongst our fishermen; they are a class apart, intermarrying, having their own peculiar customs, modes of life and thought, and mixing but little with people outside their own little communities.

Duke of Edinburgh 1883

The above quotation emphasises both the occupational and residential aspects contained in the concept of community: it is rather ironical that it comes from an article which establishes that the high death rate amongst East Coast fishermen at that time was due to the system of fleeting which at Grimsby employed hundreds of apprentices and ex-apprentices drawn from workhouses all over England and whose lives had no connection with the occupational or residential world of their parents. That was, perhaps, something of an exceptional phenomena, and fishing areas have usually recruited local labour or migrant fishermen and might in general be considered traditional communities.

The essence of 'community' is that it is a self-enclosed occupational and social world, but more than that it was a single-stratum world, and earlier commentators (Jenkins, cited in chapter 1, expressed concern that the 'community' would be split into 'employers' and 'employees') saw the widespread ownership of capital as the keystone of this community. This view was supported in a more recent essay which argued that 'community' existed in the traditional inshore and drifter industries but that trawling created a new class of fishermen 'so different from those of the boat-owning or sharing, village-dwelling hereditary fishermen'.[1] On the other hand it is precisely these town-dwelling trawlermen which some contemporary sociologists perceive as near-perfect exemplars of occupational community: '... and the studies of Hull fishermen by Duncan, Horobin and Tunstall match the criteria exactly, and if it is supposed that to qualify as an occupational community the social relations among workers must meet all three criteria unequivocally, coalmining and trawl-fishing may be unique'.[2]

The three criteria are those defined by Blauner (1975) and we will return
to his view in more detail below. The main criteria are that men (*sic*)
socialise off the job and that workplace relationships pattern non-work
behaviour. In other words the pattern of social community is determined
by the occupational conditions of the male workforce.

That there is such fundamental disagreement on which aspects of
experience create a 'community' even within one industry points to the
difficulties in using the concept for there is 'serious conceptual disagreement about whether the community is a geographical area, or a sense of
belonging, or non-work relations and so on'.[3] The substantial issues
concerned in establishing the criteria for defining the boundaries of a
community are discussed in detail by Bell and Newby (1971) and are too
extensive to be rehearsed here. My concern is with those aspects relevant
to the main purpose of this study. That concern is with work experience
and its link with the residential community ashore regardless of how that
might be delineated.

My own view is that the concept of community has little analytical
value, however it is defined.[4] One of the most detailed attempts to use the
concept as an explanatory variable is by S.M. Lipset who suggests that the
large and important role played by the printers' 'occupational community'
is the main determinant of the high level of democratic procedures in the
union organisation.[5] He claims that the individual worker is more
involved in his work than the worker who lacks 'occupational community',
and as a result of this higher level of involvement he participates more
actively in the affairs of his trade union. As this involvement is held to
check oligarchic and communistic control Lipset is in favour of 'occupational community' and the concept is normative as well as explanatory.
The factors which actually compose an occupational community are only
briefly described. The two major factors are the high status of the printers
compared with other manual work and the irregular hours of their
employment. Because of their status printers prefer to associate with other
printers or higher status occupations, their irregular hours mean that they
are at work and at leisure at different times from the wider society and are,
therefore, more likely to share their social life with workmates who share
the same structure of employment.

In one brief footnote Lipset undermines his own argument. In
commenting on other industries which are also occupational communities
(which incidentally raises the query as to why the printers should be 'the
one permanently deviant case among American Unions') he states of the
longshoremen: 'The East Coast Union is one of the worst dictatorships in
American unionism, whereas the West Coast Union, though Communist-

controlled on the international level, is very democratic.' But according to his own analysis the crucial difference in creating this extremely sharp distinction between the two unions is not 'occupational community', but the structure of the industry. On the West Coast all the men were employed on a rota system and no favouritism by either employers or union officials was possible, whereas on the East Coast 'the hiring boss, who is often the union official' (Lipset 1956:132), selected the men according to his own inclination. Under such *market conditions* the East Coast men were obliged to support the existing 'oligarchy' in order to secure employment. Given that these extremes of union democracy could flourish in one occupational community it is difficult to view it as a crucial determinant.

Robert Blauner's development of the concept emphasised the importance of 'work satisfaction' rather than the status as defined by wider society and is more useful in looking at the experience of the fishermen. His observations that 'For its members the occupation itself is the reference group: its standards of behaviour, its system of status and rank, guide conduct' and that 'in such worlds one's skill and expertise in doing the actual work becomes an important basis of individual status and prestige'[6] isolated major factors in the social perceptions of the East Anglian fishermen. They do not give much salience to the status system of non-fishermen and this may explain their lack of conflict imagery. But his approach remains essentially descriptive rather than explanatory for his factors apply equally well to occupational communities such as mining where conflict is an essential part of the experience.

Allcorn and Marsh (in Bulmer 1975) identify dock workers, railwaymen, shipbuilding workers and steel workers as industries coming closest to being occupational communities after coalmining and trawling. But once one moves into these multicraft industries it is not clear whether it is *occupation* or *industry* that is being identified. Shipbuilding workers, for example, have manifested bitter inter-occupational conflicts over demarcation lines in spite of their shared sociability and wider solidarity. It is an example which could be multiplied. Allcorn and Marsh identify further aspects of the concept, among which earnings, method of pay, small group control of the workplace and the role of formal organisations are particularly relevant to the fishermen:

In printing it would seem that to imagine the removal of the Chapel and the multifarious activities associated with it would leave virtually nothing of the occupational communities which have been described, whereas in fishing the sudden disappearance of the Fishing section of the TGWU would leave the occupational community virtually intact. (Bulmer 1975:211)

It has already been shown that the community of the East Anglian
fishermen did not depend on formal organisation and we will go on to
show that there was a shared social identity. It has already been demonstrated that even within one section of the industry at one time union
activity and strike action occurred according to the action of the employers. It was not changes in the community which caused this activity
and one of the dangers of concentrating on the occupational features of
the workers is that it tends to overlook the changing structure of capital
and the prevailing market forces in the search for an ahistorical set of
'values'.

As much of the concern with communities stems from an interest in the
sources of solidarity and wider class consciousness it would appear more
constructive to study these directly, for what the concept of community
lacks is a satisfactory explanatory link between the industrial values of the
workplace and their transfer to the residential milieu. It might be argued
that the common economic experience of a pit village or single industry
town creates a shared material experience for families based on male
occupation, but this would hardly explain the existence of community
networks in mixed occupational areas where personal fortune is more
varied. I would argue that the greater part of what is subsumed under the
heading of 'community' is simply the class experience of women: it is the
sum of reciprocal acts and obligations necessary to ensure their own and
their family's survival given the degree of direct exploitation experienced
by the main wage-earner. As such it is not an ahistorical set of values
formed at one conjuncture but a variable which can appear, or disappear,
in a variety of locations. This is not to argue that continuity and tradition
have no impact on the shaping of perception and experience, that they do
is an underlying assumption of this text, but my own view is that
'community' can be short-lived and/or established in a generation. Each
new person is socialised by their parents and then progressively by schools,
peer groups and all the other wider social contacts: it makes little
difference to that individual whether the pattern has existed for hundreds
of years or is a new one, it is the only reality *they* experience. A housing
estate thirty years old could be the only place known to a young married
couple and all their peer group whose parents would be there; for their
child it would be a fully developed 'traditional' community complete with
grandparents. Willmott's study shows how something like this has
happened:

Throughout this book Dagenham has been compared with the 'traditional' workingclass community. At the end one is impressed by how similar,
not how different, they are. Local extended families, which hold such a

central place in the older districts, have grown up in almost identical form on the estate, and so have local networks of neighbours ... In part, Dagenham is the East End reborn.[7]

This in spite of spacial configuration which more nearly resembled that of middle-class suburbia than the close contiguity of the older housing areas, and yet: 'It is striking, on the whole, not how similar Dagenham's patterns are to Bethnal Green, but also how dissimilar they are from those of middleclass suburbia' (Willmott 1963:111). The comparison is an interesting one because it points to the fact that such networks are actively constructed and do not arise simply from dense housing, overcrowding and the enforced sharing of facilities. Nor, it might be added, do they arise from similar mechanical aspects such as sharing the same occupation and/or employer, residing in the same area and sharing the same public facilities because those dimensions are equally present in a company estate. If the values of communities which share similar configurations can vary so much the concept of community would appear somewhat redundant, for to understand practice one needs to examine social and political attitudes as such and little is gained by subsuming them under another heading.

6

The social structure of ownership

In most countries, increased capitalisation of a fishing industry has usually been accompanied by a change in the pattern of ownership and organisation of firms; that is, the fisherman-owned firms are succeeded by large corporations that are often vertically integrated.

C. Wadel 1972

Capital distribution is a crucial aspect for the study of any industry and the industrial and social relations which accompany it. In this case there was an additional reason for a close analysis. The fishermen recalled the industry as an open one with able skippers being able to move into ownership. Even where they were employed by companies they referred to the owner in familiar terms and perceived little social gulf between themselves and their employers. Furthermore, where ownership was by fishermen rather than by commercial companies, they insisted that this was predominately *individual* not kin nor neighbour groups as was the case in most (if not all) other regions where fishing capital was still owned by fishermen. Because the oral evidence revealed these unexpected dimensions it brought into sharp focus the problem of the authenticity of retrospective evidence: it was open to charges of unrealistic memories which over-emphasised harmony and unity in social relations based on an economic myth. The availability of documentary sources comprehensive enough to permit a thorough break-down of the structure of ownership provided an unusual opportunity to juxtapose recalled perceptions with the contemporary material reality. In fact the differences apparent in the oral evidence from driftermen or trawler-men correlates incredibly well with the material circumstances of each section. In other words, the oral evidence is of high enough quality to distinguish not simply the experience of 'fishermen' but of the sub-sections within the industry.

During the period under review East Anglia experienced increased capitalisation but without the degree of commercial ownership and vertical integration which Wadel postulated. It should, however, be noted that nationally (and internationally) herring fishing has proved more resistant to

78

commercial ownership than has whitefishing. This was in no way due to lack of capital development for East Anglia was the most successful English region (expanding mainly at the expense of the West Country) while the East Coast of Scotland followed a similar development to dominate the industry in Scotland. In Scotland, however, this expansion of fishermen-owned capital was along traditional lines with kin-linked ownership spreading to as many as six or so of the crew. Where only one individual is concerned it is clear that access to finance rather than the accumulation of small savings and collective labour must play a crucial role. The subject of our analysis must then include a discussion of the availability of finance as well as ownership.

The level of capital required by inshore fishermen was generally so low that they are not included in this discussion, as our main concern is with levels of capital and profit which could provide the basis for occupational and social stratification. It is worth brief mention, however, as a baseline for subsequent developments.

One informant (3003) bought his first boat in 1906 for £11; about that time a Sheringham crab boat complete with sails cost only £20 new. The main exception to the low level of capital outlay was in Essex where a shrimping bawley cost well over £100 and an oystersmack several hundred. With the inshore industry in decline, however, secondhand craft were available and one Harwich informant (3037) used to buy bawleys for only £20 or £30, so even in this area of large inshore vessels it was possible to start with little capital.

One of the more irrational aspects of traditional ownership was the custom of giving one share to the vessel and one to each crew member which meant that there was no relationship between the amount of capital invested and the return on it. For example, the owner of a crab boat costing £20 would take 66 per cent of the income (33 per cent each for himself, his fellow crewmen and the boat) whereas the same share system and crew numbers operated on a bawley. Indeed, on the weight of evidence it appears unlikely that the owners (or crews) of the more capital intensive inshore vessels earned any greater income than those working the less capital intensive ones. So much depended on the type of catch, the market and transport that capital investment and the level of return were simply not related.

The boat and gear seems to have been purchased outright and there was no systematic debt on the fisherman.[1] More than the fishermen-owners in the other two sections the inshore fisherman was master of his own economic effort (within the constraints of locality and market), he owned his means of production and could work according to his own judgement. The only pressure was to satisfy the needs of his family and to achieve what he – and his wife and their community – perceived to be an adequate standard of living. This could vary by custom as well as material resources. The men from Cromer acknowledged the greater success and prosperity of the Sheringham men; this was because they would work only one tide a day while the latter would often work two (3052). In this situation prosperity within any one community largely depended on contingent factors of thrift, work and family size.

One of the more notable aspects of ownership is that it was predominantly individualistic. Although in most cases there were only two men in a crew they were rarely partners; joint ownership even of the larger inshore craft was not favoured; as one man expressed it 'it wasn't often they [partners] agreed' (3048:12); nor was kinship used as a basis of ownership. Boys would normally work with their father after leaving school (although this was by no means invariable where the father already had a regular and satisfactory crewman) but as soon as he was in a position to buy his own boat he would do so as an individual, not as a 'family' owning two boats. This was unlike the normal practice in Scotland and the South West of England where it was common for each member of a crew to provide some of the gear and frequently to be joint owners of the boat. How unusual the individualism of East Anglia might have been would take a national study to decide, but within the region even with the smallest units of production the normal relationship was that of owner/non-owner rather than partnership with neighbours or kin. Part of the ready acceptance of individual ownership of larger units lay in their customary working practices.

Ownership is analysed at three key dates: 1898 just before the disappearance of fleeting, 1912 as near the peak of expansion before the disruption of the First World War and 1931 as an indication of longer-term developments.[2] Three categories are used – company, single, joint – as indicative of three different social modes of ownership. 'Company' indicates all those vessels where that designation appeared in the title of ownership, 'single' indicates one named owner and 'joint' where two or more names appear as owners.

In Part one it was shown that Lowestoft and Yarmouth developed along different lines and so produced different industrial relations; this distinction is apparent in table 8. In 1898 Yarmouth was dominated by one large trawling company which owned 162 vessels, by 1912 trawling had virtually left the port and the largest drifting company had only thirty vessels; but the reliance on companies rather than fishermen ownership is still apparent. During the interwar decline company capital withdrew more quickly than fisherman-ownership. By contrast Lowestoft demonstrates the early predominance of single ownership which is progressively replaced by com-

Table 8 *Type of ownership by percentage of units at Yarmouth and Lowestoft*

	Yarmouth			Lowestoft		
	1898	1912	1931	1898	1912	1931
Company	51	51	35	3	23	37
Single	49	39	48	85	55	33
Joint	1	10	17	9	22	30
Number of cases	(375)	(217)*	(125)	(364)	(591)*	(432)

* Lowestoft 1912, 26 per cent missing information, Yarmouth 1912,
10 per cent missing information from the total number of cases.
As the information is from a total universe it is still at least
a three in four 'sample'. Circumstantial evidence suggests that
it is mainly single ownership which is missing.

panies and joint ownership. In view of the considerable expansion of capital between 1898 (with the introduction of the steam drifter) and 1912, it is surprising that less than a quarter of ownership was in company hands. Even that percentage of company boats exaggerates the degree to which commercial capital was replacing fishermen-owners, for during the first decade of this century fishermen began to register themselves as companies, so these figures inflate the impression of the degree to which the industry was penetrated by outside capital. The separate experience of Lowestoft and Yarmouth is conflated in table 9.[3] This offers no support to the assumption that fisherman capital was traditionally owned as a joint enterprise to be

Table 9 *Regional ownership by percentage of units*

	1898	1912	1931
Company	27	31	37
Single	68	50	37
Joint	5	18	27
Total number of cases	(739)	(808)*	(557)

* See note to table 8 above.

Table 10 *Small ownership as a percentage of total ownership*

	Yarmouth			Lowestoft		
	1898	1912	1931	1898	1912	1931
Owning one or two boats	28	32	55	63	52	38
Owning one to five boats	35	52	75	90	84	61

replaced by companies with increasing capitalisation. On the contrary, in the crucial period of rapid expansion before the war joint ownership accelerates. The continuing postwar trend shows that it is individual ownership which declines. Never, at any period, however, does company ownership take a predominant position.

Another development which reveals changes in the structure of ownership is the proportion of the industry owned in small units regardless of the type of capital formation: this is shown in table 10. What constitutes a 'small' owner is a moot point but if ownership is averaged across the three dates at both ports over 43 per cent of vessels were owned in units of one or two so ownership was predominantly small scale. It might be noted how from the widely differing position between the two ports in 1898 regards the comparative percentages of small owners and company ownerships they draw into a more common pattern by 1931 which suggests that the dynamics of contemporary developments exerted a more decisive influence than their very different historical origins. It is also apparent that there was a social and economic difference in owning a drifter rather than a trawler: the former cost up to three times that of the latter so this is the more crucial section in examining access to capital. Between 1898 and 1914 the sailing drifters were replaced by steam and by my estimate the capital value of the fleet grew from £300,000 to £1,400,000 (this being an annual compound investment rate of over 10 per cent for the sixteen year period over and above the replacement rate).[4]

Loans came to the driftermen from a number of sources but fish salesmen were by far the most common source of credit. These salesmen had a key role in the industry: the most obvious of their activities was to auction the fish, but they did much more than that: they provided owners with a great deal of white-collar service. Fish salesmen kept the accounts for the fishermen who dealt with them. They paid the bills which the fishermen ran up during the season, for food, fuel, harbour dues and ship's chandlery. The salesmen's representatives sold their client's catch when they went to Scotland in May or to Penzance in January. They settled all the fishermen's bills and accounts in these away ports as well, thus relieving the skipper/owner of a burden of paperwork – and some of the older skippers were illiterate – this service was paid by a commission on sales. This meant that the salesmen made proportionally more money from providing these services to a boat earning a lot of money: it was also much more profitable if their representative in an outport was auctioning for a number of vessels. In other words they wanted to act for as many high-earning vessels as they possibly could. By common report in the oral evidence any successful skipper was able to obtain a loan from the salesmen, indeed, might well be solicited to do so. Naturally, having provided the opportunity for a skipper to become an owner, the salesman would manage the boat and have the loan repaid out of the income. A relationship thus established would commonly last for as long as the fisherman was working – although one owner pointed out that there was no legal commitment to do so.

The first name mentioned by informants as a source of finance for fishermen is usually Norford Suffling. According to the fishermen he 'was a nice man' (3004) who would 'help anyone to get on' (3008). Whatever the truth of the financial and economic advantages he might have received from his loan activities, it is in itself significant that he is remembered with respect and good feeling and not with distaste as a loan-shark or exploiter. The most convincing reason for his being so forward in providing loan facilities is that he was not a boat owner in his own right. He needed the loyalty of the small owners in order to maintain his volume of business. His situation was in contrast to salesmen such as Westmacott or Bloomfield who also were amongst the largest boat owners in Yarmouth, thereby being their own source of work for the salesman side of their organisation. This, of course, begs the question as to why some salesmen did not involve themselves in direct ownership as the boat-owning side of the business was profitable. One can only speculate on this point. There is no doubt that fishing of any description was a high-risk business and capital put into boats and gear could not be easily realised if there was a slump: but that is true of other industries and in any case many capitalist firms did invest in fishing boats. The oral evidence, plus the rate of expansion, leads me to believe that competent skippers were in such short supply that they were given access to credit in order to secure their services. This happened in Scandinavia, and Wadel[5] identifies community values and expertise as dimensions which promote fisherman-ownership. He notes how successful skippers were offered extra shares or the opportunity to 'fish in' a partnership by non-fishermen-owners who were anxious to secure the services of a successful man. That same system was used by the firm of Bloomfield who recruited and held good skippers by allowing them to take a third share of their vessel.[6] This was, in effect, capital conceding a substantial proportion of its 'rightful' profits in return for expertise. It meant that a skipper was given title (and the accompanying debt) for a third of the vessel and repaid that with the third portion of capital's share that had become his immediate entitlement. With several firms being willing to finance successful skippers they had access to credit that could put them in possession of their own vessel provided their success continued.

Even where salesmen financed a fisherman outright they gained a considerable advantage, first from the normal commercial rate of interest on the loan and secondly their 5 per cent commission for operating as salesman to the vessel. The fish salesmen operated a business that involved large sums of money but which required very little in terms of fixed assets – a wooden portable office was the extent of their plant.[7] Thus by loaning their money to skippers they built up their business while at the same time ensuring that their capital was not locked into direct ownership of a capital asset with a high level of depreciation. Their capital was spread more widely than if it had been invested in a few vessels owned outright.

Even so, the proposition had to be sufficiently attractive and realistic to persuade fishermen to go into considerable debt in an attempt to achieve ownership which could put at risk their not inconsiderable earnings as skippers. Here the very volatility of the market and the random nature of the size of the catch ensured that the reality of ownership was bound to come to some men. The essential uncertainty of the operation meant that if fishing operations were to continue most boats had to make a profit most years. That very fact was enough to ensure that one or two would make enormous profits, in some cases repaying the capital cost in one year, as was instanced in the section on shares. Wadel, too, noted that some vessels would earn ten times that of others and that fishermen pursued fishing to the edge of bankruptcy because 'Herring fishing offers the only opportunity to rehabilitate completely in the course of a single season – if one is lucky' (1972:116), and although in his period fishing methods were different, the same basic factors applied to the pre-war herring drifting in East Anglia.

It was, then, the uncertainty of the whole operation which kept the share going to labour reasonably high and also kept the route to ownership open. The 'lucky' boats that gave their crews big earnings also repaid their capital very quickly indeed.

None of the fishermen interviewed were owners before 1914 but one informant did take ownership in 1924 of a vessel costing £1,000 for £100 pounds down and the rest on loan from a fish salesman. According to him there were at least four fish salesmen in Yarmouth competing for business and willing to stake any likely skipper who wanted to own his own vessel. It might have been a sign of the less certain 1920s that he was obliged to give the deeds of his house as collateral. Two years later, however, he needed nets costing £1,100 and was able to provide half of their cost in cash while the salesman again financed the rest thus enabling him to gain a large discount on the purchase price. He had cleared his capital (£2,100) of debt in five years: he was then still only twenty-nine years old.[8]

Ownership of Scottish drifters was financed in very much the same way during this period and provided a useful comparison, for M. Gray takes a very different view as to the reality of ownership. He gives figures to show that of the 783 Scottish steam drifters registered in 1912, 403 were owned by fishermen, 115 by landsmen and 265 by a mixture. He continues: 'But this conveys an unduly favourable impression on the independence of these fishermen who, even when they were nominally complete owners, were without doubt heavily in debt' (Gray 1978:157). He states that of the 624 vessels in which fishermen had some part of ownership 556 were still mortgaged. These figures provide an interesting check to my more optimistic impression of the position of the fishermen gained from East Anglia, but his interpretation of the data may be too pessimistic. He indicates that the cost of a steam drifter rose from £1,500 in 1900 to around £3,000 in 1912 exclusive of nets, so the amount of capital to be acquired was considerable. Yet in 1912 38 per cent of those drifters were five years old or less and 88 per cent had been built within the previous ten years.[9] That sets an absolute limit to the age of the debts and if an average debt of £2,000 is assumed, then to pay it off in ten years required the fishermen-owners to be able to clear £200 (plus interest charges) over and above normal running costs. That 11 per cent of the vessels where fishermen were involved had already discharged their debts suggests that ownership was a realistic prospect. In East Anglia £2,000 would have purchased a dozen houses: to acquire wealth on that scale was an aspiration open to few manual workers before 1914.

The difference in the trawling industry is quite marked: here the prevailing impression is of low profits and tight margins. This impression is confirmed by a survey of all the bankruptcy cases involving Lowestoft fishermen reported in the local press between 1894 and 1913. If the number of vessels working each year is divided by the number of bankruptcies, trawlers have a bankruptcy rate five and a quarter times that of drifters for every unit of ownership throughout the period. Any conclusions based on evidence drawn from public failures must be viewed with some caution, but it is informative and triangulates with the oral evidence and the known development of the industry.

It must be remembered that Lowestoft trawling reached its peak (in terms of vessels) in 1908 and there was a decline in numbers until 1914. Earlier than that the industry had reached one peak in 1894 and the number

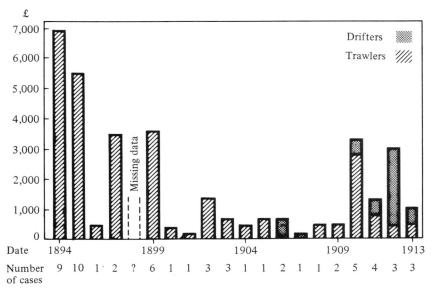

Figure 5 Bankruptcies of Lowestoft boat owners 1894–1913

of vessels had slightly declined between then and 1903 when it began to climb to the 1908 maximum. The evidence on bankruptcies is tightly congruent with this picture: bankruptcies were at their highest in 1894 when the decline started and were heavy for the next four years, they were then at a moderate level until there were none in the final two years before the peak was reached when they started again. Numbers involved were small but this is a total universe, not a sample. All the evidence, therefore, supports the view that this was a period of difficulty for the in˙ ˙stry and in an industry dominated by small owners with little capital and low profits a great number of failures are to be expected. Figure 5 shows the values involved. Besides the tabulated data the cases provide valuable qualitative evidence and this suggests that there was a certain amount of nomi⌐al ownership in trawling. Indeed, one debtor stated that he had never intended to pay any of the principal which reduces 'ownership' to a system of perpetual hire. There are two cases where the bankrupts claim that they had always been insolvent and that while 'owners' they had been paid a 'wage' of £1 a week by the mortgagee to whom all earnings were paid. Perhaps one of the most extraordinary cases comes in 1895 where the bankrupt owner was a shipwright with no experience as a fisherman who had no capital of his own. He took a smack for £500 with a full mortgage from J.H. Knowles. A few months later he took another smack at £600 on a full mortgage which he said he did not want and claimed was a wreck worth only £100, yet he took it 'as a favour to Mr Knowles'.[10] In about two years of operation he paid off £290, the boats were then valued at only £200 together. In another case from the same year a man whose occupation is not given but who appears to have been a working skipper stated that the mortgagee had 'sent for him and ask him to take the smack'[11]; in five years he had paid off £250. Those are extreme examples, but it was a common complaint in court that a smack had been bought at an inflated price and that had been the cause of the trouble. One man claimed that he bought the smack without seeing it for £750 and it was worth only £450.

It is difficult to accept such accounts as serious attempts of working fishermen (or auxiliaries) to achieve ownership. Oral evidence shows that fishermen were keenly aware of the qualities of different vessels and any man who would buy a smack unseen is not likely to be a business success, nor are those who take ownership as a favour to others. Nominal ownership, however, gave the mortgagee a method of avoiding payment of debts incurred to various suppliers; if any tradesman made the 'owner' bankrupt the mortgagee took back the smack; if the nominal owner did begin to work out the debt he could foreclose and retain the vessel. Such cases, however, are a thin fringe and most cases appear genuine with the most common cause of bankruptcy being unusually heavy losses of gear, and the usual run of human misfortunes, illness, accident and shipwreck. Two of the bankrupts claimed in court that there were 'wheels within wheels'[12] when it came to selling their smacks and the prices they received. They seemed to be implying a 'ring' which kept the re-purchase price low. Given that only a minority of businessmen would have had the ability to pay cash-down at auction such an arrangement might well have been expected. The evidence as a whole, however, suggests that it did not operate consciously as a ring, but unconsciously through market forces. That assertion is made on the grounds that of the total of sixty-four cases the bankrupt was a different individual in each case and there were sixty-eight mortgagees. Of the mortgagees ten were identifiable as kin to the bankrupt, mostly boat-owner fathers and there are thirty-seven other named sources. Of these only one occurred four times, Mr Hame, described as a ship owner; Messrs Lacon, brewers and J. Sladdern, salesman and smack owner, were each involved in three cases; three names were involved twice but all the others were involved in only one case. The sheer number of the people involved in giving mortgages reduces the credibility of the idea that there was any systematic concealment of ownership, although there is a strong possibility that the men who took on smacks with no capital were charged inflated prices for the opportunity.

The bias in the bankruptcy data has one positive advantage in that it provides some hard evidence about the two ends of the business spectrum, namely lenders and borrowers. Occupations are not given in all cases but fish salesmen and smack owners predominated as lenders. The surprising fact is that the borrowers showed a substantial overlap with the lenders. Fifteen of the bankrupts were described as salesmen, fish buyers or smack owners. There were also fifteen identifiable as being working skippers up to the time of buying the smack and another five working skippers who were already smack owners. One less expected group was that of the seven skilled craftsmen ancillary to the fishing business such as shipwrights and riggers.

My final impression of the trawling ownership from these sources is that it substantially involved skippers and ex-skippers[13] while also involving men who had other occupations connected with the fishing business such as salesmen or buyers. Such men were in a particularly good position to combine the two occupations: in fact it made sense for anyone to do so. If one had to be down at the fish docks to supervise one's smacks or merely to wait for them to come in, the time might be profitably exercised in buying and selling fish. It would be interesting to know how many of the men described as salesmen or buyers had been skippers and/or smack owners before dealers in fish rather than the other way round.[14] The cases involving relatives (mainly father and son) showed that 'ownership' tended to become a family business. This is to be expected given that the industry was beginning its long decline. Capital was being worked out rather than accumulated and this was bound to give strong advantages to those who had reached a position of ownership at an earlier stage of the industry's development. Even at this late date, however, a high proportion of them were ex-skippers and practical fishermen.

At least two very firm conclusions emerge from the foregoing: one, that the recall of the fishermen with regard to the capital basis of their industry was soundly based; two, that the economic situation of the owners of drifters and of trawlers was very different, and more on this issue will be presented in the context of their social images.

One reason why the fishermen continued to achieve ownership was that it was part of their expectations. For underlying the discussion on ownership there is the assumption that fishermen desired ownership and would attain it where possible, and also that businessmen/capitalists were equally keen to obtain ownership. That they did not do so more widely is ascribed to the low profitability in trawling and to the share system and the unpredictability of drifting. The modern herring fishing industry although now using different techniques still shares some of the uncertainties of the earlier period and Wadel's (1972) study of the Norwegian industry in the 1960s revealed a large proportion of the boats still owned by fishermen although when equipped for fishing each one cost between £75,000 and £125,000 at existing exchange rates. He estimated that one fifth of the fishermen owned some share of a boat or its gear. The family and community links that he reveals have much in common with Scotland: Gray (1978) estimates that in 1912 some third to one half of Buckie, Peterburgh and Fraserburgh fishermen working on the steam drifters had shares in them. This is quite different from the pre-1914 situation in East Anglia where the norm of ownership was individualistic, so even if their ideal had been fully realised only 10 per cent of fishermen could be owners at any one time where boats have a ten man crew. Given that the East Coast of Scotland boats and the East Anglian boats fished the same two seasons for the same markets it is not unreasonable to suggest that their respective expectations as to the appropriate way in which fishing capital should be owned actually affected the shape of ownership while not being fully worked out in either case. There is, however, some evidence to suggest that common material realities were forcing a degree of congruence, for we know that joint ownership and fishermen companies increased in East Anglia and those financing the Scottish fishermen increasingly disliked dealing with traditional Scottish multiple ownership.[15]

The realities of ownership must be viewed through this screen of expectations if one is going to comprehend the social imagery of the fishermen. The 'facts' demonstrate that less than 5 per cent of East Anglian fishermen achieved ownership, but as their ideology allowed for only 10 per cent if fully implemented the actual situation was perceived as an open meritocracy. Why East Anglia showed a preference for individual as opposed to some form of shared ownership is left an open question but there can be no doubt that they perceived ownership as widespread, owners as being fishermen like themselves (even where some of the second generation had not been such). The fact that much of the means of production was owned by members of the occupational community undoubtedly complicated the fishermen's perception of exploitation. As J. Rule points out 'the worker/ employer relationship is only one expression of the ways in which a prevailing socio-economic system conditions the lives of those who are subject to it. Men can be exploited by consumers, and they can also be exploited as independent producers' (1973:61). My own assessment – based on the primacy given to the market in the oral evidence – is that the fishermen saw the commercial system ashore with its fluctuating prices and sharp practices as the location of their exploitation. They saw owners as very much sharing in that situation although also being aware that some owners were exploiting them.

7

Images of social structure

There were no class distinctions, you just had a bit more money.

3012

Although there is one sense in which the facts of oral evidence speak for themselves they do not, unfortunately, place themselves into categories. Space precludes the long extracts which are often the best way to demonstrate the authenticity of the evidence and the appropriateness of the interpretation,[1] but the above extract and the following one serve to illustrate my contention that although the fishermen were well aware of material distinctions their perceptions of stratification were frequently weak and confused:

I was wondering what sort of place Yarmouth was in those days, people often talk about the different classes in society, rich or poor or working class.
No, to tell you the truth I never did hear – no distinction in any class or anything, not round about where we lived – there. No, I never heard nothing. I mean – a chap well off – well, not well off, but what we call well off them days he'd go about along with a chap what's very poor, and there was no difference in 'em, you know, they – there would be no difference in the two of 'em, the one wouldn't be stuck up and the other one not, there was no class distinction I don't think, very little.
What sort of man would you describe as well off?
Well – I should say – I mean now well – I can't explain it to you nicely what we call well off, but we'd call a well off like a – chap in business perhaps, you know, got a shop and that. Chap what – boat owners, or boat owners' sons like and that and – different things. We know they'd got a bob or two to lay their hand on but – I should class them as like a – class above us class like down in Middlegate Street a bit ... But I mean that didn't make no distinction on them. Not as regards to mixing along with the other class, like. No, they wasn't – I mean your idea would be to think that we mustn't go out with 'em no more, he – he's one of the downchargers like, he ain't got nothing, they're poor – there's none of that you know. (3024:59–60)

His last sentence shows that he was aware of the sort of class separation that I was expecting but he remained firm in his view that the fishermen's social world was a unified one.

90

There are many pages of such information in each interview and its very richness with shifting terminology and emphasis tend to convey the informants' feelings on class and its significance while leaving boundaries imprecise, even shifting according to context, and difficult to fix and relate to conventional models. My main concern in evaluating their class images has been to establish their class model and their own location in it. Figure 6 illustrates their image of wider society. The figure is divided horizontally into upper, middle and working classes. These 'objective' class boundaries were arrived at through a mixture of collective perception, pragmatic evaluation of the data and historical common sense. The category working class comprises all manual workers; clerical workers and small shopkeepers are placed in the middle class. This is because most informants perceived a significant division between those groups. The division between the middle and upper classes is less clearly established. In the interviews informants often placed 'small' landowners or businessmen into the middle class and 'large' ones into the upper class and the relative sizes cannot be established by any consistent criteria. The one firm benchmark in the figure is that the professional classes are placed at the top of the objective middle class. As my major concern is with the perceptions of the informants' immediate social boundaries this imprecision at the top of the social scale is not a crucial disadvantage as the main point there is to establish whether they perceived two or three classes rather than the exact boundary.

Each basic class division is separated into three to illustrate more clearly where each informant's subjective boundaries were drawn.[2] For example, the three who perceived a large working class while holding a three class image are shown as perceiving the working class extending into the lower third of the 'objective' middle class because they included clerical workers and small shopkeepers in the working class. Similarly, those informants whose two class image extends the working class to the top of the 'objective' middle class are thus shown because they included doctors, small businessmen and farmers in the working class. In addition to this symbols indicate the informants' self-ranking and those which held a conflict model of society.

It is one of the commonplaces of surveys to find that many manual workers rate themselves as middle class, indeed one study (Young and Willmott 1957:101) found that 48 per cent did so. Now this may have been the reality of the time and place but the experience of oral history interviewing demonstrates how crucial it is to record the terminology of the informant and to place it in context. The following informant had already described a very poor childhood and yet when asked a direct question of their class position responded:

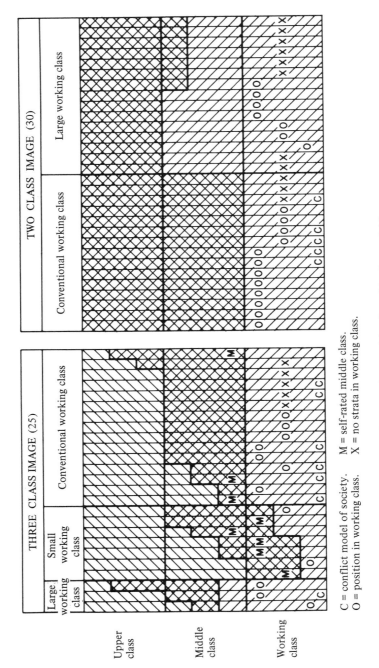

Figure 6 Objective class position by subjective social image

C = conflict model of society.   M = self-rated middle class.
O = position in working class.   X = no strata in working class.

Well I should think that we were called middle class.
What sort of class would you say were under that?
Well then there was the poor class, you know. But – oh when I think [...digression...]
What sort of life did this poorer class below you lead?
Well, him that used to go about with a organ, grinding the organ. Their names were Friday. Well, she used to go out with a big pillow round her as if she were pregnant everytime. And that *is* the truth. Well that's how they used to go and collect money. (3029:24–6)

Now unless her self-rated 'middle class' is placed in the context of her subjective social hierarchy the fact that she actually rates herself in, and identifies herself as part of, the objective working class is completely lost. There is no point in simply recording what people say, it must be placed in the context of what they mean. She appears on the figure as the only self-rated middle class to be found in the middle of the objective working class, her middle-class boundary extends only to the top of the objective working class because she called clerical workers and small shopkeepers *upper class.*[3] If self-rated class can be extracted from the content of the interviews without too much difficulty the same is not so in assessing them for a 'conflictual' model of society, and here an example of categorisation will have to serve to show the standards applied:

Was there much difference in the working class in those days?
Oh yes. Yes, God that was wicked. You had to call everybody sir or – you know. Expected you to call 'em that.
Was it any different when you went to the fishing?
Yes. That stopped all that. There were no sirs then.
(3005:39–40)

This informant went on to establish a conventional three class model and there are no other indications of class conflict. He is, however, categorised as holding a conflict model on the resentment apparent in his youthful perceptions of the village class structure.

One danger of what is essentially a *post hoc* attempt to relate these rich subjective images to the conceptual framework and concerns of the social scientist is that of over-interpreting the evidence, but its advantage is that the evidence is embedded in context and because it has not been pre-shaped it can serve question assumptions even if it cannot provide proof. The *shape* of the class imagery here does question that

the assumption that power and conflict imagery must go with dichotomous imagery leads to a search in the wrong direction: to much one-eyed and simple minded a search when attempts are made to understand and classify social imagery. It leads to a very mechanical kind of count of the number of classes, or strata, or what not, which are recognised and given tags by individual respondents in surveys. To count up in that way is to miss the point. The real question is not the number of categories which people distinguish; but the nature of the relations which they recognise between them, and the basis of the differences which they see. (Westergaard, in Bulmer 1975:253)

Certainly the distribution of conflict imagery in the interviews is less distinctive by perception of class numbers than by class shape. Of the trichotomous group, seven (28 per cent) held a conflict model against five (17 per cent) from the dichotomous group: but of the thirty with a conventionally sized working class eleven (37 per cent) contained conflict imagery whereas of the twenty-five which perceived either a large or small working class only one (4 per cent) had any conflict imagery.

The reasons for these perceptions are pursued below but in reading the interviews it is noticeable that some of the sharpest awareness of class boundaries and antagonisms came from the most prosperous informant and came mainly through her own experience of being rejected as a social equal by the local middle class because of her working-class/fishing origins and culture. I suspect, too, that her consciousness of social conflict was sharpened through her father's active involvement in local politics. She, for good material reasons, rated herself as middle class although she denied any social gulf between her boat-owning father and ordinary fishermen. In most cases, however, those who ranked themselves middle class did so because of their incredibly limited social horizons.

If the data is analysed according to section as in table 11[4] it is clear that inshoremen had the most dichotomous view of class. At first this is somewhat surprising as the majority of them had contact with the rich as crewmen on luxury yachts or as wealthy summer residents. This made them aware of a social class above their own social hierarchy. But it was their contact with the very rich which gave them their distinctive evaluation, for they tended to place doctors, farmers and similar middle-class positions in the working class on the logical grounds that they too had to work for their living. Their imagery comes close to separating society into workers and drones. Once again the shape of the class model groups informants more coherently than numbers, for over half the perceptions of a large working class come from the inshoremen who are only just over a quarter of the sample. This, however, did not lead them to a conflictual image of society, for, as will emerge in the section on politics, the yacht crewmen in particular valued the rich as a class.

The inshoremen's image of society, however, is a dual one and internally inconsistent. For although, when asked about *social class*, they have this image of a large working class which includes professionals and businessmen; when asked about their *own position*, they actually use only other manual workers as a point of reference. They, far more than any other group

Table 11 *Informants by number of classes perceived*

	Two (%)		Three (%)		D/K (%)		Totals
Driftermen	41	(9)	41	(9)	18	(4)	22
Trawlermen	50	(7)	50	(7)	–	–	14
Inshore	75	(12)	25	(4)	–	–	16
Non-fishermen	25	(2)	63	(5)	13	(1)	8
Totals	50	(30)	42	(25)	8	(5)	60

– 70 per cent of them – perceived themselves at the top of the working class when talking about their position in this class and, in this context, no longer include the working middle class as part of their comparison. It is this double standard of comparison which may account for their harmonious view of class.

How typical the fishermen's class imagery is of the rest of the manual class of the region and period is impossible to say, but the implication is that it is liable to vary quite markedly by occupation, for where driftermen and trawlermen shared an occupation with many structural similarities which gave them broadly similar class perceptions, the unique experience of the inshoremen places them apart. In fact the evidence reflected structural positions with some accuracy, for example, all the skippers who rated themselves as only 'middle' working class were trawler skippers whereas every drifter skipper rated himself higher; similarly the only crewmen to rate themselves as 'top' of the working class were all driftermen. It is clear that fishermen were reliably aware of their comparative economic position and although their views of wider social class are complex and even contradictory there is no reason to doubt that they are reliably recalled.[5]

The qualitative evidence on class shows that the fisherman has a weak sense of stratification and a strong sense of occupational identity. Particularistic relationships within small scale industry are usually considered in terms of the effects which close employer/employee contact have on the social and industrial attitudes of the employees, but of equal interest is the effects of such relationships on the employer. Here the dynamics of historical development are crucial, for the brief period of capital accumulation meant that those in different strata had shared origins. It is quite unlike the situation in, for example, agriculture where usually both landownership and landlessness were inherited: an inheritance which also imposed very different educational, cultural and social experiences. Even where material stratification was taking place there can be few industries which impose such a degree of common culture as fishing.

Going fishing as a boy took the son of an owner out of any distinctive influence which might have been emerging as a result of material prosperity and placed him back in a very onerous working environment. He not only worked but ate, slept and shared his leisure with the crew. During his early and most impressionable years he would be obliged to cook, clean and run errands for them. They were the patterns for appropriate behaviour and attitudes and by the time he became an owner (even if by inheritance) he, too, was indelibly working class; even more crucially he was a fisherman. Having worked on the share system, having had his cut of the crew perks and fiddles, there was no area or dimension of the workplace not known to him. Such an experience can have two quite contrary effects; one is that once an owner this knowledge can be used to eradicate such practices, the other is that it imbues an acceptance of the relations which exist. That the second course appears to have held good in the fishing industry is due primarily to the level of control it was possible to apply. The fact that so many owners had worked under the existing share system and customary practices made them essentially conservative and helped to stabilise industrial relations through a period of rapid technical and capital change. Owners did not have a sufficiently pure managerial attitude to push for a readjustment of the share system in favour of capital. This industrial identity has an obvious input into social perceptions.

The situation of the trawler and drifter owners is illuminating because not only was there a different level of prosperity between those sections, but because in both sections the fishermen-owners shade imperceptibly into the local commercial and business elite. This merging was a double movement with fishermen becoming prosperous through ownership and with local businessmen diversifying into ownership of fishing capital so blurring the social and cultural lines of ownership, and through that who was part of the fishing community or of another class.

The low level of class conflict had different sources according to section. The trawlermen frequently mention the low profit level of the smacks, the high risk of loss and the number of owners who 'went broke'. The following example starts with a leading question trying to establish the degree of geographical separation:

Today the manager of a factory will live in a posh house away from where the workers live? Ah – ah. Factories, I expect they do. Yes, I reckon they live in a posh place, the

factories, but the owners of fishing craft they were – they were as poor as – nearly as poor as what we were.
They'd live in the same streets would they?
Yes, live in the same streets, yes. Well, you know, they'd come down and lend a hand rather than put anybody on, they would come and lend a hand to get the work done. (3036:17)

The work referred to is unloading the fish. Other informants referred to the smack owners in the same terms, and the economic difficulties of owners who lived in the same terraced housing as themselves produced little envy. The perceptions of the driftermen, however, were rooted in a very different material context. Kessingland was a fishing village which supplied owners (sixty-seven of them in 1912) and men for the drifters based in Lowestoft:

I was trying to get a picture of the community, were there any rich?
Well the boat owners were the ones. They were the rich people.
What sort of class would you call them, upper class or middle class?
Oh no. They were alright, they weren't uppish or ought like that, they were just – they were just people. If you were going to Lowestoft and they used to go to Lowestoft in a horse and cart, or horse and trap, and if you were a-going they would pick you up and give you a lift home ... They mixed with you. And if any on them what were in really serious trouble they would help them. (3014:37–8)

Thus although boat owners are spontaneously mentioned above local shop-keepers and tradesmen as the wealthy they are identified as part of the fishing community. Confirmation of this view comes from Winterton which was also noted for the number of owners and men who worked in the drifting industry. The informant started work for the employer mentioned as a beatster in 1907:

Did the boat owners in Winterton employ servants?
No, their income wasn't enough.
Oh, I thought that they would be quite something as boat owners.
No, no, see, – now, hear me out – the little boats on the beach they didn't have enough coming in to keep themselves, but the drifters what went out at Yarmouth – I don't believe there was one but that got on. My meaning is, he began with nothing and he kept going by going up the ladder as I might say.
Did the man you worked for have a big house?
No, their wife kept a little shop next door to us, and he had a daughter lived at home, and mother and daughter done what there was to do, she would have somebody come in to do the washing weekly because there was the shop, and to keep washing and wiping your hands wasn't too nice a job ...
So apart from having this weekly washerwoman in they would live much the same as the fishermen?
Yes, yes. Very little difference. You see well, they had got to get out of debt. And that took a time, if they didn't earn a lot of money ... (3025:59)

According to the documentary evidence this owner had one vessel in 1904 and by 1912 owned two and was part-owner of another two. Clearly he was prospering very rapidly. But it is obvious that it made very little difference to his outward circumstances; there was little or nothing to distinguish him and his family from their neighbours, for the informant's family also kept one daughter at home to help with the housework. It is significant that this was not an 'opinion' remembered from the past, but a simple account of who lived next door and an observation as to their way of life. Notice, too, how the informant carefully separated my loose question on 'ownership' into ownership of inshore 'boats on the beach' and of 'drifters': a good example of the commitment to accuracy and a desire to communicate their memories with precision which is the hallmark of a good informant.

Wadel identified a similar situation in Norwegian fishing communities in the 1960s where working fishermen would own assets of up to £125,000 yet still lived in a style much the same as their neighbours:

Their consumption patterns are related to the fact that they reside in small fishing communities along with ordinary fishermen who are their neighbours and often even kin. Most of the skippers and net-bosses (as well as fishermen-owners) have worked themselves up and have kept their previous standards of living. Moreover, excessive consumption of goods threatens their personal relations with fishermen, and is regarded as foolish and the topic of much gossip when it occurs ... On the other hand, ownership of fishing vessels and/or gear carries the highest prestige in these communities, especially when combined with active participation in the fishery. The community structure thus favours 'conspicuous ownership and production' rather than 'conspicuous consumption' (see Erasmus, 1961).[6]

Although there are similarities between Scandinavian fishing communities and English ones our evidence suggests that *village community* is not the crucial factor. One Lowestoft informant's father owned four drifters and was a local councillor, pillar of the church and was generally active as a (small town) 'middle-class influential'. Her mother 'entertained ladies most afternoons', but in spite of this, and of living in a substantial five-bedroomed house, they had not one living-in servant. This must be virtually unprecedented in a business home of this standing before 1914. The house had its business premises adjoining and a certain amount of help was taken from the workers there:

Did your mother have servants in the home?
We had Totty, but she used to work in the beating store and then she used to come in and help. And then we had Annie sometimes come and help when my mother's spring cleaning. And my eldest sister was at home.

Was the washing done at home?

Oh yes. Well, my mother used to send some to the Lowestoft Steam Laundry, send the sheets and – you know, big white table-cloths and serviettes, we had our own serviettes and they went to the laundry, but the towels and things like that, there was the old fashioned wooden mangle and she used to have the man from the net-store come and turn the mangle. (3030:6)

Throughout this interview one is aware of the strange mixture of affluence and local importance with a working-class cultural pattern. Her father continued at manual work with his workers and, given the large element of working-class culture in a prosperous employer's home, it is not surprising that material advantages did not create a social gulf. This owner sold up his business in 1920. Having severed his links with the fishing industry, he then retired to a 'posh' part of the town, and employed a living-in housemaid.

If social distinctions are to arise along the lines of occupational class relations, then the income provided must not only be large enough to make those distinctions manifest, it must also be permanent and reliable. In certain circumstances the differential need not be large, for the systematic receipt of only a few shillings a week extra can, in a large town, lead to socially stratified housing areas. There is evidence to show that this was happening in Lowestoft just before 1914:

This was the area where most of the fishermen lived was it?

Yes. Well then of course they built houses right up Worthing Road and – that was when the herring industry was a little more prosperous – and all the known skippers went to there, 'cos they called that the Skippers' Row. Yes. Worthing Road they called Skippers' Row. (3006:25)

Clearly after the initial period of capital accumulation there was an opportunity for this wealth to start the process of separating members of the fishing community into economically defined locations. Comments from some of the younger respondents who spent most of their fishing experience in the postwar period also suggest that there was some sharpening of class perceptions in the 1920s and 1930s.

You don't think that there was much difference between the fishermen and the owners on Lowestoft then?

Well, no. Not the old ones. But as the sons came along they seemed to have a more – more poshy way about them, if you know what I mean. But the fathers, now you take the missus, she knew Old Coventry Capps, she knew all the other Capps, she knew practically all the owners and they used to say good morning to her or that, when she went in the office to get the pay – but you get the sons, they get a bit posh that's my opinion of it. But the old men, they were proper old tops, but rough, rough, rough. But they bought their children up, and a lot of them only bought up in a little old cottage on the Beach.

So they didn't live in big houses?
Oh, no, no. I can remember Capps living in a house called 'Wilde House', that was at the bottom of Wilde Score, on the Beach. And then they shifted up to Worthing Road, a bigger house, called 'Vigilant House', and that's where he died. But I knew 'em when they all started and they were all brought up on Old North Beach.[7]

This element of personal acquaintance with the local business and commercial elite obviously delayed felt social differences and there is no doubt that the growth of the fishing industry and its prosperity turned local shopkeepers and small businessmen into something rather more substantial. It is a process that was common to a number of areas at a certain stage of their development and a similar development is reported from mid-nineteenth-century Tyneside:

> The process of segregation which was slowly cleaving the community into an up-street aristocracy and a down-street anything, had not long set in, and the lines demarcating the several strata of social position had not been definitely drawn. The professional man, the lawyer, the magistrate, betrayed in errant locations the thinness of his educational veneer. The well-to-do shipowner had hardly cast-off the manner and bearing of the skipper and, despite his wide-skirted blue surtout, was recognised by the altogether unawed populace as Captain So-and-So, who had lived not long ago on the banks of the river, or in the long 'narrow street' itself. (Haswell 1894:137)

This process was particularly evident in Lowestoft where, in round figures, the population expanded from 19,000 to 34,000 between 1891 and 1911 (Yarmouth 50,000 to 56,000). The degree to which outside capital financed this is beyond the scope of this study, but it is evident that there was enough local involvement to legitimise what capital came into the community. This paraphrase of an interview demonstrates the point:

> There were no companies then. I knew Mouse Catchpole, he had twenty or thirty boats. He was 'a proper gentleman' although you wouldn't think so to see him in his fisherman's clothes. He was worth thousands but 'would talk to you as one of your own'. I sailed for him on the *Beacon Star*.[8]

In fact Catchpole owned only two boats in partnership and the *Beacon Star* was owned by the Star Drift Fishing Company Limited which owned six. Whatever outside capital was involved in the company it clearly remained Catchpole's in the eyes and attitudes of the local fishermen. The company was registered in 1902 with seven subscribers with 500 shares each. G. Catchpole (Mouse) was managing director, the others were A. Goulby his partner in their private boat-owning business (also an ex-fisherman), W.W. Greaves fish merchant, G. Thurston ice merchant and A. Spashett shopkeeper. All were from Lowestoft which establishes the local nature of most of the capital and the control of the company. W. Stuart of Esk Mills,

Musselburgh, manufacturer (probably a net supplier) and F.H. Phillips a herring exporter of Newcastle-on-Tyne represented outside capital, but also commercial connections which might be assumed to have been of benefit to the local owners. Clearly the position of Catchpole as the active manager not only preserved the impression of fisherman-ownership and personalised industrial perceptions, it doubtless preserved the actual operating style in a manner familiar to the fishermen.

In both communities, Lowestoft and Yarmouth, ownership was a complex web and many of the non-fishermen investors were locally known businessmen, so status was interactional and class boundaries not clear. An extract from the letters column of the local press contains many clues to class relations:

It is astonishing how our buyers of fish are becoming buyers of houses and shops; and, in fact, are becoming great landlords to such an extent that it seems a great mystery where they get their money for it, as they say, they cannot give more money for fish than they do ... [They] by their avaricious ways and prices are surely bringing us to starvation, while they are like lords of the land, and can afford to give fifty guineas for a ring to adorn their fingers while packing fish in the market.[9]

The image of prosperous landlords with expensive personal jewellery still packing fish on the market neatly encapsulates so much. That such a man was still visible in a manual capacity in one of the more menial jobs illustrates how slowly the wealthy members of the business world assumed a separate cultural pattern. In this situation of comparatively small but expanding and prosperous communities the upwardly mobile were known to many of the rest of the population. These aspects of new wealth, mixed residence, kinship links and known individuals blurred the distinctions that newly acquired wealth might have created. The elements of cohesion lay partly in the shared experiences and *memories* of the participants, for a number of the interviews mention having been to school with, or were relatives of, the owners and small businessmen. Common knowledge and shared culture allowed considerable property distinctions to occur without serious loss of social cohesion. People were known as individuals rather than by their class position so their images are a fusion of class, status and, indeed, cultural boundaries. Figure 7 summarises their position. This is compatible with their perception of exploitation in which fishermen – both owners and crew – are collectively exploited by the organisation of the market ashore. The majority see themselves as part of a broad working class with only a minority perceiving themselves as either poor or middle class.

If the most powerful impression conveyed by the data is that class consciousness was peripheral to the ideology of the fishermen it in no way reduces the significance of those social images. That they reveal particular

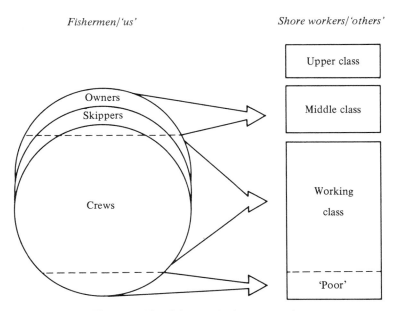

Figure 7 The fishermen's class perceptions

aspects is only to be expected, for as David Lockwood has written 'the industrial and community milieux of manual workers exhibit a very considerable diversity and it would be strange if there were no correspondingly marked variations in the images of society held by different sections of the working class'.[10] The three broad types he delineated provide a useful framework for a final consideration of the fishermen's place within the wider working class:

> ...first, the traditional worker of the 'proletarian' variety whose image of society will take the form of a power model; second, the other variety of traditional worker, the 'deferential' whose perception of social inequality will be one of status hierarchy; and, third the 'privatised' worker, whose social consciousness will most nearly approximate what may be called a 'pecuniary' model of society. (Bulmer 1975:17)

He reminds us that 'The "traditional" worker is, of course, a sociological rather than an historical concept' so it is not surprising to find that the fishermen do not neatly fit those categories. Nevertheless, his ideal types do provide complexes of social experience which illuminate aspects of the fishermen's identity.

The work aspects of the traditional workers (proletarian and deferential) are held to be dominant (high involvement, comradeship through occupational culture, this carried into leisure) and linked to residence – workmates often neighbours and kin, living in solidary communities. These all apply to fishermen with some slight reservations on the 'solidary community' because some still lived in agricultural villages, but even here there were usually a number of them from each location. These circumstances, Lockwood argues, give rise to values focused around mutual aid, moral density and limited horizons. The question of mutual aid and moral density in the community will be dealt with in Part three, but clearly the moral density of the workplace and the limited class horizons are amply evident. Historically, only the fleeting section of trawl fishermen fulfilled the further dimensions for proletarian traditionalists, which include working in large establishments and holding a 'them' and 'us' view where 'they' include their employers.

The typology of the deferential traditionalist is more complex but the focus on location (small-town/rural, autonomous communities) and work (small-scale, pre-industrial, unique position in a job hierarchy and so forth) apply to most of the fishermen. But if their industrial and political behaviour falls within the form delineated by Lockwood's model their perception of social class does not. The inshore fishermen provide the clearest example, for they do not conform to the model by perceiving two classes rather than three; not only that, they include their own local status hierarchy of farmers, businessmen and professionals in their own class. This was, in part, due to the general indifference to the social hierarchy ashore already noted, but here it takes a particularly unusual form because of the disjuncture between work and location. Lockwood points to the importance of the seamlessness of experience in shaping the deferential traditionalist with their hierarchical views:

The persons who exercise authority over him at his place of work may not be the same persons who stand at the apex of the local status system, but the structural principles of the two social orders are homological; and from neither set of relationships does he learn to question the appropriateness of his exchange of deference for paternalism. (Bulmer 1975:20)

In the case of the inshoremen, particularly those who served as yacht-hands, their contact with wealthy members of the *national* status system lead them to evaluate their *local* hierarchy on less customary lines. They conflate the middle to the working class because they also had to work in contradistinction to their employers who would spend an entire summer yachting. Their social perception is based on a more fundamental distinction of leisured and non-leisured classes. This devalued the significance of their own local hierarchy.

This view is apparent in a number of the fishing villages which serviced large yachts or had wealthy visitors. The distinction between wealthy/non-wealthy almost conflates in their minds with outsiders/locals:

What sort of village was Mersea in your young days, were there any posh people in it at the time?
Yes, yes, there were quite a few posh people about there.
What sort of people were they, what sort of occupations?
Well, people from London – business people from London – or retired people from London. (3047:28–9)

Not that I would ascribe this perception entirely to real material difference in the degree of wealth between the outsiders and the local hierarchy. It would be obtuse to consider the relations between perceived status hierarchies simply as how they affect the working class and not dialectically. Part of the effect of local systems based on small-scale employment and ascriptive knowledge is that socially and culturally the elite have a greater identity with the workers: it may be a hierarchy but the perceived gap in terms of education, cultural pursuits, leisure and so on can be quite small. Employers who still worked as many hours and as many days as their labourers and who spoke with much the same accent and vocabulary were not perceived as, nor could perceive themselves as, so different from those employed, however much economic power they wielded. Lockwood writes that

Workers in such environments [small isolated country town] are unlikely to change their patterns of consumption as they are their political loyalties, because in both cases they are encapsulated in social systems which provide them with few alternative conceptions of what is possible, desirable and legitimate. (1975:21)

Here he is delineating the very conditions which apply to that local middle class.

Part of the collective social identity of the fishermen, regardless of their material wealth, was also due to the way in which the rest of society perceived fishermen. The failure of the rest of society to accord as much social status to owners of fishing capital as they did to holders of other forms of capital inevitably tended to prevent such status (and class) differences being accorded significance within the industry. This can be seen in the following extract from the informant whose father was the owner of four steam drifters, a Conservative councillor and so on:

I can remember once some visitors coming along and they were working on the Denes, and he [her father] had on a tan jumper and I suppose they thought he looked like an old man you see. They went up to him and he explained to 'em about it and they gave him a bob tip. And my brother Victor said 'What do you think? The old man put it in his pocket, he never gave Bob and I sixpence each'. (3030:20)

It is difficult to visualise such a prominent worthy being willing to pocket a shilling tip from a visitor in any other occupation. Indeed, given that his assets were around £10,000 before 1914, it is doubtful that such an event would happen to many other businessmen. Part of the fishermen's sense of social unity came not from factors within the occupation but wider society's perceptions of them.

The third category of 'privatised worker' was drawn mainly to encompass the modern worker engaged in large-scale mass production whose work is 'repetitive and lacking in autonomy'. This alienation at work is reinforced by the 'social structure of the council, or the private, low-cost housing estate'. As a result of this pattern of work and residence these workers develop only a minimal sense of class or group affiliation and judge others merely by material possessions: 'Basically, the pecuniary model of society is an ideological reflection of work attachments which are instrumental and community relations which are privatised' (1975:21). Comment on the social situation of the fishermen is in Part three and comment here is restricted to one or two aspects of the work situation, for, in spite of their being polar opposites of the privatised worker in terms of work satisfaction and a common identity, they have a number of values in common with the privatised typification.

The fishermen commonly held the image of a large class and they held a pecuniary model of class. Of the informants, 58 per cent gave 'money' as the basis of class distinction compared to the next highest category 'behaviour' with 13 per cent, the other categories being 'status', 'power', 'occupation', with 5 per cent 'don't know'.[11] That these traditional workers held such a view points towards a complex layering of attitudes to be found in working-class communities. It might not be unreasonable to assume that pecuniary motivation has existed at least since the introduction of waged labour. The difficulty for deferential workers (working in similar scale production to the fishermen) was that they could not make demands on their employer without coming into direct conflict with their own social ideology. But the prevalence of the share system which gave fishermen a proportion of the product removed one point of conflict, and allowed a different ideology. There was no inconsistency in a fisherman being committed to his work and his workmates while being deferential and holding a pecuniary model of society. After all, the more he produced the better he served his mates, his employer and the more money he earned for himself. It is a mistake to assume that job satisfaction does not coexist with financial inducements.

This points to the relations of production, rather than the actual nature of the work task, as inducing alienation; putting such workers on a share of the product might well change their level of involvement. Moore has observed that '...the proletarian outlook is relatively modern'[12], and it could be a stage in a change from systems of small capital ownership, craftsmen's ownership of their tools, share systems and various forms of piece and task work. But whatever role the standardisation of wages and methods of payment may have played in changing perceptions Lockwood has postulated that the pecuniary model of society receives expression only where social conditions allow, and it is the community ashore which forms the final part of this study.

8

Political attitudes

... for elections held after the passing of the Ballot Act in 1872, we cannot make precise correlations between the electoral behaviour of small localities and the appropriate statistics of personal income, occupation, religious affiliation and so on ...

H. Pelling 1967

In spite of the difficulties noted above Pelling typifies the 'marine population of the little coastal ports' of Essex as mainly Conservative, thus going against the grain of the Liberal tendency in the area. This was true also of the Suffolk and Norfolk inshoremen. He states that the deepsea fishermen of Lowestoft and Yarmouth were split, with the trawlermen being Conservative and the driftermen Liberal over the issue of Free Trade.[1] The aggregated interview data largely supports this description.[2] Pelling's complaint about the difficulties created by the 1872 Ballot Act was made before the widespread collection of oral history interviews. These now provide a potential source of correlations which are known to exist because income, occupation and so forth are united, not by statistical inference, but through the coherence of personal experience. As the informants were resident in eight different constituencies it would require many more of them, even if space permitted, to contribute to understanding the political history of the region. Our main interest is not which party held power but how the political values of individuals are related to their industrial and social position.

The interviews contain a substantial amount of information on the politics of farm workers as well as of fishermen. A recent study of East Anglian farm workers noted that they have 'customarily been regarded as the epitome of the deferential worker, together with servants'.[3]

Deference is another concept which has been applied to a rather wide range of phenomena, but most significantly to account for the fact that a substantial proportion of the working class have voted for political parties which primarily represent the interests of capital and management rather than those of labour. This pattern of voting has been explained in a number of ways but among those most relevant to this study are an acceptance of the

107

hierarchical social system and the influence an employer has over his work-force in situations of small-scale employment.

The difficulty in looking at historical behaviour from this perspective is that it is often impossible (through lack of appropriate evidence) to see whether a particular pattern of behaviour was due to deference – a belief in one's 'betters' and a readiness to accept their lead – or whether the behaviour was due to powerlessness – a fear that unless one behaved as the economically and socially powerful expected one would be penalised. In his study Newby (1977) makes the point that, in fact, the rural areas of East Anglia have a long tradition of rural protest and trade unions and that behaviour interpreted as deference has been powerlessness.[4] Our accounts confirm that point.

It is evident from our interviews that pre-1914 farm labourers showed a determination to hold their own politics in spite of overtly deferential economic and social behaviour. The clearest example of such links is a family where the mother had been a house servant to the farmer before her marriage and still helped in the house as required, the father was a plough-man but worked Sundays as a groom and gave similar personal services, sons worked on the farm and there was virtual total dependency and yet:

Well father was a Liberal. See that was all Liberal that time of day.
I wondered whether with being so closely connected with the big house and that whether he would have been Tory?
No. Father wouldn't be that way don't you see. See the – the farmer he was Conservative. And – we were Liberal, we went – we didn't make a lot of noise about it. But father went and I know he always voted Liberal. But [his employer] never ask him where he was going and father never went to no meetings. (3007:58)

His father did not make a show and in many interviews there is an implicit fear of revealing one's politics. One (Conservative) informant (3011) when asked if employers ever put pressure on employees replied that he had heard stories of it happening but that he did not believe them. On the other hand he did not know the politics of his father, who was a regular voter, but he did know the politics of an uncle who lived in the village. Significantly his father was a farm worker while his uncle had a smallholding and was independent of such pressures. This ignorance, however, is frequently recognised as being due to the employer's power:

Well, I never voted when I was young you know – and I never did know how my father voted, he wouldn't tell you. He wouldn't tell you what he was.
Do you think some men wouldn't say how they voted because they were frightened of getting the sack?
Oh yes.
Was there much of that?
Yes. Because – some of these farmers – 'course they were nearly all Conservative at

that time of day. They'd sometimes ask the men how they're going to vote, or something of that. Of course they wouldn't never tell 'em. No. Because nearly all the farm labourers that time of day were Liberals, see. (3005:63–4)

The general tone of village politics is secretive and covert and is set in a matrix of more general social control. A number of interviews state that farm workers had to attend church on Good Friday morning otherwise they would not receive a day's pay for the holiday; 'And there was one farmer in the village, that on his travels Good Friday, saw one or more of his men doing gardening, and he issued orders then for the following year that I'll pay you to have Good Friday off as a holiday, but there must be no gardening' (3011:34). The interesting fact is, however, that in spite of the continuous power which was brought to bear on them they maintained their commitment to the Liberals even where the pressure was so strong that they were afraid to let their own family know how they voted. These interviews bring into sharp focus the distinction between deference as a social act and as a political one: the farm labourer observed one, but not the other. If Conservative voting is taken as an indication of deference in agricultural workers then other evidence suggests that deference has grown with the second generation who would have started voting in the 1920s and 1930s.[5] This is congruent with Newby's argument that changes in the social dimension of farm work (fewer workers, closer working contact with the farmer and so on) rather than any basic change in the power relationship have caused changes in the contemporary farm worker's social perceptions.

The evidence from the fishermen reveals a very different political consciousness and one which varies according to their particular sectional experience. Yacht-hands were the most deferential both from direct pressure and through their own perceptions and attitudes:

I always used to vote Conservative. Well what your father was nearly all the boys was the same.
Do you think that it had anything to do with mixing with the people on the yachts?
That played a lot of it. I mean all those yachting people were well-to-do people weren't they? They're all Conservatives, I mean they were nearly all very rich people that owned these yachts. That's how it came about really.
Would any of the old skippers take any notice of your politics?
Some of them would, and some wouldn't. Some of them would say 'Well you do as you like'. But some of the old skippers they'd try and get the governor votes, the owner you see, and if you didn't – well you went the next year if you voted Labour and he was a Conservative you wouldn't get the job. That's how it used to go on. (3059:13–14)

That this sort of political pressure was of long-standing was confirmed by a man born in 1872 who was away yachting in the 1890s. He stated that yacht captains would not take you if you were of the wrong political complexion.

Another, born in 1879, described the importance placed on voting by the employers: 'But often we were away in the summer, away yachting. And a lot of the men used to come home to vote. Might get a week off, the governor used to give 'em a week for to come and put their vote in' (3038:49). On the whole this pressure to vote seems to have coincided with the political preferences of the inshoremen who were overwhelmingly Conservative. But one interesting dimension of the oral evidence is that it reveals that this practice continued well into the 1920s and 1930s and that such pressures were put on women voters once they obtained the franchise:

Were most fishermen Conservative do you think?
Well the majority of 'em were. The majority of 'em were – for this reason. All the men in these – they had to rely on yachting. They were moneyed people. And they had to be Conservative to get a job. Now – I can remember when I first got married in 1928, I – my wife was never a Conservative, or I think she had an open mind about politics really, I don't think she was more for one than the other. But I know I was yachting at that particular time and there was a woman – that I know – she was chairman of the Ladies Conservative Party, and she stopped my wife in the street one day and she said – you don't come to our Conservative meetings do you. So my wife said no. Well look, she said, I think that you should, because if you don't become a Conservative your husband will never get a yachting job. See, it just shows you, I mean they had to be Conservative. (3045:58)

This final extract from the inshore section overtly expresses the perception of self-interest which has been explicit in some of the other statements:

Were many of the fishermen Conservative then?
Most of 'em on here. That's the best for us for yachting, yes, 'cause if you get a Liberal or a Labour government half of them wouldn't pay – I don't trust 'em.
So you reckoned that it looked after your job a bit better?
Oooh lots! Lots better for us. Crikey yes. (3058:12)

The pressure from their employers appears to reinforce their own perceptions of the necessity of a wealthy class and the existing property relations to preserve their employment.

The driftermen were mainly Liberal voters but it would need more interviews to ascribe their motives with any confidence. Many spent their life in agricultural villages where the community tradition of Liberal politics would have been an influence; as the drifting section was supposed to be Liberal over Free Trade, a deferential vote for their employer would also have been Liberal. It is also apparent that local politics were much more complex than the simple national issue of Free Trade. Many of the men who stood as local councillors in the Conservative interest were connected with the herring industry, and local alignments were clearly associated with local issues.[6]

Political perceptions are complicated by the fact that in Yarmouth the practice of paying for votes continued well into this century. It seems to have been quite widespread in so far as half of the twelve Yarmouth interviewees mentioned it spontaneously. There was the well-documented case in 1906 when the Conservative candidate Arthur Fell was fortunate to retain his seat when his election agent was found guilty of bribery under the Corrupt Practices Act. The mood of the voter was reported by one of the recipients who stated in evidence that he would not vote '... until he got some money ... he was out of work on election day, and he got the best price for his vote, which he certainly would not have given had he not received something for it'.[7] This attitude has affinities with the pre-Reform view of the franchise as a piece of property which should be of direct financial value to its owner: a sentiment still apparent in the interviews:

Now say me and three or four more are sitting in the pub, we're having a drink see. And they close at eight o'clock the polling booth. Well about half past seven a couple of these blokes come in, said 'Have you been and voted yet?' No. 'Come on you have to come and vote. Come on' he say 'it's worth half-a-crown each for you if you come and vote.' Well, he'd give half-a-crown each and away they'd go and vote. (3024:54)

Two other respondents remembered people coming to the house to solicit and to pay for their fathers' votes:

In those days they used to come after you to go and vote. And you'd hang on 'til the last minute. If my father was in from sea he'd hang 'til the last minute – and then they'd come to the door after you, 'cos you'd get five bob if you went and vote. And I'll tell you who that was for – Fell. (3019:53)

The other related a similar story, he stated that his father received 2s. 6d. from Fell, although he added that his father was a Tory anyway so it is conceivable that the corrupt payments did less to affect the way in which votes were cast while serving as a necessary inducement to get voters to the poll.[8] This was a practice which continued beyond the 1906 election:

How long did this paying for votes carry on in Yarmouth do you think?
Oh dear, not in these latter years. No. No, it's a good many years since that was given.
But it was quite a common practice was it?
Yes.
All the parties used to do that?
Yes. My brother used to say, 'Don't give 'em the two bob Beany, give 'em a shilling.' They used to be given the money to give out. 'Course what they've had to spare they've been in this very room and shared it. They have. (3012:23)

As the informant did not move into that house until 1916 this indicates that paying for votes continued into the 1920s. This may be a unique constituency in this respect but it raises the question as to how widespread were these practices at a time when most historians have considered them defunct. As with a number of areas this is more likely to be revealed retrospectively to the oral historians than to contemporary commentators.

The trawlermen might be seen in many ways as the antithesis of the yacht-hands. They lived in urban Lowestoft and had no contact with the very wealthy, even their employers were not perceived as middle class and yet they were quite content to follow their political lead:

Do you know what your father's views were at that time?
Oh he was always Conservative. Yes, he was a Conservative.
Was this true of most fishermen do you think or not?
Well – it all depend on the candidate, I think, more than anything. And it then – it more or less – depended on your employer. You see, I think that your employer used to expect, well of course they did, they never knew but they used to expect that you would do what he voted for. Particularly if he was a good employer, a good ship owner and that, well you didn't worry, politics didn't worry you, whichever one you voted for didn't bother. Never took it as a serious thing ... (3012:23)

This is an indication that the concept of 'deference' is more complex than its usual application as the subordination of one class to another: according to the trawlermen's social perceptions these smack owners were very much social equals and sometimes neighbours. According to Newby, deference involves an hereditary element as well as being 'the subscription to a moral order which endorses the individual's own political, material and social subordination' (1977:118). In this case, however, political deference appears as an intra-class phenomenon – although given to those with power to hire and fire. In the interviews it is difficult to determine whether political allegiance was deferential or simply pragmatic:

Did your husband used to vote at all?
He used to say – I'm trawling for Westmacott so I shall go and vote Conservative. (3029:33)

As an employee in the trawling sector he may have perceived Conservative policies in his self-interest independently of the wishes or politics of his employer. Given the small-scale nature of much of the ownership and the common cultural roots it seems just as likely that the employers' politics would have been influenced by their close cultural identity with their workforce as the other way round. Certainly the influence on voting does not fit into the usual concept of deference. Paul Thompson (1977) has raised the issue of the effectiveness of the political system as a means of social change and how this was perceived and there is much in these interviews to support his categorisation of the Conservative working-class vote as a matter of pragmatic self-interest, apathy or indifference. Two other commonly perceived threads in political deference are that sections of the working class hold the view that familiarity with wealth and power are essential to those people running the country, and the other based more in terms of traditional social hierarchy with the Conservatives perceived as the true leaders of nation – or Empire.[9] The idea that the wealthy involved themselves in politics as a public service, and that wealth ensured a personal disinterest, is also apparent in the interviews:

My opinion about that lot [present MPs] is that they don't do anything only help themselves, there ain't a man Jack there what is doing it for your benefit. They're all holding out their hand for nearly five thousand pound.
Do you think it was different in your young day?
Yes, because there was several of them, used to go there, and they didn't take the money what they used to pay 'em. (3010:42)

I mean, years ago, when that come to being a candidate for Parliament, them what went in for it done it for the honour of the country didn't they. They didn't get a very big salary. (3014:55–6)

I remain unconvinced, however, that 'deference' is the appropriate designation for their values. Those who were most continually under the influence of the traditional ruling class and/or the capitalist farmers were the most firmly committed to their political independence. That the fishermen were not was due to indifference not deference.

The political temper of Lowestoft was quite different from Yarmouth. This reflects their social and industrial distinctiveness as Lowestoft grew from the inflow of small fishermen-owners and the expansion of local businessmen rather than the movement of large-scale capital as with Yarmouth. Politics in Lowestoft were much more personalised and had a sharper edge than in Yarmouth; the one shared feature is that they also had something of an archaic flavour which serves as a reminder that even at this period the ballot box and party voting did not comprise the whole politics. The following is abbreviated from the *Lowestoft Journal* for 19 January 1895:

In the neighbourhood of the Town Hall the street was in a very congested state, and the passage of a vehicle occasioned some amount of squeezing, so closely packed were the crowd. Under the circumstances, prudent tradesmen put up their shutters to preserve their windows from breakage, owing to the pressure ... But everything comes to those who wait, even unto effigies, and about half past seven the strains of a band were heard, and in a few minutes torches and flares proclaimed that the procession was coming. And a fearful and wonderful procession it was! Torch bearers, to the number of about a dozen, walked in front, and flanked a couple of men, who bore aloft a hugh halberd, fashioned out of tin, with bills, bearing some kind of undistinguishable wording, depending from the shaft.

THEN CAME A BRASS BAND

perched in a wagonette ... Their hirsute disguises, however, must have affected their rendering of what was supposed to be the 'Dead March', for more excruciating strains it would be difficult to imagine. Following this was a cart, in which was a live donkey, although what this had to do with the case was not very clear. Next was what all Lowestoft and his wife had come out to see –

THE EFFIGY

This was crude and inartistic in the extreme – and it might equally well as served for any other individual who wears a wideawake hat and has grey hair. The crowd, however, were content to adopt it as the effigy of one man, and as such greeted it with loud yells and hooting. The wondrous figure had on a hat of clerical cut. Its hair was white, and it wore an antediluvian frock coat. On its back was the legend 'Stout V Pigs' and on other parts the figure displayed such soul-raising words as 'Old Tom Gin', 'I'm a Christian', and 'I've Shilling Charity'. In the cart with the effigy was a young fellow attired in a white smock and with a mortarboard on his head, evidently intended to represent the chaplain accompanying the aforesaid effigy to the stake – quite an elevating picture?

In spite of the question mark, the report relishes every detail of the evening's events leading up to the final burning. Mr Adams [the effigy] is described as 'the chieftain of the Lowestoft Liberals' a temperance worker, Methodist lay preacher, Borough and County Magistrate, member of the East Suffolk County Council, Guardian of the Poor and so on. He was the town's best known public figure and there are hints that 'Tory gold' financed what was purported to be simply an expression of the community's moral censure of his behaviour. The episode arose out of Mr Adams accepting a two shilling charity ticket in part payment for rent from cottage tenants on Christmas Eve. The reaction is an example of the social temper of the community where actions and motives were based on personal knowledge and direct relationships. The fact that the area was weak in trade unions, Labour politics, effective formal organisations and manifestations of opposition to the local business and political elite should not be taken to indicate that local employers and administrators were free to pursue their own ends without hindrance or opposition. The form of the protest would not be out of place in one of Hardy's novels, nor, for that matter, would be the response to it. The next issue of the paper a week after the effigy burning notes that Mr Adams gave his 'annual dinner' to all his tenants and of the 150 invited 120 attended. The fact that an annual dinner was given for tenants by a man whose fundamental business seems to have been a grocer – although he was involved in smack owning, the Steam Laundry and other local business – is indication of the social mood of the town and I suspect that the number attending after such a dramatic vote of censure can be read as a vote of support from his tenants.[10]

That this was not an isolated incident but part of the temper of local politics is confirmed when the same man was mayor two years later:

On Saturday morning over 100 unemployed waited upon the mayor at his residence ... a deputation had interviewed the mayor on two occasions earlier in the week ... [He] ... promised to bring the matter before the Town Council on Tuesday evening, and then gave them assistance, for which they gave him hearty thanks.[11]

Relief given at his residence on Saturday morning can have come only from his own pocket and the episode has strong overtones of mob pressure on a local worthy. The final point is that in straying into these accounts of local politics it is impossible to know to what extent fishermen were engaged in these activities, although there is some circumstantial evidence that they would not have been involved in the latter incident to any extent.[12] Unfortunately the full story of Lowestoft's politics cannot be pursued here, for it would require a separate study to identify the role of the fishermen, so their political temper will have to stand on the weight of the oral evidence.

PART THREE

The family, social practice and belief

Introduction

Generational reproduction involves biological reproduction, the regulation of sexuality, and the socialisation of children, while day-to-day reproduction involves numerous tasks of domestic labour such as shopping, cooking meals, washing, cleaning and caring. The two forms of reproduction of labour power inscribe biological, economic and ideological components, which are the tasks of domestic labour. The family is furthermore involved in the reproduction of the social relations of production which are in capitalist society both class relations and gender relations.

V. Beechey, in Kuhn and Wolpe 1978

Although this book is concerned with an exclusively male workforce and the effect of occupation on industrial and social attitudes, it would be incomplete without a consideration of domestic life and the values transmitted in the home. The family is the first social experience for most people and it is there that individuals learn the use of language and through this, and the actual experience which gives it meaning, an implicit ideology which precedes entry into the workforce. The acquisition and modification of meanings is a continuous process which can lead to the rejection of earlier values later in life but it is not unreasonable to postulate that there will be the least change in the significance of early experience where there is the greatest continuity and articulation of domestic, communal and industrial experience.

Class and gender relations are experienced and internalised first in the family. The fact that their occupation removed most fishermen from daily contact with their family brought into focus the prime role of the mother as the exemplar and mediator of class relations to the child. The first practical experience of our class position comes through the particular set of social relations which arise out of the local ensemble of the relations of production and the resultant specific social structure. Most children are still ignorant of the authority relations, and so forth, of their father's workplace long after they have absorbed their social position from the temper of their mother's contacts with landlords, shopkeepers, schoolteachers and all the similar contacts through which their mother's praxis inculcates social knowledge.

The same argument can be presented regarding gender conditioning and the attitude to the division of labour. Practice in the home shapes expectations as to what is 'normal' domestic practice and what the proper fields of activity are for men and women.[1] This final section, therefore, attempts a brief consideration of the domesticity of the fishermen and the relations of the family to some social practices and how those practices illustrate aspects of their values and beliefs.

In order to place domestic labour in context and to consider the input of wives, husbands and children one needs to consider the input of women into paid labour. As our interest is limited to the families of fishermen the evidence used is largely oral, although given the well-known under-reporting of women's paid work in documentary sources this probably leads to a more complete account.[2] Although this indicates wage levels and opportunities (or lack of them) open to women of the period our main concern is with work as a supplement to what all, including themselves, considered their main role as housewife.

9

Female waged labour

The fishwife lends a hand, overhauls the nets, counts the fish into tubs and baskets, and keeps a keen eye on the payments. All the boats have come in now, and Yorkshire men and Cornishmen jostle each other round the fish buyers; bids are rapidly offered and taken, the wife puts in a last word, and the bargain is made.

Joseph R. Bagshawe 1933

In many traditional communities women collected shellfish for bait, baited the lines and repaired net   their involvement in the commercial dimension is revealed in the extract above describing Whitby around the turn of the century. Similar accounts can be found in many contemporary sources and one Cornish working fisherman who had a paper published on mackerel fishing in 1883 wrote of the share division between crew, nets and boat 'We leave all that to the women.'[1] In other words the pattern of production was markedly pre-industrial with women and the family as a unit of production. But just as the East Anglian fishermen showed local peculiarities – working on Sundays, individual ownership and so on – so the work pattern of women did not conform to the traditional role of women in inshore fishing communities. Very few women had any direct connection with the fishing process through collecting or preparing bait and fishing lines nor even through preparing or hawking fish. Indeed, it was exceptional for them even to make or mend nets save as employees in the netchambers connected with the drifting industry. This non-involvement is most noticeable in Essex where they only occasionally did some network. In Suffolk, interviews from Southwold and Aldeburgh reveal slightly more involvement although it was claimed that it was not general for wives to repair nets but that they would occasionally boil shrimps and sell those to shops. The picture for Norfolk is similar up the coast as far as Cromer where the cooking and dressing of crabs for the hotel and holiday trade as well as preparing bait for the fishermen's lines are reported. My own research did not extend further north, but other accounts suggest a growing involvement along the north Norfolk coast.[2]

There are technical and geographical reasons why women were less

121

involved in East Anglia than in other areas. The flat shelving coastline and hinterland is in marked contrast to the West Country and Scotland where steep cliffs or rocky inlets greatly increase the amount of labour involved in getting gear and fish ashore.[3] The absence of musselbeds accessible from the shore prevented women from collecting bait and East Anglian fishermen frequently used net-caught fish as bait. Because of the nature of the grounds and type of fish long lines requiring a great deal of intensive hand labour were less frequently used than in other areas. Within East Anglia this situation began to change along parts of north Norfolk. Shrimps caught from the small beachboats of Suffolk and Norfolk had to be boiled in the home, so women could perform that task: in Essex the larger specialised shrimp boats had boilers on board and the fishermen cooked them before landing them. None of these reasons offer a full explanation, however, for in no case does it explain why women did not take a greater part in hawking the fish.

The trawling industry centred at Yarmouth and Lowestoft provided virtually no involvement for women in the period under review. Fish was landed at the fish docks, packed, iced and transported by male labour. A few informants report that their mothers used to braid trawlnets at home, but this was apparently by the turn of the century a defunct industry.

Only the drifting industry generated work for a considerable number of women: as beatsters and in kipper curing, to be considered in a moment, and as gutters preparing and barrelling herring for export. The season for the gutters was the same as the Home Season for driftermen, September to December, and at its peak in the years up to 1914 employed some 5,000 women at Lowestoft and Yarmouth.

Few local women were employed in herring gutting; the vast majority were Scottish 'girls'. Although the work was extremely tiring with long hours in exposed conditions it did offer the chance of comparatively high earnings in an area of low pay and on the face of it it is strange that more local women were not employed. That local women had worked in the industry and valued the employment is evident from an account taken from the *Aberdeen Weekly Journal* 11 December 1901, which reported the return of a fishworkers' train with some 300 to 400 girls who had been working the season at Yarmouth: 'The girls complain of having received a boisterous send-off from the English girls amongst whom a considerable amount of jealousy prevailed during the last season owing to the curers preferring the Scottish girls.' The impression from oral and documentary sources is that by 1914 there would be hardly enough English girls employed to give anyone a send-off.

The exclusion of local women might be explained through patronage in the system of employment, for most of the curing trade was in the hands of Scottish firms. As the Scottish girls would have already worked the summer season in Scotland they may well have been quicker than the local women, as the essence of piecework is speed through practice. One might also suspect that migrant labour was more desirable because it had no domestic commitments and could respond more readily to the fluctuations in the working hours. Not that the migrants were an entirely docile workforce, and as the result of a strike nine fishergirls were sued for breach of contract by their employer in 1910. The evidence[4] reveals the difficulty of establishing the contract of work, for according to their employee they were to 'work whenever required, day or night – any to work "green" or fresh herrings. Sometimes they worked from 10 am to 4 o'clock the next morning', whereas, in their defence, one defendant stated that it was her seventh season in Lowestoft and that she had agreed to return 'on the same terms as last year', and those restricted work to between 6 a.m. to 7 p.m. with time for meal breaks. The absence of written contracts did not prevent them from being found guilty and fined. The nature of the work is clearly described by one of the informants:

My father was a Yarmouth fisherman, my mother a Scottish fishergirl. They met in Lerwick, but she'd been down to Yarmouth. They used to run special trains years ago from Aberdeen and all the Scottish ports. They were part of the community. They were as natural as the leaf on the tree, they were seasonal, they were part of the business. They used to work jolly hard in all weathers and ninety percent of them were not under cover. They used to work in the open. They used to wear oilskins just above the elbow and their arms used to be red, absolutely red, with the salt and the wind and that. They were real hard, tough girls – at the same time they were good girls. They used to work terrifically long hours, seven or eight in the morning 'til eight, nine and ten o'clock at night. (3017:2–3)

At least one contemporary report (McIver 1906) is less certain of their hardihood and comments that working fourteen hours a day in cold and ice led to many illnesses and that the girls often fainted. He states that a team of three girls could do up to thirty-three barrels a day and were paid 1s. per barrel. That is a potential income of well over £3 for a five and a half day week. A cooper in the herring industry for over fifty years puts their capacity even higher:

What sort of money could the girls earn?
Oh, very poor money. Very poor. Eightpences per barrel. And there is three in a crew. Every barrel they packed, and there might be thirteen, fourteen hundred herring in a barrel. Eightpence for one barrel, and it had to be divided out between three girls. When I was in Gorleston with her [indicating his wife] there was an overglut of herring so we worked a whole week, worked right up to Saturday

teatime, that was working every night 'til nine. And I used to mark their barrels and I marked 298¾ barrels for the wife's crew. They were a dandy crew. Oh it was a fast crew. (3055B:39–40)

In spite of the reduction in piecerates[5] his wife earned 66s. in that week, although one must appreciate the exceptional output. But the fluctuation in catches which affected the driftermen also affected the women and even in 1913, a year of very heavy catches, the local paper reports on the 4th of October that the gutters had been idly waiting for two weeks with no fish at all. Taking the amount of herring landed and the estimated number of girls working as very crude indicators suggests that the girls may have averaged 25s. a week before 1914.[6] This is still higher than many local male rates, and even carters who during the herring season worked six days of unlimited hours with no overtime pay also received only 25s. a week.

The other branch of herring processing which provided work for women was kippering. Filleting a herring for kippering is a much more painstaking task than gutting one for pickling. To be kippered a herring has to be cut down the back close to the backbone and gutted while preserving the skin intact to keep it in one piece. The fish are then threaded on to speets through their gills and placed in layers up in the smokehouse and smoked overnight. Next morning they are ready for packing and dispatch. The industry was small scale and I have no reliable estimate of numbers employed – but hundreds rather than thousands. Nevertheless, by common account it seems that there was a converse set of circumstances to the gutting, for most of the labour force was local women who also travelled for their firms.

They were paid a fixed wage and had a fixed weight of herring to kipper every day. The wage rates are established from a report[7] on an agreement made by 'fifty of the principle firms from Lowestoft to Stornaway' at the end of the 1904 season. This constituted a wage reduction due to 'a decline in the market price of kippers', wages previously running from 17s. to 21s. a week were reduced to a flat rate of 16s. Firms were to employ one learner to every ten women and pay them 12s. a week. Two crans of herrings were to be split, tentered and packed as a day's work. In local terms still a good wage and one confirmed by a Yarmouth informant who started in a fish house in 1901 aged sixteen having worked the two previous years as a silk factory winder for only 7s. a week:

In the fishing time, before me and my mother used to go to work, six o'clock in the morning, we would go to the Star Hotel on the quay and have rum and coffee for twopence.
That was a very hard job wasn't it?
Lovely work. We enjoyed every hour. Every hour. There used to be about eight women at a bench. We'd all be singing or chatting away, telling jokes. Well the

happiest days of my life that was, in the fish house. You got a weekly wage, twelve shillings. (3029:2,19–20)

They worked five full days a week, from 6 a.m. to 6 p.m., and Saturday mornings to pack the kippers which had been smoked overnight. This apparently took three or four hours. The other attractions of the work are apparent in this account of the 1920s:

But we loved it because we were all a happy crowd you know. When we went to Hull you had the Iceland herring. They used to be all frozen stiff, if you cut yourself you didn't know it, your fingers were nearly frozen. We used to go up to Peterhead, Scotland. See as they had their seasons we used to travel round. We used to work hard but we used to go out night time after the boys, and chase them around, or they used to chase us. It was hard work but it was a free and easy time, you weren't restricted like – you know, in a factory where there were bosses, you had to work hard mind, no stopping, but it seemed freer. There used to be so many crans come up and put on the bench and we used to just slog in and get 'em done. (3060:19–23)

These two extracts raise a number of industrial and social points. That the work was 'very hard' is repeated three times but it is accompanied by a sense of no bosses and of freedom. The industrial relations were not unlike those of the fishermen themselves in that the work was a collective enterprise so the group would control slackers as the less one did the more others had to do to finish the day's task. The absence of machinery or noise, the physical layout of the work meant that the social interplay was very high. There was also social freedom. Travelling to different places, living together in lodgings, the rather tough image of the job all no doubt helped to create the same independent attitude in women as it did men and leave an ambivalent memory of whether they chased or were chased by the boys. Certainly their work experience was as much one of an occupational community as any male occupation.

The most respectable and skilled occupation connected with the fishing industry was the repairing of the herring nets. In 1912 there were 570 drifters registered at Yarmouth and Lowestoft and as each one provided constant work for about three women it was a comparatively widespread occupation:

Would women be employed regularly all the year?
Oh yes, all the year round, they used to work from eight in the morning 'til six at night. They were long hours in those days and from September to Christmas, if they liked, they would work overtime 'til eight 'til nine at night.
What sort of wages did they get?
Well they used to do about a shilling for the first year, one and six for the second

year, and then they could make about eight shillings a week when they came out of their time. They were two years serving their time. I don't know what they made when they worked overtime. (3030:5)

That account refers to about 1912 and the wages indicate the very low regional levels. One informant who started as an apprentice beatster in 1907 confirms the wage as being 8s. a week but states that she was paid 3s. for the first year and 4s. the second. She saw this as a welcome escape from domestic service and presumably got the opportunity because her grandfather was the ransacker in that netchamber. It employed three women and two apprentices. Sometimes they would be put on piecework when apparently they could earn 10s. or even 12s. a week. She was married in 1915 and worked at home after marriage: '... when I came up here [1920s] I had two children, and the man in the shed knew me, I knew them well, and he said would I do a net. Well I was highly delighted. I used to stand at my shed hours – and sometimes I'd earn five shillings and six pence [in a week]' (3043:4). Other accounts stated that women would take babies and young children to the netchambers with them and it is clear that working arrangements were quite flexible. One account indicated that it was work where children could help:

When you were a child did your parents play games with you in the house?
No. When I was a youngster my mother used to have the nets at home and mend. I would sit and thread the needles for her while she did it. Well then I got so I used to learn to mend what we called 'sprung', that was two meshes broke into one. I learned to mend them and then I learned to mend what we called 'crows feet'. That would be three meshes broken. That's how you used to learn the men to beat. Pass the time away, there weren't no real games – I mean you used to play marbles and that – but there weren't nothing for the children that time of day when I was a kid. (3014:58)

One interesting feature of that extract is his comment that 'the *men* learnt to beat' at this childhood stage. A man's ability to beat nets added to his value as a crew member as some mending was done during the voyage and could secure him a job in competition with a man who did not have the skill.

The great advantage of the occupation for women is clearly that it provided a comparatively well-paid and regular occupation (by regional standards) and one which could be followed on a piecework basis as outwork after marriage. It was undoubtedly considered as a skilled trade by the local community and as superior in status to both factory work and to fish preparation. It was the elite of manual work inferior only to superior shop and white-collar work. It also had the considerable, if unassessable, psychological advantages of providing work in the community of origin and keeping a girl at home as a member of her family. As a beatster she was very much part of the fishermen's world.[8]

In spite of the jobs created by fishing, domestic service was still the most common occupational experience for single girls. Experience of domestic service after marriage, however, does reflect certain local aspects. The coastal towns and villages of the region were holiday centres and this generated a demand for lodgings and intensified the demand for daily cleaners and washerwomen. The extent to which domestic washing was engaged in is suggested by this extract from a letter in the *Lowestoft Weekly Journal* 2 March 1889 protesting against plans to form a company to build a steam laundry in the town '... hundreds of women earn a livelihood by taking in washing, and I may safely say one third of these are widows'. The same newspaper records on 30 August 1913 that the Kirkley Steam Laundry (Lowestoft) sued an employee who left without giving a week's notice. It was a sizeable concern with sixty employees and her wages were 6s. a week. This makes the 1s. 6d. that is usually cited for 'a days washing' seem almost generous, especially as most of the daily washerwomen were given lunch as well. The wages of 6s. weekly in a commercial laundry in Lowestoft in 1913 verify the account from a Harwich laundress between 1909 and 1912:[9]

Oh yes, and then I went to the laundry. I was head finery ironer when I left. I used to do all the best, all this lovely linen for the ladies you know, and I used to take an interest in it. We used to do the ordinary irons then, not electric ones. We had a great big thing, all the irons were put round – and then you'd take them out, whatever iron you wanted. I used to do all the silk work. And I had four bob a week when we first started. Then I went to six. Six bob. And we used to go eight of a morning 'til eight of night. Monday 'til Friday. That's a long time ain't it. (3039:29)

By this period the fishing in Harwich was in a very depressed state and there was hardship in the fishing families. As one male informant stated of the fishermen's wives 'Some of the poor old devils used to take in washing. Lot of 'em used to say that Harwich men killed women at the washtub like' (3037:21). Certainly commercial laundry work at 1½d. an hour could hardly prove more life-enhancing.

At Lowestoft and Yarmouth the practice of letting rooms was widespread due to the influx of Scottish workers during the ten week season between September and December. With an influx of about 5,000 girls and some 600 or so male workers, some 2,000 local homes were needed to provide lodgings so it was a general experience:

Of course our rooms were big, you could get two beds in one room. But we took

these six girls in, they came from Fraserburgh. And they bring in their big boxes
you see. Well, out of courtesy you'd let them have a table to put their things, but
they'd sit on their boxes. You've got to supply them with heat and lighting and
what do you think it was for each girl per week? Three shillings. Now thats
eighteen shillings. Of course, if they were good girls they would give the landlady
another two or three shillings 'cos they used to work on the bonus then they did.
And if they were good girls they would give the landlady more, if you looked after
them you see. But you had to be strict with them, run the rule over 'em when you
first take them in, say now – ten o'clock. No men in the house. You'd stretch a
point on Saturday night, 'cos their husbands used to come down in the drifters,
they'd come down with the buyers. Well of course if they had their sweethearts or
anything come my mother said that's all right. But look out if it isn't. Out you go
lock stock and barrel. (3006:22–23)

The work of the gutters was mainly out in the open during some of the
worst months of the year and there is no doubt that there was a great deal
of upheaval in having them, as their working clothes were permeated with
herring and even the problems of coping with six oilskin outfits and so on
caused problems in the small terraced houses. If there was a room which
was large enough for two double beds, however, the 18s. a week was
equivalent to the gross wage of a third hand on a trawling smack and more
than the full wage of many male adult workers ashore. Letting to holiday
visitors was even more profitable, and although this was practised in
surprisingly cramped houses, on the whole it was most frequently
practised in one of the respectable streets of terraced housing. A distinction can be seen in this interview where the woman first lived on the
'Beach' (the old area of Lowestoft) when first married in 1907 and later
moved to 'here' (i.e. a four roomed terraced house):

I used to do that a good deal in the summer, yes, bed and breakfast.
This is the house on the Beach?
No, its when I'm here. I've had Scotch girls when I lived on the Beach. Three.
Actually three in a bed. Nice girls they were though my husband didn't approve of
it. He liked his own house for himself. Mind they [the houses] had only two
rooms, little living room and the other room, and they had to come through our
room. I was glad of the money. That was only three shillings each, nine shillings.
You'd got to find them a fire at night; I used to do all the cooking for the nine bob.
(3016:15)

The husband was a trawlerman and would therefore be home for one
night a week. His objection is echoed in other interviews and the woman's
determination to earn money in this way was sometimes a matter for
domestic friction:

I let like the devil here. Me and my children [two] used to sleep out in the shed
when my husband was away. If he come home and I had people he used to have to

sleep in the front room on the floor. And he used to mutter, he used to jaw like mad. I'd think to myself, my word I wish he weren't at home.
So did most of the fishing women earn a bit by letting?
Well, they did, yes they did. We used to charge ten shillings a room. We thought we were well away you know. We supplied the bed and did all the cooking. You know cooked their breakfast and all that. They used to go and get the stuff for their dinner and bring it in and we would cook it for 'em. (3043:7–8)

That informant was married in 1915 and let intensively in the interwar period. Perhaps her description of letting 'like the devil' establishes her level of activity as atypical. If this spouse objected to little effect some women state that they did not let because their husbands objected – although in one case the spouse cooperated to the extent of taking their two sons to sea for a month so that there would be another room free to let:

Well, my mother used to let for summer visitors, to help her, you know, through the winter. Well, there was no room for you, so he used to take us boys, me and my brother, in the summertime when we was out of school, to sea with him. I always used to go to sea with my father. (3022:7)

This expansion in paid domestic labour – possible within the house as a result of the growth in the numbers of holiday-makers and of seasonal workers – may well have provided an alternative source of income to herring gutting, which was in any case monopolised by the Scottish women. It would certainly be a source which would interfere less with domestic duties and be available for a longer period of the year.

None of the other occupations engaged in by the kin of fishermen merit detailed consideration. Single girls were obliged to work although the oral evidence reveals that of the twenty women interviewed seven did not enter the workforce immediately after leaving school but were kept at home to help their mothers with domestic labour or were withdrawn from work for considerable periods for the same reason. The situation after marriage is more interesting. For although only a third of mothers, wives and informants (120 cases in all) worked outside the home another 40 per cent made a financial contribution through the various forms of homework detailed above. Thus, in 70 per cent of the homes children witnessed the woman engaged in paid labour and if the location of the majority of it did not challenge the view that a woman's place was in the home, it at least undermined the image of the male as the sole breadwinner.

The attitudes to women working showed a considerable range in both male and female informants. One man expressed the view that although married women did not normally work, 'a woman would have to work if she had a lazy husband or something like that' (3008:45). Another man stopped his 'wife' from working as soon as they became engaged because he felt that he was earning enough that there was no need for her to go out. The reason given for not letting wives work was that it let the home go. It is possible that the high percentage of women earning money *in their homes* muted what might have been a stronger attitude. As the extracts indicated, a number of women were determined to earn money in spite of their husbands' opposition, others were given credit by their husbands for their financial contribution, while the feeling that a woman should not work came from female informants too:

Did you do paid work after you married?
No, love, no, no. I'd enough to do to keep me house clean and the children hadn't I. No. Never been to work, no never. And I didn't care who came into the little old house. Though I say it myself it was a little old palace. (3019:79)

Housework itself had its own, and for some, sufficient satisfactions, and the issues relating to role divisions are discussed in the section on domestic life and family relations.

10

Domestic life

The husband was not only mean with money. He was callous in sex, as often as not forcing a trail of unwanted pregnancies upon his unwilling mate. He was harsh to his children. He was violent when drunk, which was often.

M. Young and P. Willmott 1957

This travesty of working-class family life encapsulates an established sociological view of the father in the 'past'; the past is then used as a history-as-progress analysis to show that a more equal partnership exists in the present. We have questioned this view elsewhere[1] and our informants' evidence denies the generality of that account. This evidence is quite crucial in relation to the debate on male domesticity because the results stand in such sharp contrast to Tunstall's study of the Hull fishermen of the 1950s. And while not questioning the validity of his findings that in the 1950s 'Some fishermen quickly come to regard their wives merely as providers of sexual and cooking services in return for a weekly wage' (1962:162) our evidence refutes the thesis which links tough male-only occupations with heavy drinking, domestic indifference and brutality.

The difference in period, place and work patterns prevents any detailed comparison between this study and Tunstall's. My impression from reading his book is that his fishermen resented the comparatively easy lives of their wives compared to their own, whereas the East Anglian fishermen were quick to acknowledge the heavy burden of domestic work and responsibility shouldered by their wives and mothers. This impression is congruent with the material reality. The Hull fishermen of the 1950s were fishing in arctic waters, working a hundred hour week and doing so in some of the most dangerous and severe conditions in industry. By contrast, for that generation of housewives, the amount of domestic labour was beginning to decline with smaller families and more convenient homes and services. The contrast between the input of each spouse into maintaining their family must have been one of the sharpest in the country. In the earlier period in East Anglia, however, both parents were required to work around a seventy hour week to complete the amount of labour (waged and

Table 12 *Domestic work in the home*

		Regular (%)		Occasional (%)		Never (%)		D/K (%)		Cases
Father		25	(15)	13	(8)	28	(17)	33	(20)	60
Children:*	male	40	(16)	28	(11)	18	(7)	15	(6)	40
	female	45	(9)	25	(5)	–	–	30	(6)	20

* I.e. the informants' own childhood experience.

unwaged) required to support their family. Many of the interviews convey a sense of partnership in marriage.[2]

This sense of partnership extended (in a different form) to the children, and the family formed an effective economic and emotional group. Certainly there is no evidence in these interviews to support the thesis that the family relationships emerge largely as a result of individual bargaining power. This is not to deny that, in general, family norms and relationships were not a valuable source of exchanged services and mutual economic advantage: what is not accepted is that the family contacts depended on economic individualism; indeed, it is not even accepted that the family is a collection of individuals. Children are born into and socialised by the family, they are not simple individual members but part of its unique product; whether they accept or reject it they can no more not be part of it any more than they cannot be part of their own self. For most people early socialisation within the family imposes a web of affections and loyalties which become the basis of praxis; for affection, or even a sense of right action, can provide stronger constraints and rewards than a marginal few shillings.[3]

Family socialisation has an enduring importance, and its general importance in the acquisition of language and, through that, ideology has already been stated. This point will bear some elaboration, for the material reality of working-class life of the period was bound to provide a barrier to dominant ideals no matter how widely they were propagated. Children may have heard or read that a woman's place was in the home and that the man was the breadwinner but the majority of this group experienced their mother earning money and their father helping in the home as a matter of course.

Table 12 shows that boys as well as girls were expected to help with domestic chores. There was a degree of gender patterning in the duties performed, with the boys doing most of the outdoor jobs such as errands and cleaning outside yards and toilets. They often did weekly cleaning jobs, such as shoes or cutlery, although many had their share of washing-up and similar tasks. Girls were more involved in the routine of cleaning and even simple cooking. Even so, a quarter of the female informants claimed that what help they gave in the home as a child was voluntary, and there are only two examples of children being over-burdened and turned into drudges.

Although there was gender typing this was secondary to the need to have tasks fulfilled. Thus there are examples of boys who stated that they had little time to play because they always had to mind numerous babies,[4] and of girls who had to run errands: roles usually reserved for the opposite sex.

In this the father's example must have been significant. This informant insisted that it was customary local practice for men to help in the house before 1914:

Was it a bit unusual in those days for men to help in the house?
No. No, the men always used to do some housework more or less.
A lot of people say that's a new thing, helping in the house.
No, not here. Because lots of them used to do things in the house, you know, to help the women out, because they most all had families, five or six was moderate – and eight and nine was – so they had to help more or less when they were home. Of course, they weren't home much. In the summer they used to go away – yachting. (3054:49)

It is worth making the point that domestic work is a flexible procedure according to the standards maintained. And although the overwhelming majority remember their standard of care and feeding with satisfaction there are only two interviews which reveal the obsessional scrubbing and polishing that feature in accounts from northern areas. And in one of those the standard was maintained by the male:

Yes, he was a good father and a good husband. My children never knew what it was to get their own water in the morning to wash with. Before they went to school he'd clean their shoes.
Would he do any other jobs around the house?
On Friday night he used to say to me and my dear old mother – go in the other room I'm going to clean through. And he'd clean through my kitchen. I had a big cooking stove in there, with big white plates at the back, and he'd make that shine like a bit of glass. (3029:29)

As this informant married in 1904 it would seem that the experience was pre-1914 or at the latest in the early 1920s. Usually the male approach to housework was more pragmatic and restricted to necessary tasks. The contribution made by the men should not come as a surprise, for some contemporary observers at least were aware of it: 'Men of the working class are as libelled as fathers as working-class women are as cooks, nurses and managers. In countless homes the busy, many-childed mother breathes freely for the first time in the day when her husband returns from work.'[5]

There was a great deal of domestic labour to be done, for the fishermen had large families. Family size ranged from one to eighteen, with eight as the mean average and median and ten as the mode. Table 12 shows that the majority of men for whom there is information helped in the home.[6] The number of don't knows and their distribution made it impracticable to tabulate the results by occupation but it does appear that the driftermen gave most help (in terms of the range of tasks they would do) in the house, and this is what might be expected given their work pattern of long spells without work or the need to look for it. The pattern of work, however, does not have as great an effect as might have been expected, and helping in the home appears to have been a regional norm, for even in those cases where the man did not help in the home this is usually reported as being because the mother would not allow him to – usually on the grounds that he had worked hard enough. In only two of the interviews does the lack of contribution to domestic chores by the man appear to have been based on objection in principle by the male. The major value which comes through these interviews from both male and female, is that of reciprocity and equal effort.

The sense of partnership in work (both contributing to domestic and waged labour) was paralleled by the attitudes to money. The norm was one common purse managed by the woman. There is no comparison with the situation Tunstall found where the fishermen's only contact with those ashore is seen through the cash nexus: 'All his intimate contacts on shore may involved him in backhanders. He is likely to give them to his wife, his children, his father, his friends and the agent of his employer. These human contacts all involve the passing of money and silences' (1962:155). It is not clear what is meant by silences but if giving money to wife and children and, at times, to others near to one it might be fairly stated that all wage-earners are involved in backhanders. There was no trace in East Anglia of the Hull fishermen's practice of treating the weekly allowance which wives could draw while the men were away as the wives' wage and the lump sum of share money paid at the end of the trip as the man's pocket money:

Would your husband bring the money home all right even though he liked his drink?
Oh yes. Yes. He used to come home – and bring it and we'd share and share alike. Oh yes, we never had nothing no different then. (3032:7)

What happened when he was trawling, did he have the stockerbait money as his pocket money and you have the rest?
He would bring it all home to me and I'd give him – what I liked.
So you always managed the money did you?
Yes, yes. Yes. (3029:42)

Among the trawler and inshoremen the 'share and share alike' was a more typical response than total control by the woman. This situation clearly reflected the short absence away from home of the man, but even so the woman usually held the family income. This situation was greatly reinforced in the case of driftermen with their absences lasting several months and the total surrender of all money to the wife was the more normal procedure even though the men were about to have several weeks at home:

What about the share money when you paid off, who used to look after that?
Well – well my wife. Used to give that to the wife, yes. Oh yes. Yes, give that to her, certainly. If you took thirty pounds that was a bloody big lot of money – you done well for yourself if you took thirty pounds at Christmas –
Did you discuss how the money was spent?
No, left that all to her, she was father and mother. In fact she brought them all up herself really speaking. (3034:46–7)

Did you ever discuss with your husband how the money should be spent?
Oh no. No. He used to come home at the end of a voyage, he'd come home and if there was anything to take, he'd come home and lay it all on the table. (3042:39)

How did you manage money matters as you were away so much?
I never did see after the money until three years ago, I – the wife got so deaf and couldn't see – I always give her the money. I came home from the fishing one year – I think that was about 1921 – any rate, I shuffled the pound notes out to the wife, I gave her fifty-two, enough to make a pack of cards. Now, I said, I don't see no more of it. She knew how to look after it better than I did. (3007:73–4)

This giving of the money to the wife to control was accompanied by a keen appreciation of the size of the family burden shouldered by the wife and just how essential a capable wife was to a fisherman. One who was not efficient could bring hardship and difficulty to the family involved:

Did you used to leave your wife to pay all the bills and manage the home?
[She] Done everything. I don't know what went on. They had to be good managers. They did. If they weren't, that was your hard luck. I know one skipper I was with, he had a bad manager, she was always running him into debt, he had to cry – what they called cry her down. You know what that mean? Used to put the name in the paper and tell all the trades-people that if they allowed her credit without his signature, they wouldn't get the money.
So the fishermen's wives had much more responsibility?
Yes, they had to see after everything. Pay rates, pay rents, and – and see after the children, bring the children up. (3021:86–7)

With the man away the women were left in charge of the lump sum needed to meet the bills over the following months and there is one example of a woman who was conscious of her own inability to spend money slowly using more stable kin as a check on her own activities:

Well, the most my husband has ever taken in the fishing is sixty golden sovereigns. And he used to give me the lot. I used to give him what I thought. And I used to give it to my brother to look after and when I asked him for five pounds he would say, what do you want that for. He used to give me one pound at a time. (3029:26)

The general control by the women over the family purse fits the description of fishermen from other sources and P.F. Anson noted that this attitude was common to Scottish and French as well as English fishermen and described them generally as 'Under petticoat government.' 'They ruled their husbands in just the same way and kept a firm hold on the money.'[7]

As the domestic picture that emerged is so unlike the one Tunstall found it can only be concluded that domestic relationships he found are a recent development or the specific result of the distant-water trawling industry. In the East Anglian trawling there was not the separation at the psychological level that Tunstall postulates between work and home:

See, what we used to do that time of day, mother – before we went to sea, she used to pickle beetroot and onions, things like that see, and we used to take them to sea with us. Well, when we had emptied the jars, whelks, which were things we used to throw away, we used to boil them, cut them up, put them in vinegar, put them on the ice, and they'd be mother's delicacies. Be what we brought home to her you see. So there was a two way traffic with that. (3012:10)

The smacksman's life may have been male only, hard and dangerous but there is no evidence to support the view that it devalued wife, children or home.

Most informants were at a loss to explain how their parents maintained discipline although most of them reported that they 'had' to do as they were told. By far the most common means of control was verbal admonition, 'stop means stop, go means go, yes means yes and no means no' were the only necessary rules governing children according to one informant although his own childhood was marked by unrestricted playtime, the freedom to join adult company and, as he put it, 'to voice an opinion in any conversation' (3011). For the majority childhood was fairly unrestrained and free from fear although many informants whose parents never used corporal punishment reported that their mothers kept a cane on display as the ultimate threat.

As there are so many lines of explanation relating to socialisation one must be particularly careful in attempting to derive any interpretation from structuring the evidence. Nevertheless, the oral evidence had an internal coherence, for the children of non-fishermen and inshoremen report that only 3 per cent of their fathers had no role in shaping their conduct compared with 32 per cent of driftermen and trawlermen. This should not be interpreted as a sign of indifference but as a pragmatic response to the structure of employment. It was essential that the woman be capable of maintaining control of the family in the husband's absence, no amount of support while at home would control the activities of children during an absence of weeks. This was evident in one man's life for he had to leave the fishing because his three boys grew too unruly for his wife to control (3007). In all 50 per cent of the informants stated that they were chastised occasionally in their childhood, 37 per cent that they were not and 13 per cent are not known. Our main interest, however, is with which parent actually applied corporal punishment and this is shown in table 13. Two aspects most apparent are the fact that more mothers chastised children than did fathers and that this chastisement was more common in urban than in rural areas. In the rural group children living in fishing villages had least fear of punishment in spite of the more constant presence of their fathers. The informants seemed to accept this as a norm of society: 'I was never punished – and not many of the other boys were either' (3059:23). 'I don't know any of our family ever got hit – I don't remember any children being hit about here at all' (3003:24). Yet another from a different village in Suffolk relates how the inshore fishermen disliked children playing around their boats, but that if the fishermen shouted at them the boys used to retort 'Come near us and we will throw stones at you' (3014:4). That in itself was a jest for the beach was pure sand without a stone to be found. Stephen Reynolds (1910:79) who lived and worked with a fishing family in Sidmouth around the turn of the century notes, without much approval, the fishermen there were also reluctant to rebuke children for playing on boats and gear. He ascribes this to fear of becoming involved in conflict with neighbours. This may well be an element in the behaviour, although in a small community this intimacy could just as easily result in tight control of children by all adults.

Various explanations might be offered for this difference between the level of punishment according to location. There is the simple fact that urban children had less space to play without coming into conflict with adults and that the urban areas were better policed than the rural ones. Also the rural child was more often involved in working with parents during non-school time; domestic duties of gardening and fetching water as well as earning money through blackberrying, mushrooming and similar activities as well as directly paid seasonal work on the farms. If, through examining the actual incidents which resulted in corporal punishment, attention is focused on the action rather than situation, it becomes evident that corporal punishment came mainly as a result of activity which brought the offender's family to the attention of the authorities or in conflict with their neighbours. The stricter discipline in the urban areas was clearly due to offending

Table 13 *Administration of punishment*

		Chastised (%)	(%)	Did not chastise (%)	(%)	Had no role	D/K	Cases
Urban:	mother	53		28		–	19	32
	father	22		34		22	22	32
Rural:	mother	29		57		–	14	28
	father	21		54		11	14	28
Totals:	mother	42	(25)	42	(25)	–	17 (10)	60
	father	22	(13)	43	(26)	16 (10)	18 (11)	60

public rules rather than domestic regulations and this helps to account for the apparent distinction between the agricultural and fishing villages. In the agricultural villages the children of the working class were liable to incur the disapproval of farmers and other employers whose power was much less evident in the fishing villages.

As was found by N. Dennis *et al.* (1956) interfering with the domestic routine could bring punishment but this was always less likely to result in corporal punishment. Domestically, honesty was undoubtedly seen as the major virtue. Honesty, that is, in terms of telling the truth to one's parents rather than a strict acceptance of the wider society's definition of property rights. Children could often escape punishment, even for quite serious transgressions, provided they confessed their culpability in good time.

Any conclusions on the reasons for punishment would need a great deal more evidence, but what is here suggests that the amount and degree of physical punishment is linked to the parents' ability to cope with the cost of misbehaviour (for example, broken windows, fines for playing football in the street) and social pressures. Social status and poverty appear to be the main reasons for parents resorting to chastisement and not the wilfulness of the father, drunken or otherwise.

11

Leisure

It is hardly too much to say that the right to dwell freely in a grimy street, to drink freely in the neighbouring public house, and to walk freely between the high-walled parks and the jealously preserved estates of our land owners, is all that the just and equal laws of England secure to the mass of the population.

W.S. Jevons 1883

The charge that the working man in general, and occupational groups such as miners, dockers and fishermen in particular, spent their leisure and the family income selfishly on drink is common: the main focus of this chapter is on those drinking habits. At the anecdotal level other forms of leisure are mentioned but the public house is the only facility to be found in every location throughout the region. People from Lowestoft and Yarmouth attended music halls and theatres, but on the whole leisure seems to have been a matter of doing nothing in particular, walking in the countryside or on the beach, or occasionally visiting relatives. The work pattern of drifter-men and trawlermen precluded any regular attendance at a club or institution. Thus, although a substantial proportion of the fishermen owned and played musical instruments none are reported as belonging to a band. The existence of continuous and formal organisations require a regular home-based workforce and any mention of leisure time being exercised as part of a collectivity or team is very rare. Their leisure was unstructured and this degree of 'privatisation' accounts for its nature. Driftermen frequently took the whole family out for a day's pleasure when they came home and then dropped into the rather aimless behaviour of the unemployed, killing time until it was time to return to the next season's fishing. Indeed, a number of men from the drifters used to go to Grimsby after Christmas and work from there until May and the start of their own summer season. In the larger towns where there were fishermen's missions some men would use the facilities but there is little evidence of any form of leisure pursuits or culture particularly their own.

The nearest to an exclusively fishermen's leisure culture is where lifeboat sheds provided an occupational 'club' in a few locations.[1] A more detailed analysis of the data would undoubtedly reveal some structured difference in the use of leisure, such as inshoremen having allotments and occasionally belonging to some group or team, but the generalisation about leisure being mainly a matter of the local pub and of doing nothing in particular is basically sound. The one time when there was any collective activity was on a regatta day: but these were frequently organised with considerable involvement of yachtsmen and other 'outsiders' so they were by no means an expression of fishermen's group activity, indeed the purely fishing villages appear not to have held them.

The oral evidence is taken from a period which saw a noticeable decline in drunkenness among fishermen.[2] There was a large temperance campaign in Yarmouth in the mid-1880s as well as the formation of the Mission to Deep Sea Fishermen which attempted to prevent drunkenness at sea. Work routines were responsible for the pattern of drinking and the greatest excesses were prevalent under the fleeting system of trawling. While the fleets were in operation they were attended by floating shops, 'copers', sailing from the Continent which sold the fishermen duty-free tobacco and spirits. These could be paid for in money, fish or ship's gear and the owners were concerned with their losses through barter. A number of men and smacks were also lost as the direct result of drunkenness. It is claimed that as a result of the work of the Mission (which undermined the copers by selling duty-free tobacco themselves) and the International Conference at the Hague in 1886 drinking at sea was stopped.[3]

At first the smacksmen were opposed to it for the first Mission ship joined the fleet in 1882 to the jeers of the smacksmen. In 1884 the Blue Ribbon Army received very rough treatment at the hands of the Skeleton Army. Their Gospel Hall was mobbed by a crowd of thousands and the magistrates advised the Blue Army not to parade; when they did the magistrates charged them with 'causing an annoyance', and their parades resulted in brawls and serious injury to their leaders.[4]

The Mission grew in strength and in 1898 was listed as owning ten vessels registered at Yarmouth and working with the fleets. An account of the work of the Mission published in 1890 was already claiming: 'Drunkenness has been reduced to a minimum at sea, and while there are still drunken fishermen to be met with in the eastern seaports, yet all are agreed that an enormous change has been wrought in the general life of the trawlers both as men and as citizens' (Gordon 1890:53). Although temperance workers are not the most reliable source on these issues the oral evidence taken from the childhood homes of the 1890s confirms that in general drinking was moderate.

The evidence for Lowestoft suggests that drunkenness was less of a problem. The local newspaper was attacking the Liberals for having introduced a Local Veto Bill motion in the Town Council in 1893 and for their activities on the Licensing Bench the following year. In 1899, however, there were two meetings to form a branch of the Suffolk United Temperance Council which drew a maximum attendance of nine people including the organisers. The difference in capital structure and work patterns of the industry between the two towns can hardly fail to be relevant. But there are indications that the level of drinking did decline. The local paper commenting on the end of the herring season in November 1907 claimed that there had been a change in the patterns of drunkenness amongst the driftermen with local men offending less and the hitherto sober Scottish fishermen becoming the main offenders. Their hypothesis was that the steam drifter had undermined the character of the previously hard-working Scotchmen – although they failed to explain why it had the opposite effect on the equally hard-working Lowestoftman. (If their observation was correct the same paradox would rule out the demands of rapid capital accumulation and similar material explanations which I would be inclined to suggest.) The general and growing sobriety of the men, however, is confirmed by a report the following year from Penzance Petty Sessions which noted that in spite of between 1,000 and 2,000 East Anglians (mainly Lowestoftmen) in the area throughout the mackerel season there was not one case of drunkenness before the magistrates.

The East Anglian fishermen were noted for commitment to work and while they were fishing away from home leisure was something of a foreign concept. Contemporary sources referred to the driftermen as being intensely hard-working, matter-of-fact men who worked through Sunday even where it was contrary to local custom. The Scottish season was an exception, for there Sunday fishing was prevented by law but even there there was very little drinking, while away from home. A few men might go to the huts of the gutting girls for impromptu dances or a few drinks, and the Mission to Fishermen used to hire a hall in Lerwick for smoking concerts:

... but very few people ever went ashore, in the latter years I went to Lerwick I never went ashore myself. I have been there fifteen weeks, never gone ashore, only on the quay, you know, just on the quay.
What about Aberdeen and those places?
If you went to Aberdeen, you might call there one night perhaps, go ashore and have a few drinks but – on the whole they weren't a very boozy lot. There was exceptions, they'd have a drink now and again, but there was none of that. (3017:27)

There was always a few rough pubs, a few fights about. But the biggest part of the people weren't in that line at all. You see, the skippers didn't want them people, you had so many people want to go to sea you could get your crews without – you could always find – you knew decent people don't you see. (3007:26)

Thus the fishermen themselves did not have a hard-working 'tough' image of their occupation but perceived it as an occupation for sober hard-working men.

Two patterns emerge according to the pattern of work. The driftermen worked long seasons away from home, and although we do not have direct evidence on the level of fathers' drinking during the voyage, the accounts of the informants' own experience as driftermen, plus the documentary evidence cited, suggest that any drinking during the voyage was moderate. The main occasion for drinking was pay-off day. It was pretty general for the men to get drunk that day and then to disperse to their homes. For most men that would be the end of heavy drinking. An exception to this seems to have been fishing villages where whole crews came from the same village and where there was a lifeboat shed to provide a centre for card-playing and drinking during the afternoons. Here the celebrations appear to have lasted several days:

What about when your father was home, did he go out much in the evening?
No. No, he sometimes used to go, perhaps a dinnertime, to have a pint of beer and a game of cards in the Ship. Where all the fishermen, they all used to meet there. But that was all. They never went gallivanting on – pub crawls and things like that. But the day when they finished their voyage, what they call paying-off day, well, all the wives knew what to expect. They'd all come home tiddly. But my father was so funny when he'd had a drink that he'd make you laugh. Mother used to get very annoyed with him. 'Sit down there' she used to say to him. But we didn't care, I mean he never sort of frightened you. You know some men – I mean my uncle next door, he was violent. My poor cousins were terrified of their father because he'd had too much to drink. (3051:38)

That typifies the experience from both reactions to drink. But after the one day – when the men paid off in Yarmouth and then returned home – they would settle down to kill time and any drinking usually took place during lunchtimes when yarning over a small quantity of beer seems to have been the norm. Indeed for many of them the lunchtime sessions were very few:

Father didn't go out much. Perhaps he'd go and get a pint Sunday dinnertime and then he didn't go any more. The later part of the time when we were getting off his hands he might, I mean, at that time of day he daresn't go and spend money on beer – what about food. (3008:28)

This prudent attitude to the amount of money spent in the pub undoubtedly reflects their pattern of work as that informant stated they knew how long they were going to be out of work and they just had to 'equalise' their money so it did last. Table 14 is an attempt[5] to present a synoptic view of parental drinking habits. The high level of don't knows weakens any comparison between male and female but another fourteen females might have been

Table 14 *Parents' drinking usage*

	Customary (%)		Moderate (%)		Occasional (%)		Never (%)		D/K (%)		Total
Father	18	(11)	32	(19)	23	(14)	13	(8)	13	(8)	60
Mother	3	(2)	10	(6)	7	(4)	22	(13)	58	(35)	60

categorised with some confidence with a final result of 26 per cent drinking, 39 per cent not drinking with 35 per cent don't knows. If male drinking is considered by section, two trends appear. One is that trawlermen are mainly categorised as 'occasional' compared with the driftermen as 'moderate' and that the majority of the 'never' (on principle) come in the inshore section. Many of the trawlermen, however, came very close to never drinking:

> He never drank a glass of beer or anything like that, he never had the money to buy beer. He might have a drop of whisky if the owner took him in. He wouldn't go in of his own … if he got any stockerbait, he'd call and bring some oranges home for us. And that would be all he would do. (3006:5)

This moderation of the deepsea fishermen contrasts very markedly with the more recent findings on the Hull fishermen. Tunstall explains the hard drinking there in terms of trying to buy status and in trying to obliterate the harsh reality of their working life. This may well be so, but given the very different pattern in East Anglia it does seem that there must be some other variable at work. One thing that suggests itself is the balance of time at sea and time ashore. The driftermen were ashore for a spell of three to four months which in itself would, at some stage at least, necessitate a moderate and rational use of alcohol and clearly did lead to a disciplined use of available resources. The trawlermen were at sea for only five days with then one and occasionally two nights in. This gave them a more continuous contact with their families and their locality than the distant-water trawlermen whom Tunstall studied where the average voyage at that time was three weeks.

The evidence from the trawlermen shows that they kept in contact with their families and that all the earnings the men had were part of the collective purse rather than as Tunstall found the stocker money being the man's spending money. The last extract is typical in that the stocker money was usually spent on non-essentials such as sweets for the children, or an evening out with their wives. This view of the fishermen came equally from the females as well as the males in the sample. This informant, who was born in 1885 and married a trawlerman in 1907, applied the following view to both childhood and marriage:

So you could tell a fisherman by his dress could you?
Oh, you could then, you can't now. And their roll. The trawlers – fishing smacks, they all used to have a [mimed roll] and there weren't no drunkenness and that like there is now. They'd go and have a pint before they came home but you never heard of a fisherman round here being drunk. Mm. (3016:6)

And this is typical of the accounts from wives that their husband would have a drink during the day after docking and landing the fish, but would never or seldom go out in the evening to drink.

The position of the inshoremen was somewhat different from either of the above groups because their form of fishing gave them no structured time away from the pub:

Of course in them days you see the pubs used to open here about seven o'clock in the morning. And the chaps'd get in there and they wouldn't – you wouldn't see 'em before they chucked 'em out at night.
Was there very much of men going down intending to fish and then not bothering?
No. No. But if there was a breeze and they couldn't get off, they'd go in the pub and that was – they were finished. (3050:26)

The ever-present opportunity to drink may account for the fact that the inshoremen provided most of the confirmed teetotallers. The need to make provision for bad seasons, for the winter period when little fishing was possible in many areas and to have a reserve to pay for lost and damaged gear, must have served as a counter pressure to the attractions of leisure time and free spending. The general impression of the inshore fishermen is of prudent self-discipline in most aspects of life.

The pub was the main leisure centre for all sections of the fishermen yet they indulged with moderation and due respect for family circumstances. Women also drank but more frequently this took place in the home. Nevertheless, the pub is mentioned by a few informants as the place where they met their wives, and the female fishworker who reported regular visits to the pub with her mother for rum and coffee before starting work also remembered the pub as a place for evening entertainment as a single girl: 'You'd go in if you wanted a drink, there was always somebody to treat you. Well you wouldn't want no money to go in with, not a young woman wouldn't any rate. You wouldn't' (3029:27). Still, as one would expect, the public house was mainly a resort for men and, less frequently, men with their wives. In fact married women seemed to have very little leisure. Most informants claim that their mothers simply never went out, and that chatting to neighbours and visits to nearby kin were the extent of their leisure activities while their husbands were away.

When the fathers were home they were the ones who took the children out, not the mothers. Quite often this would be a trip to visit relatives, a day at the seaside, and often included a day shopping for new clothes – and even this took place without the mother. Such events are obviously exceptional but many report simple routine days with their fathers while they were home and this seems normal for the region as such reports also come from non-fishermen homes:

Were you ever taken out with your parents, round the shops or any sort of outing?
I used to go along with my old man every Saturday night ... And – I tell you we used to walk from Oulton Broad [to Lowestoft] – perhaps he'd get a quarter of sweets for the old girl [mother] and – get perhaps half a pound of tomatoes for him and the old girl – and we used to get the nine o'clock train home. (3020:36)

When he was home did he take you out?
Oh yes, we used to scrounge about, you know, on the beach. We used to walk through to Yarmouth and he used to have a couple of lines out, used to put the lines out and walk up towards Yarmouth and there used to be a big hut there, used to sell sweets and all that stuff, we used to go in ... walk back again. Well, I used to play about in general on the sands. (3031:44)

Compared with the 25 per cent who reported having days out with their father alone only 4 per cent reported having days out with their mother. This is rather surprising in view of the number of men who were away for considerable periods but that is the content of the evidence. Even more, 33 per cent reported that they used to go out as a family group with both parents:

Did he have any dealings with you children or did he leave all that to your mother?
Oh no, we'd – my family was very close. We would go out, sometimes he says, in the afternoon, might be on a Saturday afternoon when there's no schooling – if they happened to be in on a week-end – come on, he says, I'll take you for a ride. Used to get on the trams and we'd ride to the top – Kirkley and up the other end, and that was really an enjoyable day out that was. Just a little tram ride with father and mother and probably we might get an ice-cream during the day. (3012:6)

More typically family outings were visits to relatives. Once again to focus on the driftermen, for whom reporting is more complete, 38 per cent report days out with their father alone.

This sociable contact outside the family had its counterpart in the home:

Did you have any musical instruments in the house?
Yes. Me and my father played the accordion. He taught me to play ... He used to play and me and my mother used to sit and sing hymns. (3054:10)

– father used to go out every night, he was a teetotaller and he used to go to see his brother every night, but before he went out – they'd put the big table back – and he used to put a big chalk circle on the floor and play marbles with my brother. Yes, every night, except on Sunday. (3052:12)

Would your parents join you in these games?
Yes, oh yes. Mother would help you and father, especially ludo. Dad used to love to do it and snakes and ladders. (3051:39)

Some 25 per cent of the informants specifically mention their father playing a musical instrument and having social evenings with the family. This area of experience correlates with, and confirms, the accounts that most men drank only at lunchtime and so were indoors during the evening when children were in from school and play. Even where actual recreation was not shared the impression is of affectionate relationships: clearly fathers were comparatively home-centred and neither brutal nor alienated from domestic life.

12

Religion: practice and belief

Where did you used to go when you were courting?
Well, they'd have to go and get where they could, there was no pictures at that time of day you know. The wife and I used to go to church on Sundays to Aldeburgh or – wherever we thought best.

3003:50

Religion is taken as the final dimension because it forms something of a link between the family, leisure, work and the community. Although the fishermen were largely secular in their outlook religious institutions were as ubiquitous as public houses, and, whatever the degree of individual commitment, were social institutions of considerable influence. Every person interviewed attended somewhere during their childhood. Organised religion was also actively involved in missions to the fishermen and through the testimony of our informants it is clear that they also sent church visitors around the homes in at least some areas. It will be argued, however, that religion did not play a very central role in the lives of the fishermen or their families.

The findings were anticipated in the secondary literature. Contemporary comment particularises the East Anglian fishermen as the one major group of driftermen who would fish on Sundays, and as the trawlermen were away for four or five days it was accepted that they would be at sea and working on Sundays and this caused little comment. In contrast to these deepsea fishermen, inshoremen tended to preserve Sunday as a non-working day and were often committed to various non-conformist sects. This general picture is reflected in the interviews, and table 15a shows that about a third of the whole group attended church or chapel whereas when it is divided by male occupations the higher attendance of the inshoremen is quite notable.[1]

If the pattern of behaviour shown in the retrospective evidence was anticipated from the contemporary sources what was not anticipated was the discovery that the church did not play a more significant role in the lives of women, who were so much alone and who had so few other social outlets. But table 15b shows that only about one third of mothers attended services,

147

Table 15 *Religious attendance*

	Yes (%)	No (%)	D/K (%)	Totals
a. Fathers only				
Deepsea	14	50	36	28
Inshore	55	30	15	20
Others	25	66	8	12
Totals	30	47	23	60
b. Parents				
Fathers	30	47	23	60
Mothers	30	45	25	60
Totals	30	46	24	120
c. Informants: domestic observance as children				
Males	40	28	33	40
Females	40	25	35	20
d. Informants: attendance during teenage years				
Males	20	28	53	40
Females	55	5	40	20

and membership of sewing circles or similar church-based social functions almost invariably occurred in the period of their lives after all the children had become adults and had left home. That this was not due to the apathy of the churches is suggested by the following two extracts which establish that the Church of England was active in trying to establish contact:[2]

Did you ever go on the Parish?
Oh no, my goodness no. The church people had what they called a district visitor come round with a magazine once a month – that's the Church of England – and she

was supposed to ask how you all were and all the rest of it you see, and they were supposed, if anybody was ill they would give a milk ticket, shilling, that'd pay for a week's milk I suppose then, or a half a crown I think it was for groceries – and something else, whether it was for coal I don't know. But I remember father being ill, in bed, when one of 'em came round, this lady came round and my mother said – could she have a milk ticket – and she wouldn't give it to her. That was nothing to do with her, she wasn't paying for it but she wouldn't give her it. Whether it was because we didn't go to church because we were chapel, that was what my mother thought. But it was humiliating having to ask for it. (3052:29)

On Saturday night, after we had our bath mother used to wash our clothes out, and dry 'em and iron 'em and air 'em for us to put on Sunday morning. Never had a second change. One pair of shoes. And years ago you know they used to come round with tracts – women used to come round voluntary with tracts. And my mother said to the tract woman once, do you think you could get me a pair of shoes for one of my children? She turned round and she said, no I don't think so, your children always look nice and clean when they go to school, I don't think they need any shoes. Mother said, well take your tract and keep it and don't you come to mine no more. (3029:14)

The resentment of the control of charity by denominational religion in the first extract and the rejection of visitors without practical help in the second shows not only an attitude to religion by the women but something of their social attitudes.

One service that all mothers used was the provision of Sunday schools. Attendance varied from those children who attended two services on Sundays to those who put in the minimum number of attendances necessary to qualify for the annual treat. Some rebelled against it but for most it was simply as immutable as any other custom or rule imposed by adults:

I went to Sunday school 'til I was about fourteen I reckon, 'til I went to work. Went to Sunday school morning and afternoon, never missed, and chapel service. We had to go. It was instilled in us; so much so that we took it as we did the ordinary day school. Sunday you go to Sunday school and Monday we go to the ordinary council school. (3057:11)

That account from Essex speaks for most of the respondents, particularly those from rural areas or from 'respectable' families. At the other end of the scale of childhood attendance was the more self-directing pragmatic attendance of boys who – although not compelled to attend by their parents – put in a selective attendance:

Oh yes, we went to Sunday school – if you were clean enough and if your clothes were alright to go with – but the time came when your clothes weren't even fit to go to Sunday school with, and they wouldn't fetch you into a Sunday school. That all depend how well you behaves, you see, the well-behaved boys went to Sunday

school and the others didn't. But we nearly always managed to get into a Sunday school before Easter, you see, then you'd qualify the next few weeks to go on the treat.
Which one did you go to?
I went to several, wherever paid the best dividend. I went to St Peters, and I went to one in Fish Street, the Gospel Hall. Oh, I went to several of them, and you know they used to have Bible classes in the evening, well, some of them used to give you a bun and a mug of cocoa. (3017:46)

That account is from one who spent his boyhood in the old Rows of Yarmouth and he points out they were not entirely welcome due to the state of dress and, by inference, the state of their cleanliness.

Most children, however, were compelled to attend by their parents but this universal attendance in public was not reflected in domestic practice. Only 40 per cent (table 15c) reported any form of religious observance such as grace at meals or bedtime prayers at any stage of their childhood. It seems clear that the parents did use Sunday school as a means of discipline and control or simply as a means of ensuring themselves a period of peace and privacy during the one day they were together. The element of control becomes apparent in the gender difference in the pattern of reported behaviour during teenage years (table 15d). During this part of their lifecycle boys had greater freedom simply to go out with no clear purpose whereas girls were more controlled. Where boys did attend after starting work it seems to have been for a limited period until they could be accepted into the company of men and entry to the public house. This varied with the locality and the higher attendance in rural areas was clearly related to the lack of alternative places of entertainment:

Were the fishermen mainly church or chapel people?
Oh there was – they were both, there was people went to church, too, fishermen. And – there was no service in the church in the afternoon, only Sunday school. Well, a boy of fifteen, sixteen to twenty wouldn't know what to do [with his time] so they'd come to our chapel half past two, and that chapel used to have lots of young people there. (3025:50)

One brief extract from Norfolk and another from Essex show that this attendance by bored youth was something of a mixed blessing for the incumbents, however much they may have felt it was an opportunity to reclaim the unredeemed:

What happened after you left school, what did you do for leisure, did you still attend church?
Yes, well – after I left chapel – I used to go, a lot of us young 'uns used to go up to Happisburgh Church you see, and go in there and kick up a row. That's all we went for. The parson, Hitchcock, he had some pear trees and they hung over the wall into the road and we used to go up these trees and get these pears and take 'em to church and eat 'em, chuck the cores all over the place. (3005:63)

I used to feel sorry for the poor old soul sometimes – couldn't hear himself speak you know. We were talking during the service, during the sermon, he very often used to have to stop and ask you for quiet. But eventually they put two men up there. We were playing about, wouldn't listen. I don't think that there is anything like that now. He was a nice old devil, as I told you before. But you couldn't get a seat, that's the truth, in them days. All us young fellows courting girls used to run up to the church, or you couldn't get a seat. (3038:51)

That teenage behaviour was something of a bane to church authorities at this period is confirmed by accounts in the local press in 1911 of youths being fined for 'indecent behaviour' in Kessingland Church (Suffolk) very much on the pattern reported by our informants including 'throwing apples at each other'.

A number of the interviews reveal the class separation of the church and chapel. There was too, an element of bowing to authority if one attended the Church of England and those with economic power did not scruple to enforce at least occasional observation:

And Good Friday, all these people – well all – nearly all these old farmers, they went you see, you went too – you had to go to church on Good Friday morning. If you didn't go you didn't get paid. These old farmers, they'd go and they'd see if you were there. And if you weren't there there was no money for you the Friday, they'd cut you off that day. But if you went you'd get paid for the Good Friday. (3005:33)

The rebellious and disruptive behaviour of ex-chapel youth to the church by law established may have been a form of class rowdyism not entirely displeasing to their parents.

In the section on work we argued that the structure was such that it released many of the fishermen from much of the social control experienced by other workers, particularly those in rural areas. But where there were large numbers of men working away from home they were often the target for evangelical work and the fishermen were no exception. The activities of the Mission to Fishermen has already been noted in the chapter on leisure. By the 1890s it was undoubtedly welcome for its humanitarian services as was the North Sea Mission which was started by the vicar of Gorleston in 1895. The reverend Tupper-Carey of St Margaret's Church Lowestoft, earned the name 'the fishermen's parson' for his work among the driftermen and is mentioned with some affection in the oral evidence. But the religious effect of his work, and that of the others, seems to have been somewhat limited as even the special thanksgiving services held annually at the end of the herring seasons attracted disappointingly few fishermen.

The East Anglian's custom of working on Sundays led to the Newlyn Riots in the spring of 1896. The Cornishmen and women stoned the crews, dumped their catches and damaged their gear; troops and naval ships were required to restore order. The issue had been festering for years and the Cornish fishermen had previously called for boycotts on salesmen handling fish caught on Sundays. Three years after the riot the editor of the *Whitby Gazette* deploring the port's decline published a letter from a Cornish fisherman explaining that West Country fishermen no longer voyaged to Whitby because of Sunday fishing: 'The greed of the Lowestoft owners has destroyed Whitby, and nearly destroyed Newlyn. There are over a dozen Lowestoft boats on the side of right, but they need sympathy.'[3] At this date a dozen amounted to less than 5 per cent of the Lowestoft fleet which confirms how rarely men from this region observed the Sabbath.

The objections were not based in religious bigotry but in that Sunday-caught fish pre-empted the Monday market and so disadvantaged those who did not work. The church recognised the crucial role of the market and through the efforts of the reverend Dickenson, vicar of Christchurch, Lowestoft fishmarket was closed to Sunday trading early in 1899 and the Great Eastern Railway agreed to run no more fishtrains. But this ban was circumvented because fishing boats could unload their catches on Sunday and within a few years full-scale fish handling and packing started promptly at Sunday midnight. The attempt to make the Lowestoft driftermen observe the Sabbath by coercion failed.

This refusal to let religion interfere with the business of earning their living is most apparent in the driftermen because the structure of their employment did not require it and because it was contrary to practice elsewhere. Their attitude reflects a deep pragmatism found amongst all sections of the fishermen: 'My old father used to say, no need to prepare for the next world, we got to live in this one. That was his version of it' (3037:22).

Evidence on the practice of and belief in superstitious ritual, however, has a very different quality. It not only reveals a much deeper commitment to its practice than in the case of religion but the degree to which it was practised can be related directly to the work situation of the three sections.[4] The practice of superstition was not related to the community or the level of belief ashore. Because of this the evidence has been structured to bear on Malinowski's[5] theory of magic which proposes that the economic uncertainties and personal risks inherent in fishing will lead to attempts to control and influence irrational and unpredictable forces. There has been a considerable debate as to which of those two — economic anxiety or personal risk — are the major cause of superstition. My own analysis supports the former.[6] What is more I would argue that the structure of fishing in East Anglia provides a crucial test between the two because there are three types of fishing within one cultural area. The inshoremen were the least superstitious, the trawlermen were a little more so, while the driftermen were the

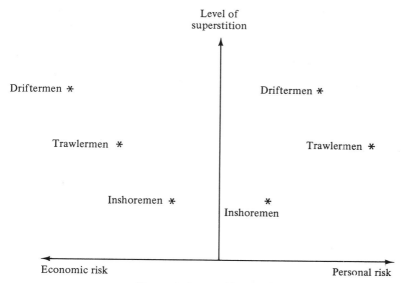

Figure 8 Superstition and risk

most superstitious of all. The death rate, however, follows a different ranking, with the driftermen having double the death rate by marine misfortune of the inshoremen while the trawlermen had a rate more than seven times that of the inshoremen.[7] We have already demonstrated that the inshoremen had only a small capital investment and modest expectations, the trawlermen had a higher level of capital investment with a fairly steady if low return while the driftermen had a high investment with a potentially high return with a highly volatile market and an uncertain resource. If these three elements are presented visually (see figure 8) it is apparent that the practice of superstition correlates with economic anxiety but not with personal risk.

This difference in practice can be demonstrated with accounts from the three sections of the industry:

Well in my younger days superstition was a hatch turned upside down, if anyone turned it up with the bearers across – bad luck. I don't believe in that. The old fishermen were, not my generation, my father and all them, they was very superstitious.
Can you remember any others that they had?
Yes. There was Poll Brock, she had a cast in her eye, and they always used to say that she was bad luck. They'd go out there and not have a very good catch, and they'd say, 'I knew I wasn't going to do any good' – but there was nothing else on the boat they were superstitious over. It was just the hatches upside down. (3001:21–2)

That is typical of an inshore interview. There is usually a recall of one or two items but they are related as things known of rather than as things practised.

The trawlermen, however, clearly had practice and belief. The following account was given by one of the crew:

And if that was a calm, he used to climb up the rigging, up the mast head with a chopper – said he'd chop the Lord's head off if he didn't give him some wind. And when you were hauling in the mornings if there weren't enough fish to his liking, he used to scoop 'em overboard, he'd say there you are you old bugger, he say, you can have them for your breakfast. And yet with all his, what do you call it – badness? I used to laugh to myself when I used to stand on deck and look down the skylight and look at him, he sat there, and get the Bible out, and get his glasses on, read the Bible. 'Cor he was a wicked old sod. Called the Lord all the names you could think of. (3021:28)

'He' in this case was the skipper, who generally invoked superstition and ritual where they were used. Another common practice amongst the trawlermen was to 'buy some wind' and this was a matter of firm belief. The next extract shows how selective men were in the superstitions in which they placed some credence. We had been talking about the driftermen's practice of trying to 'buy the herring' of which the informant was quite scornful:

Were there other things like that?
No, wouldn't make any difference, they used to do it just to buy the herring, but that didn't make no difference. But I will tell you what did. When they've been laying in a calm – over with a bob and buy a shilling's worth of wind. And they knew it. Yes. If you bought a shilling's worth of wind it's ninety per cent certain you were going to get a gale of wind. (3014:17)

This scepticism about the ability to influence the size of their catch through luck was common to smacksmen. They recognised the existence of luck but placed skill of seamanship, application, knowledge of the seabed and the tides as the main reasons for any individual's economic success. Their magic ritual was mainly concerned with influencing the weather.

Although they were the most modern, prosperous and dynamic sector of the fishing industry the driftermen were undoubtedly the most superstitious. They constantly reiterated the importance of 'luck' in the herring fishing industry. They had far more superstitions and held them with greater conviction than other fishermen. A rather lengthy extract will serve to convey something of the quality of the difference:

Of course superstition did weigh tremendously heavy along of practically every boat, and every one of the crew, in the fishing industry. For instance if one skipper saw a black cat, that was a bad omen, or another one saw something else, that was a bad omen, while for others it was luck. There were two – very lucky skippers. And one of them I was with, he would not allow a pack of cards aboard his ship. The other one – to go to sea without a pack of cards aboard his ship he might as well have left his nets ashore. That – that's perfectly true.

So there wasn't any sort of agreement on what was lucky and what wasn't?

No. Now to go back again to personal experience. I was along of one of the tip-top skippers. He was a man then could always demand what ship he liked, you see. Every firm was eager to employ him. 'Cos he always carried such an amount of luck. Well, all right. We got sent home. We were round in the Minch, Hebrides. So we duly arrived, and I was mate then. Skipper lived at Lowestoft. He went home to Lowestoft, he said to me tomorrow morning, he said, get the crew together Herbert he said, and start rigging out the *Ocean Toiler*. [The next morning] the ship's husband stood on the quay, he said you aren't going to have the *Toiler* Herbert, you're going in the *Lassie*. Well the *Lassie* had a very, very bad reputation. Nobody had earned any money in her – for years. And all our own hearts dropped, and it was a case of had there been any other ships available, we would have throwed her up. But it was the end of the season then you see, all the others were ready, and crewed up. That was either that or walk about, so we went aboard. We got her ready for sea. Now I want to tell you the perfectly true story because there'd be no sense in saying otherwise. We went to sea. Everybody round about us could get good shots of herring. We got nothing. One week we earned twenty-five pound. We went the next week. Same again. Surprising how people are alongside there, easy within talking distance, can get a boat load, and you in the middle got nothing. Incredible, but perfectly true. We went three weeks like that. Well in that three weeks these men that I've been telling you about on the wharf – they're also ex-fishermen and rank with superstition. They kept saying to me – as I landed what few herring we did get, there's something unlucky aboard her. If you do see anything or do find anything throw it overboard afore you get out to sea. Well I used to laugh at 'em. I was superstitious you know, myself, but I used to laugh at 'em, say, that's the luck – can't believe in such stuff as that. That's just our luck. Well now – the true story is this – I hunted up and down, in and out, I couldn't see anything wrong. But eventually I opened a little side door on the engine casing, and I did see something there that was wrong, and I thought to myself, oh that's going overboard before I get out. I wiggled my way aft, nobody see me, nobody see what I did, I threwed it over the side. Honest truth, we went to sea that night, we filled her full of herring, we come in and landed, we went out again, we filled her full of herring again, we come back again. We did so that three nights in succession and of course when you got these big shots that was necessary to call these people in to lend you a hand to clean nets, and busy cleaning our nets and getting the herring out the conversation was, somebody's done something, somebody's done something. Altered her luck, altered the luck. And I amongst them you see, don't talk so silly there's no luck. And none of the crew knew. Well it was remarkable. Remarkable. But we went then from the lower ship to the tip-top ship before the season ended. And was almost half the season over before we started. Then again ...

What was the unlucky thing that you threw over?

Oh, that was what we call a scutcher, it's a wooden scoop that you have to unload herring. They don't cut 'em you see. Held about a stone of herring, each scoop you see, and it was upside down. Strange thing about this superstition, if you shot you see, and you'd got four baskets in the kip you'd get four baskets in the herring nets in the morning. Very very unlucky to put them there. And it often happened so, you see, and all these sort of things. Never put anything upside down. This thing was upside down. Over it go you see. (3011:46–8)

That story has a wealth of detail from personal experience and he was about to launch into other examples before telling me what the unlucky object was in this specific case – and even then his reply to that question adds another superstition to be observed. His account contains not simple generally accepted superstitions but starts with the specific luck carried by individual skippers and their personal superstitions. This focuses attention on the fact that social practices are manifest through the actions of individuals and that:

Each individual is affected to a different degree by the beliefs of his culture. Since magic beliefs usually arise in situations of stress and since individuals differ in their ability to withstand tension, the ones who have the greatest need will internalise magic beliefs to the greatest extent. (Mullen 1969:219)

Whatever the variations in the individual ability to withstand stress, there was one individual whose position in the industrial structure determined that he would undergo more stress than the rest, namely the skipper. It is noticeable that it was always the skipper who maintained the level of superstitious practice: it was always the skippers who resented any non-observance of ritual by their crew as these brief extracts show:

I've been told that a lot of fishermen didn't like it if you mentioned rabbits at sea?
Oh dear, blast me, no. They don't. The oldest ones. The younger ones now, like my age, we didn't pay no regard to it. I was along of a skipper – in a drifter – he was a mild sort of bloke and we was fishing out of North Shields. I come on the deck this here morning, he was in the wheelhouse looking out of the window, and he weren't getting many herring see. And we knew he didn't like that. And we were singing – and then there would be one shout out, pigs! rabbits! ferrets! Cor blast, he slammed the wheelhouse door and he ran aft out of the way. We laughed. Yes, oh he was dead against any mention of anything like that. (3021:54)

It might be noted that that respondent was born in 1888 and that men twenty years his junior gave full accounts of superstition at work, so his ascription of superstition to the older generation is an inaccurate generalisation. In the following extract it should be appreciated that any mention of 'pig' was completely taboo:

I know we were laid in at Lerwick one fishing. We weren't getting many herring – (the skipper was ashore) – and one of them say who can draw a pig? I said I can. They say dare you do it? I say yes, give me a pencil, and I drew this here great big pig. And then I painted it. When he [the skipper] came aboard, he got into the wheelhouse, who drew that on there he say? He said, keep that mooring fast, I am not going to sea. He said, if I knew who did that I would give him a good hiding. (3014:21)

Crews generally showed greater willingness than skippers to mock at super-stition and ritual. Two informants relate how when the skipper said 'Are you ready together? All right cast in the name of the Lord' someone in the crew might shout out the name of a well-known local prostitute or the name of the local parson just as the skipper got to 'in the name of ...' (3017:18, 3019:71). But in both of the above accounts it is noticeable that they mention quite incidentally that they were not getting many herring, and presumably the skipper's authority was suffering as a result of this failure to produce the catches upon which everyone's income depended.

The level of superstition in drifting was reinforced by the unknown pattern of behaviour of the herring. Unlike most other commercial species of the time its movements and breeding cycle were unknown so fishermen could not build up a level of personal expertise as could men involved in the whitefish industry. And this degree of mystery was apparent in the highest echelons of the industry:

Some months we cannot find them [herring] at all; we do not know anything about them. We have had boats out, and we have tried to follow them after December ... what brings them in the season I cannot say. There is no particular food that we can find in the water ... Just now we have not the remotest idea of what becomes of the herring. Some people think they go down the Channel; others that they go over to Norway. It is a most extraordinary thing. Up to a certain date as the moon falls, say the 15th of December, we can go out and our boats will come in heavily laden, and a day or two after there is not a herring on the ground.[8]

The uncertainty left the drifter skipper in a situation of great anxiety with no apparent rational method of ensuring continued success. There is a close similarity between the skipper of a drifter and a gambler, and the great variety of superstitions and rituals reported among the driftermen seems to indicate that the skippers were not only keen to observe the traditional forms of ritual, which are mainly prohibitory and designed to avoid bad luck, but had their own individual observancies which can only be described as gamblers' fetishes, or as good luck rituals, and were not part of socially maintained beliefs. This extract is from a man who became skipper and owner in the early 1920s, and although personally very successful all his life did not ascribe this success to skill or ability:

Why do you think that some men were so successful?
Well that's what we call the luck of the sea. They would know – they had some other instinct. Not long experience, I don't mean that, now my younger brother when he went skipper two or three years after me, he was just about the top boat in his first year. But he wasn't always after that. ... (you go to sea and decide to shoot your nets) ... The water don't look bad, you look at the water, see if there are any birds about. And about a dozen of you would all shoot down alongside each other. One of those would get a big shot, two or three a reasonable shot, and a couple would get very

little. And yet they all drifted about twelve miles backwards and forwards with their nets over the same ground. I can't explain it. But it must be some instinct they have because it went on so much. But I think life's like that ... (3027:44–5)

He continued with an account of a particular crew member who always won at cards, or in sweepstakes or raffles – 'He was always winning' – and compared his strange facility to win with the facility of some skippers always to have a prosperous season.

Once again the much higher level of superstition practised by drifter skippers when compared with the trawler skippers serves to indicate that the higher belief, or practice of superstition by skippers was not purely a result of their position of authority or responsibility. If this were so one would not expect to find such a difference between the two groups of skippers. The 'economic anxieties' of the drifter skippers were much more acute than those of the trawlermen.

The degree to which these practices were internalised within very specific industrial contexts and were not the result of some unstructured personal psychological need or general community factor is aptly encompassed in this final extract. The informant was basically a drifterman who worked deepsea from May to December but had an inshore boat which he worked in the intervening months:

Did you do anything?
Ah, we used to chuck a penny overboard to buy 'em. Cast the nets in the name of the Lord always. Always, when you used to shoot, and you always shot the nets the side the Lord shot his. What he told the disciples, you always shoot your nets the same side. Yes. And that's one thing I will say about a fisherman. In the name of the Lord, pray God he send what he think fit.
You'd say that every time?
Every time we used to shoot our – well, not everybody but – we used to. I was talking about the drifters now. Not the longshore.
The longshore wouldn't say that?
No. Just chuck 'em over. (3015:29)

Further conversation made it clear that the ritual was always observed on the steam drifters, but never by the inshoremen, although they were at times after the same sort of fish with the same type of gear. Yet this respondent appeared convinced of the efficacy of magic and gave the only account of magic at work to come from an inshore fisherman. He related how a dog caught a rabbit and laid it against his boat just as they were about to go off fishing. He was in favour of returning home and losing the day's work, but his mate urged him to ignore the omen; they sailed, only to lose two trawls over ground they fished regularly and *knew* to be clear of any obstructions. It is obvious that he gave credence to magic and yet his practice of an appropriate ritual depended upon whether he was 'inshore' or 'drifting'. This reinforces the argument that among the fishermen superstition was industry-specific to a very fine degree and not simply the property, or propensity, of certain individual personalities.

There appears to have been only a very low community involvement with rituals connected with the sea. Women not washing their linen on the day a man started a voyage from fear of washing him away is almost the only superstition which appears to have been observed. Many had heard of the superstitions against burning the bones of fish, or the need to break the shell of eggs because witches could cross the sea in them, but these were not practised or taken seriously. Nevertheless, the community lived on the season's earnings and was not unaffected by the tensions and beliefs associated with the occupation.

The driftermen would celebrate with a short drinking bout in their first few days after ten to twenty weeks of intense labour. It was also the first occasion that the tensions below the surface of the carefully maintained collective identity of the crew could be expressed:

But mind you – they used to get drunk. 'Cor, when they used to pay off I've seen the pub full and you – fight! They'd fight hand over fist.
What about?
Anything – they'd get arguing the toss about boats. There you are. Look out! (3015:15)

Alcohol provided the solution in which to dissolve the carefully cultivated control necessary to the success of the voyage. It was this rather than ideas of status as such which is the most likely reason why, during the voyage, skippers would usually drink with other skippers – there was less risk of their authority being challenged while the voyage was in progress.

Besides the release of the intra-crew conflict (and the celebration of friendship) it was also an opportunity for men from the same residential community to relate and compare their occupational experience of the past weeks and months and to re-establish contact with those they had not seen since the season started. The extreme fluctuations in the level of earnings and the pecuniary motive for going fishing have been established elsewhere, and it was a situation calculated to cause conflict. The elation and free spending of men who had a successful voyage would contrast with the bitterness and care of the men who had gambled their labour only to face the next four months of unemployment with little or no money. The concept of 'luck' served to keep these sources of conflict from growing too severe. It avoided the vast income differentials from being ascribed to skill, effort or enterprise with the consequent loss of reputation for the low earners. If low earnings were associated with laziness and incompetence this would not only affect a man's reputation among the working community but create family tensions as some wives had to pinch while others lived comfortably. As all the men involved in the industry were agreed that luck determined economic prosperity the beliefs of the fishermen not only allowed them to cope with an extremely unpredictable occupation but also served a function in muting potential conflict and dissension within the family and community.

13

Community and conclusion

What has been related about fishwives in Scotland applies almost equally well to those in England and France during the last century. They ruled their husbands in just the same way, and kept a firm hold of the money.

Anson 1965

The final review of the argument introduces some new material on community because one of the major conclusions to emerge from the study is that non-work and pre-work experience is as fundamental a location of class experience and attitudes as is occupational experience. The importance of non-work experience became manifest almost by default as aspects of the fishermen's consciousness could not be convincingly located in their industrial experience. Their working-class identity and values are unexceptional and it might be urged that they could hardly hold any other perspective given the totality of the society in which they lived. But it is the very pervasiveness of class experience which raises the question as to how it is founded and sustained.

Emphasis on the non-work dimension is not intended to in any way devalue or replace the workplace as the major location of class conflict. Industrial struggles have been the major source of class solidarity and political struggle. Indeed, attempts to politicise industrial struggle and resistance to this has been a continuous thread in trade union history. But, apart for one section of the industry for a brief period, the East Anglian fishermen did not have a trade union and they were politically apathetic. To equate working-class consciousness only with the (unionised and mainly male) workforce directly engaged in the productive process would be to predefine and limit the nature of that consciousness: even worse it might limit and misdirect the understanding needed to change it.[1] We will approach this wider consciousness through a brief summary of some of the major factors which created their industrial identity.

Location of fish stocks, coal and access to market determined the overall development of the region and the relative growth, peak and decline of the various sections of the fishing industry. This, however, does not explain the

161

different success to the two major ports of Lowestoft and Yarmouth placed only twelve miles apart. Figures 2 and 3 showed that Lowestoft was much more successful than Yarmouth although it developed later. Up until 1881 Yarmouth had roughly twice as many trawlers as Lowestoft, by 1900 it had none while Lowestoft had some 200: the gap in drifting was less pronounced although Yarmouth had a marked lead until 1881 which was lost by 1891, and by 1911 Lowestoft had some 330 drifters to Yarmouth's 220. Yarmouth always experienced sharper fluctuations in the expansion and contraction of both sectors of the industry than Lowestoft and this was largely due to the capital structure of the industry.

Trawling arrived in Yarmouth as a service base for the system of fleeting. A system by which at least one large capitalist company was needed to provide the infrastructure – fish-carriers, ice, boxes – to take the catch to market. In order to keep a large enough fleet in being to generate sufficient volume of work for these services it also needed to enter into direct ownership of trawlers. That the fish was sent to Billingsgate by sea meant that the local fish docks' easy access to railway sidings and so forth were not developed. This method of intensive fishing by a concentrated fleet with seaborne transport required greater fish stocks than the local grounds could sustain. It was not a system, however, that could easily contract to adjust to those resources. The local fishing effort depended on outside capital to provide the infrastructure and when that was withdrawn it meant the disruption of the Yarmouth trawling community. Those trawlers which were locally owned moved their operations to Lowestoft where the infrastructure had developed along very different lines.

Lowestoft grew slowly as fishermen from other ports migrated with their boats and local townsmen put their capital in fishing. Table 8 shows that in 1898 only 3 per cent of the vessels were owned by companies and by 1912 it was still only 23 per cent, and many of these companies were formed with capital from fishermen and local businessmen. (Yarmouth had 51 per cent company ownership at both dates, much of it outside capital.) That small local interests retained ownership of the fishing capital here was due to the fact that access to national markets was through the railways. The railway company developed fish docks in order to generate traffic for itself. Although this was not local capital it was fixed to the locality in the sense that railways are permanent ways and need to generate a return on the original layout, unlike the fleeting investment in fish-carriers which could move to other locations. In any case the railways did not invest directly in fishing boats and the local nature of this meant that it endured on reduced profits, it went into a slow decline, but it continued to provide jobs for people in their community of origin.

Apart from the way in which different capital structures create and destroy employment they prompt very different industrial relations. The one major classic strike took place in Yarmouth and was limited to the large capitalist fleeting companies. This was in response to managerial control of the relations of production and it was an attempt to change these, rather than the introduction of technical changes, which account for the timing of industrial troubles. This is also evident in the industrial relations of drifting. Here there is a record of trouble between employers and employees in the earlier period when payment was by a fixed payment for each last of herrings caught. I have argued that had this system been in operation when the technical changes increased productivity there is every reason to assume that these labour troubles would have been exacerbated. As the driftermen outnumbered the trawlermen in 1901 by about four to one, rising to nearly five to one by 1911, their industrial identity dominated the ethos of 'fishermen'. As we stated at the beginning the phenomenon which needs to be explained is a decline in militancy and trade unionism at a time when the intensity of labour increased.

My argument places much weight on the system of 'co-venturing'; that was, the adoption of the traditional inshore fishing practice of dividing the market price of the catch between capital and labour in fixed proportion after running expenses had been deducted. This transferred the risks of the market from the owner alone to him and the crew. This had two major effects; one, was to give capital and labour a shared interest in ever greater productivity; two, to extend what had been a short seasonal occupation for most men into a full-time occupation albeit one with a long slack season for many workers. This development took place because seasons of exceptional risk were now shared by the crew. 'Co-venturing' was an effective relationship for handling the unpredictability of labour input and profit. This system cleared the way for the acceptance of steam capstans, the introduction of steam propulsion, the restructuring of crew numbers and positions without notable conflict. I am not arguing, however, that this is the mechanical or invariable outcome of such a system. It did so in this historical instance because of the wider regional rewards and prospects for labour, the high visibility of the market process and the degree of crew autonomy. The driftermen were attracted to the industry by its high level of reward. That level of reward was visible to them daily in the amount of herring they caught for market and the price the market paid. The owner of the capital they ventured with was visibly in the same boat: his fortunes rose and fell by the same two factors. The degree of exploitation between them was insignificant in real and perceived terms compared to their shared powerlessness to influence the market. In other words their direct employer (he did have the power to discharge the crew) did not fix a rate of reward for the employees and the price of the product so as to maximise his profit but had to take his chance within the terms of the agreed split.

In fact ownership as such exercised very little control over labour or the work process. Customarily the owner hired only the skipper, and crew selection was a matter for him. Indeed, it might be noted that as the owner had to replace damaged nets and gear there was no incentive for the crew to cease fishing in bad weather when a good catch might bring high prices. As one owner stated:

They were getting bigger boats, more powerful, burnt more coal, so they would be at sea almost any weather, so there was a lot of wear and tear on gear, so that's not always the man who grossed the most money [who] left his owner the most. That's where the single boat owners had – their idea was to be a bit careful with their nets, 'cos they'd got to pay for them not the crew you see. They grossed less and perhaps – well, anyhow, in the bad thirties as we call it, that was the bigger firms which went bankrupt more than the little man.[2]

The impracticability of maintaining managerial control over capital save by being a working skipper owner may have been one reason why larger capitalists were not more frequently involved in direct ownership. It explains the motives for such companies allowing their skippers to become part-owners. It explains why the large trawling companies insisted on nets being a charge to joint crew/owner expenses in the strike of 1887.

To return to drifting, however, crew autonomy and the nature of the work removed another basic conflict between capital and labour: that of the length and intensity of the working day. The basic work pattern was determined by the habits of the raw resource. The amount of labour performed was not affected by management, it was determined by the luck of being struck by the shoals. In any case the crew welcomed intense work because it meant high income. The incredible physical demands these irregular bouts of work demanded have been documented with the clear conclusion that this was self-exploitation with the crew as eager to drive as hard as the skipper. Because of the responsibility for damage to gear the owner was often less keen to drive as hard as the men. The result of this is what might be called 'crewism': by that I mean the sense of competition that each crew felt regards other crews. This industrial situation not only explains the low sense of industrial solidarity but is one of the reasons why such a group of 'traditional' workers held a money model of society and were so privatised. And even within the collective identity which a crew needed in order to create the morale which could withstand both the stress of the daily routine of shooting and hauling with little or no reward without being discouraged, and the sudden bouts of intense labour without collapsing, the structure did not allow for a common grievance. Crew wages and status was a complex hierarchy with no less than six different rates for the ten man crew. It was, however, an open one with no barrier between moving up the scale as there was in occupations which prevented labourers from becoming skilled and the skilled from changing those skills. Few men are willing to see their differential eroded especially when they have worked their way through the hierarchy; they feel that others who want more money should do the same and do not share a collective grievance. This wage hierarchy combined with the share system and the extreme range of actual and potential earnings left each man looking to his own interests. Thus, the intra-crew team relationship had the antithetical effect of privatising the economic struggle while generating a keen appreciation of the need for united effort. This unity, however, was of a limited kind and did not provide the basis for a collective identity: on the whole trade unions were simply perceived as irrelevant rather than liked or disliked.

One must not assume, however, that the loss of trade union organisation automatically meant a relative weakening of the workforce in the face of their employers, for the conditions which fragmented the solidarity of labour also fragmented the solidarity of capital. The managing director of Hewett's fleet could control, or attempt to control, the working conditions of 167 boats; after 1900 that degree of control would have needed the conscious solidarity of (on average) over seventy owners.[3] Conflict does not disappear in those conditions but it is handled differently, and as has been shown the conflict between the fishermen and the owners over the method of paying for the capstan was settled on the men's terms.

Examples of action taken jointly by employers and employees to maintain a competitive market for their product were, however, more in evidence than conflicts. If the workforce was not part of a militant and politically conscious national working class the same might be stated about their employers and the middle class. Their industrial consciousness was limited and shaped by the same conditions as shaped their workers.[4] In this situation conservative practice predominated and it is noticeable that in both the profitable drifting section and the unprofitable trawling section the share division remained unaltered. Relationships were personalised for both groups and neither possessed the perspectives, will or organisation to institute radical change.

Although they shared the experience of working in small-scale employment there were noticeably different social and political attitudes within the 'fishermen' according to sectional experience. The inshoremen, for example, revealed an unexpected and contradictory class model. They saw society as divided into an extremely large working class which included all those normally considered middle class, with an upper class of the extremely rich or wealthy retired. The local social hierarchy of farmers and business people was clearly devalued by this comparison. Their two class model almost divided into those who had to engage in some activity to live and those rich enough to live without work. Their accounts in particular, however, revealed the difficulty of structuring a rational or consistent class model. When they referred to their own position in the working-class hierarchy they actually compared themselves only to other manual workers and not as at, or near the bottom of, the lower of their two classes. Their perceptions of the class structure altered according to which aspect of it they were considering.

Their views might be contrasted with the class model of those who perceived clerical workers as middle class, or who virtually deny the existence of class through restricting their social perspectives to their immediate neighbourhood.

This contrast underlines in a rather stark manner that it is not the mere structure of employment which is important for social attitudes but the social location of the employers. It is perhaps because Lockwood's model of traditional workers considers only the material circumstances of the workers and not the employers that the fishermen do not fit into its categorisation more completely. Where employment is small scale cultural capital enters the relationship. The agricultural employee of one of the minor gentry might be in small-scale employment but it will be a very different relationship with his employer than the one experienced by a fisherman with his employer. Their money model of society and degree of privatised social relationships may well be due to their employers' recent origins in the working class and the lack of a cultural gap between them: they could aspire to emulation.

Neither the fishermen's industrial experience nor their social perception led them to value politics and this was to be expected given their industrial and social perceptions. Industrially they could not locate an oppositional 'them' who were directly responsible for their working conditions and rewards: socially they felt somewhat distant from the hierarchy of shore employment. A weak sense of 'them' left them with an attenuated sense of 'us'. This contrasted sharply with their own accounts of rural politics. The social and occupational experience of the agricultural worker revealed who was responsible for their conditions. Because they had no hope of winning either social or industrial struggles they valued their franchise: the voting booth was the only legal opposition they could exercise without victimisation.

The hope that politics could be used to compensate for an economically weak bargaining position might be noted more widely in the late nineteenth century. It was the new unskilled unions of the 1880s which wanted to use politics to improve their occupational circumstances through legislation of minimum wages acts, eight hour day legislation and so forth. It was the skilled men with some degree of bargaining power (and differentials over their labourers) who wanted to keep politics out of the industrial sphere.

There is a hint that the usual buyable apathy of the Yarmouth fishermen may have been altered on one occasion. The Conservatives lost Yarmouth to the Liberals in 1892, although they regained it in 1895 and held it subsequently. Pelling (1967:93) ascribes this defeat to the sitting M.P.'s failure to secure the desired expansion of railway facilities, as a result of which the normally Conservative fishermen voted Liberal. The 1887 strike, however, intervened between the 1886 and 1892 elections and the only reason the fishermen could be interested in, or benefit from, railway improvements would be that better direct access to market would emancipate them from the control of the fleeting companies. The strike may well have raised political consciousness for a brief time and in a very instrumental fashion.

If one accepts the force of this argument it is apparent that the industrial experience of most fishermen provided no basis for values of solidarity, communality or class. Nevertheless, in spite of high earnings and a degree of real and perspective capital ownership they were solid in their working-class identity: there was also a network of mutual aid and support exercised between neighbours. In other words there was a form of class consciousness and class practice. This cannot simply be assumed as 'natural', if the relations of work did not create it then it must be found elsewhere.

That the pattern of domestic and neighbourhood life are affected by the work pattern of the (usually) male breadwinner is nowhere more self-evident than in fishing. Studies such as Tunstall's, however, over-emphasise the degree to which male occupation determines familial and non-work practice. We have shown that the East Anglian fishermen, although engaged in a severe occupation, did not devalue domestic life or feel alienated from their families. The fishermen's mothers and wives were not passively shaped by the pressure of their menfolk's work but were active in creating their own social relationships. Indeed, as the area lacked formal class organisations the one remaining element of class solidarity was the level of mutual aid and that was constructed and operated by women. When fishermen returned home they returned to a family and community which operated throughout their absence. If this was a working-class community it was so through the class experience of women and children.

Class experience originated in the domestic sphere. Working-class children were usually initiated into the world of work through being given a share of the domestic tasks. Work was not something which began at the end of schooling or even with the first paid labour of errands and part-time work. The large and under-financed working-class family not only consumed the wages of productive labour (earned by wives and children as well as the 'family' wage of the male), it also produced use values which required a great deal of labour. Work is the engagement of people with material reality and one should not allow it to be absorbed by capitalist ideology to signify only one dimension of that process. I would argue that the basic sense of 'us' rather than 'I' which has been the bedrock of working-class collectivist values was rooted in the struggle to survive as a family. Within the family of this class and period the individual gained very little sense of self: children had neither their own room, own bed nor often even clothes exclusively their own: survival came from sharing. Economics did enter deeply into family life but mainly as a struggle in the face of exploitation rather than in competition between its members. That sense of being part of a collective enterprise was the basic reality of most working-class childhoods and one which instilled the predisposition to respond to future experience in a collectivist manner.[5]

If the occupational role of the men entailed their absence from the family for most of the day, even in non-fishing occupations, that was not a rejection of domesticity and the family but a necessary contribution to it. The work of the fishermen makes the point wih particular clarity. It left wives, however, with an extra burden of responsibility and the sole domestic responsibility. It has been shown that they held the purse strings, that their husbands accepted domestic chores as normal and that male children as well as female were obliged to take their share of household chores. One does not want to over-emphasise the amount of housework performed by men, for, as a proportion of the total amount, it was obviously small. The interesting point of this is, however, that of attitude, for the men did not object to domestic work in principle. This it might be noted was not exclusively a pattern of the fishermen's behaviour, for the reports of childhood homes include many from rural backgrounds where similar patterns are apparent. Domestic labour is also an early source of gender conditioning; that boys saw their father had no objection in principle and because their mothers made them share domestic chores males could not believe that such work was outside their sphere entirely. There was some gender distinctions in the tasks given to children but these were flexibly applied and the need for a task to be done over-rode any assumed gender suitability.

It is evident from the accounts of women and men that few of their fathers were the selfish, drunken and violent figures some studies present as typical. Most of the informants had warm and friendly relations with their fathers and their presence in the home was positively welcomed. It is tempting to find an explanation for this in the particular conditions of fishing. After all, as a mother could not use a father as an authority figure, and threaten children with his displeasure and punishment if they did not obey her, she was obliged to play that role herself. The evidence of my study supports this view in so far as the mother applied corporal punishment more often when the father worked in drifting and trawling than when he worked in inshore or shore occupations.

This occupational explanation is made less likely from the undeniable fact that some of the easiest relationships where children were punished the least were in the inshore section where fathers were at home. A similarly positive image of working-class family life between 1890 and 1914 was found by Elizabeth Roberts' study of domestic life in Barrow and Lancaster.[6] That the negative image of working-class life was not found in two such widely separated regions and occupational structures should be sufficient to make the case for further study and reassessment of family roles and behaviour. Had the male been so selfish, drunken and brutal one would have expected his absence to have been a positive boon but the level of reported sibling mortality by our informants is lowest in those families whose father was home most (non-fishermen 8 per cent and inshoremen 7 per cent) and highest where the father was absent most (trawlermen 17 per cent and drifting 16 per cent), and if there are many other factors which could account for this difference the correlation remains suggestive.[7]

If the basic positive elements of class collectivism are apparent in the family then the first introduction into the wider relationships of class come in the local community. This is a mixture of direct experience and the mediating practice and values of the adults. Such anti-authority attitudes as the fishermen possessed are more convincingly located in this pre-work experience:

The policemen used to carry canes that time of day ... I have had a cut across the stern with this cane, and do you know the women were as good as the boys. If you were running away from a policeman and a woman see you, they'd say, come on, in here. And they'd let you go in the front door and out the back. Yes. They wouldn't let the policeman through though. Oh yes, they were good. (3021:33)

Now whether fathers approved or disapproved of the role of the police in controlling children, or their wives' attitude to the police, is of comparatively minor consequence when they are not at home: it was the women who socialised children to perceive police authority as something to be evaded. Similarly one informant (3017) claimed that women 'ganged up' against schoolteachers who were too free with the cane. The husbands of such women could be as deferential and law-respecting as any occupation could possibly make a man, but unless one can convincingly demonstrate how the father transmits those values to children he scarcely sees then one must accept that the main influence on early social attitudes is the mother.

It is through the family and its relations with the wider community that a child learns of property distribution and ownership, social class, status, hierarchy and the appropriate response to them. This process does not merely instil a knowledge of who 'they' are at an early age: through the network of mutual acknowledgement and aid it instils an indelible sense of 'us'. It is not a negative process of resisting social control but an active process of social formation. In looking at this it is perhaps worth trying to consider the experience of men and women separately.

The women appear to have lived very privately on the day to day level. There is very little evidence of women casually (or formally) visiting each other, sharing cups of tea or loaning and borrowing as a matter of routine:

We had good neighbours [but] we never made a practice of going in one another's houses. If we wanted anything – just called [verbally]. But there weren't no under-tow, like tittle-tattle or all that. (3016:19)

Did neighbours come in and out the house very much?
I don't think so. We used to speak – but I don't think my mother used to run in and out of people's houses. I don't think she did. And more neither did I. (3032:22)

Yet, reported with this rather private lifestyle is the assertion that people would always help when there was any need. Sickness and pregnancy in particular are mentioned as times neighbours would help with cooking, cleaning, washing and similar services. This duality is not the result of different experience from separate informants but is contained in single experiences:

And another thing, people were very different to what they are today. They helped each other. If your wife was going to have a baby they would come and nurse you, they would come and do what they could for you. If you were hard up they would bring sheets ... and if you were hard up any time your neighbour in the Row would lend you a pair of sheets to pawn. (3019:35)

Did you ever get neighbours popping in and out during the day?
No. My mother had only one neighbour all her life. And that was next door but one to us. (3019:59)

There is a degree of difference in the level of privatisation women practised according to their place of residence. There was more visiting of other women to sit knitting in the evenings and so forth in the fishing villages than in other areas. This may have been due to the degree of inter-marriage and resident kin, for most visiting was to relatives. It may, however, be due to the degree of gender separation, for, as we will see, men in these locations also gathered together more than in other locations. My evidence comes from too many locations to be more than suggestive but there seems to be a decreasing degree of female networks from fishing villages through the Rows of Yarmouth (the working-class area of narrow alleys where most of the fishermen lived) through to urban Lowestoft and to the rural areas. In any case there seems to have been very little use of formal networks provided by organisations such as the church.

Men's leisure activities were more home-centred than had been anticipated but the greatest degree of male-centred leisure came from those fishing villages which had lifeboats and where the need for constant look-out and preparedness provided a male-only club for leisure. Where they lived in urban areas or rural villages they were more home-centred, thus paralleling the experience of the women. As Lockwood postulated privatisation can only take place where social conditions allow. This seems to have been least possible in fishing villages and here the existence of a male-only centre outside the home may have been the crucial factor. If this is so it points to the out of work activities of the male, such as clubs or trade unions, as the location of male culture rather than occupation as such.

If one looks at the interviews for evidence of communal *mores* one is tempted to see a greater moral density in these fishing communities. A woman was driven from Tollesbury through parading and burning her effigy because she had been 'going wrong', and at Winterton public opinion felt that the suicide of a fisherman was due to his wife's nagging, and her house was mobbed at night by villagers carrying torches and an effigy[8]. That two examples of rough music are found in such a small sample demonstrates that community policing of this sort endured longer than most people might suspect. This sense of community is also reflected in the experience of children in these type of villages who would divide into 'beach' and 'street' gangs. On the other hand this type of pressure was evident in the politics of Lowestoft. And even if the parade of the effigy was politically motivated and financed the mob pressure at the mayor's home seems spontaneous. The newspaper accounts suggest that it is unlikely that fishermen were specifically included in the unemployed protests so one is left with the conclusion that this type of community pressure on offending or responsible individuals was part of the more general culture.[9]

Those manifestations of community opinion show a mixture of social and political action. It is also arguable that similar pressures were responsible for economic action in that it was the small owners who more frequently undertook the third drifter season of high risk. Their costs of laying-up for four months could have been no greater than those of the larger companies and it may well have been, as one interview suggested, undertaken as much to provide work for the crew as for hope of profit. So although I would recognise that in a particular area or region there may be a configuration of forces that one would wish, as I have done, to refer to in a descriptive way as 'community', it would seem that the complexity of the phenomenon makes it unsuitable as an object of direct study. Particular communities, moreover, can be constructed comparatively quickly, and their destruction as capital and productive processes move to new locations can be even more rapid. What endure anywhere are the industrial, social and political practices of the residents: these might as well be studied directly rather than through an assumption of a sense of unity or common boundaries.

Appendix: supplementary information on the interviews

The sixty interviews listed below are those used for all tabulations and aggregated data. Interviews 3015, 3025, 3029, 3033, 3034, 3047, 3048, 3049, 3050, 3051, 3053, 3054, 3055 and 3060 are supplemented by another person. Usually this is another member of the family such as sister, son, aunt, nephew and these directly supplement the main interview. If used for qualitative information, the interview number is followed by 'B'. There are also ten untranscribed interviews which are cited as 'Spare (untyped)'. The interviews were conducted by the author during the period 1974 to 1976 with the exception of interviews 3031, 3038, 3034B, 3054B and the initial interview with 3034A which were conducted by Paul Thompson. They were collected as part of the Social Science Research Council project HR 2656/1 'The Family and Community Life of the East Anglian Fishermen', directed by Paul Thompson.

The tapes were transcribed by Janet Parkin and the tapes and transcripts are in the Essex Oral History Archive, director Paul Thompson.

The interview schedule was the one developed by Paul and Thea Thompson for use in the Social Science Research Council supported project 'Family Life and Work Experience before 1918' but modified for this particular occupational group and region. All interviews were open-ended and designed to encourage the informant to volunteer information. The interviews average three hours of tape with individual ones varying from one to five hours. In some cases this variation is due to the life experience of the informant. For example, if they never concerned themselves with religion or politics two areas of discussion were quickly exhausted: the amount of detail recalled and the narrative skill of the informant also greatly affected the length. This approach poses problems of missing information when structuring and tabulating sections of the information but the losses in uniformity are outweighed by the gains in authenticity.

Table 16 *Profile of informants*

MALE INFORMANTS: 40

Interview number	Date of birth	Siblings	Date of marriage	Children
3001	1897	8	1923	3
3002	1899	2	1938	2
3003	1888	5	1909	2
3004	1889	8	1933	0
3005	1889	10	1917	D/K
3006	1896	10	1921	1
3007	1890	8	1914	6
3008	1896	4	1922	4
3009	1895	11	1918	3
3010	1888	17	1913	7
3011	1897	13	1917	2
3012	1899	3	1918	2
3013	1893	5	1919	2
3014	1886	12	1907	2
3015	1904	15	1930	?
3017	1906	7	1930	2
3020	1887	7	1904	9
3021	1886	8	1909	5
3022	1897	7	D/K	3
3024	1892	4	1912	3
3026	1896	10	1930	3
3027	1899	7	1922	D/K
3028	1880	5	1902	7
3031	1910	2	D/K	1
3034	1888	10	1911	15
3035	1898	13	1921	D/K
3036	1888	13	1908	2
3037	1903	10	1933	2
3038	1879	11	1903	0
3040	1902	3	D/K	D/K
3045	1905	6	1928	5
3048	1900	5	1929	2
3049	1887	12	1909	D/K
3050	1899	6	1924	D/K
3053	1903	14	D/K	2
3055	1899	D/K	D/K	D/K
3056	1897	2	1919	5
3057	1900	7	1925	D/K
3058	1891	6	1913	1
3059	1898	1	1927	1

Occupations of parents

Father	Mother before marriage	Informant	Location
Inshore	Servant	Inshore	Leigh-on-Sea, Essex
Inshore	Shop ass.	Inshore	Leigh-on-Sea, Essex
Inshore	D/K	Inshore	Thorpeness, Suffolk
Trawler	No work	Ransacker	Caister, Norfolk
Rural	Rural	Drifter	Happisburgh, Norfolk
Trawler	Servant	Ships' husband	Lowestoft, Suffolk
Rural	Servant	Drifter	Repps, Norfolk
Drifter	No work	Drifter	Yarmouth, Norfolk
Drifter	Beatster	Ransacker	Caister, Norfolk
Trawler	Factory	Drifter	Yarmouth, Norfolk
Rural	Servant	Drifter	Catfield, Norfolk
Trawler	No work	Trawler	Lowestoft, Suffolk
Drifter	Servant	Drifter	Gorleston, Norfolk
Drifter	Beatster	Trawler	Kessingland, Suffolk
Drifter	D/K	Drifter	Winterton, Norfolk
Drifter	Gutter	Drifter	Yarmouth, Norfolk
Trawler	D/K	Trawler	Lowestoft, Suffolk
Labourer	Rural	Trawler	Corton, Suffolk
Trawler	D/K	Trawler	Lowestoft, (from Ramsgate), Kent
Drifter	D/K	Drifter	Yarmouth, Norfolk
Trawler	D/K	Trawler	Yarmouth, Norfolk
Drifter	D/K	Drifter	Yarmouth, Norfolk
Trawler	D/K	Drifter	Hemsby, Norfolk
Drifter	Servant	Drifter	Caister, Norfolk
Trawler	Barmaid	Drifter	Gorleston, Norfolk
Drifter	D/K	Trawler	Lowestoft, Suffolk
Trawler	D/K	Trawler	Lowestoft, Suffolk
Inshore	Barmaid	Inshore	Harwich, Essex
Inshore	Tailoress	Inshore	Brightlingsea, Essex
Inshore	Servant	Inshore	Tollesbury, Essex
Inshore	No work	Inshore	Tollesbury, Essex
Inshore	Servant	Inshore	Tollesbury, Essex
Drifter	D/K	Drifter	Lowestoft, Suffolk
Inshore	D/K	Inshore	Aldeburgh, Suffolk
Inshore	No work	Inshore	Southwold, Suffolk
Drifter	D/K	Drifter	Gorleston, Norfolk
Inshore	Tailoress	Inshore	West Mersea, Essex
Inshore	D/K	Inshore	West Mersea, Essex
Inshore	Servant	Inshore	West Mersea, Essex
Inshore	No work	Inshore	West Mersea, Essex

FEMALE INFORMANTS: 20

Interview number	Date of birth	Siblings	Date of marriage	Children
3016	1885	8	1907	8
3018	1880	7	1911	5
3019	1894	15	1912	3
3023	1888	10	1910	0
3025	1890	11	1914	2
3029	1885	14	1904	9
3030	1898	11	1920	1
3032	1886	4	1908	6
3033	1902	9	D/K	2
3039	1892	11	1912	4
3041	1888	18	1909	2
3042	1895	4	1918	4
3043	1894	3	1915	2
3044	1890	4	1922	1
3046	1907	10	N/A	0
3047	1901	9	1922	4
3051	1906	13	N/A	0
3052	1896	2	1918	D/K
3054	1901	1	1926	2
3060	1904	10	1925	4

Occupations of parents

Father	Mother before marriage	Occupation before marriage	Location
Trawler	Servant	Servant	Lowestoft, Suffolk
Rural	Servant	Servant	Blundeston, Suffolk
Trawler	No work	Factory	Gorleston, Norfolk
Publican	Servant	Servant	Lowestoft, Suffolk
Inshore	Beatster	Beatster	Winterton, Norfolk
Hawker	D/K	Splitter	Yarmouth, Norfolk
Drifter	Servant	Clerical	Lowestoft, Suffolk
Labourer	D/K	Servant	Lowestoft, Suffolk
Drifter	D/K	Teacher	Caister, Norfolk
Inshore	Shop ass.	Laundry	Harwich, Essex
Rural	Servant	Servant	Langley, Norfolk
Railway	D/K	Servant	Lowestoft (from Buckie, Scotland)
Drifter	D/K	Beatster	Pakefield, Suffolk
Inshore	D/K	Servant	Cromer, Norfolk
Inshore	D/K	Shop ass.	Harwich, Essex
Inshore	Servant	Servant	Tollesbury, Essex
Drifter	Servant	Servant	Caister, Norfolk
Inshore	Servant	Servant	Cromer, Norfolk
Labourer	Servant	Factory	Lowestoft, Suffolk
Labourer	Splitter	Splitter	Lowestoft, Suffolk

NOTE ON OCCUPATIONAL CATAGORIES

beatster: a skilled occupation repairing the herring nets. Required an apprenticeship

gutter: a women who prepared the herring for pickling in barrels.

labourer: refers to a variety of unskilled urban occupations

ransacker: a skilled occupation in the netchambers rigging all the necessary ropework onto the nets.

rural: refers to a variety of agricultural workers.

ships' husband: a person who arranged that the vessels were properly serviced when in port.

splitter: a woman who prepared herrings for kippering.

Glossary

Note that these explanations are not intended to be full or technical. They are simply intended to elucidate the term sufficiently to be understood in the context of this study.

bawley: the name of a first class sailing vessel used in Essex for shrimping and general fishing.

beam trawl: this is described on p. 18.

boat: 'boat' is used interchangeably with 'vessel' and both terms are intended to avoid the confusion of using the technical type of boat name in each circumstance. Where the type of boat is important, for example for capital cost or similar reason, this is specified in the text. *See also* smack, lugger, bawley, and so on.

bob: colloquial expression for one shilling. *See under* money.

capstan: this term is used interchangeably with 'winch' as this was local usage. A capstan is a cylindrical object rather like a slightly concave barrel around which a rope can be passed two or three times which then provides enough friction to haul in the rope as the capstan revolves. Formerly the power to revolve the capstan was provided by men pushing on bars attached to the cylinder and walking in circles, latterly steam power was used. Usually the term 'capstan' is applied to a single vertical cylinder and 'winch' to a horizontal cylinder of which there are two, one each side of the machinery which drives them. Essentially they provide power for haulage.

carrier: a vessel specially developed to sail at speed and used to ferry the fish from the fleets to Billingsgate (or other market). They were the first vessels in the fleets to be equipped with steam propulsion for swift, certain carriage of the fish to market. They were equipped with trawls and did occasionally use them, but the main purpose of this equipment was to enable them to register as fishing vessels and so avoid regulations applicable to ships of the merchant navy.

coble: a type of small sailing boat used mainly in Yorkshire.

crab pot: a trap made of open basket work rather like a bird's cage. This contained bait and trapdoors which would admit a crab or lobster but prevent them emerging. This was usually left on the seabed for a period of time before hauling. They were usually laid in a string of twenty or so.

cran: a measure of herrings which varied according to locality from 3½ cwt to 4 cwt. Not widely used in East Anglia until 1908 when it was legalised and fixed at 3 cwt. Previously herring were counted ashore by the men picking up four herrings at a time. 4 herrings = 1 warp. 33 warps = 1 hundred. 100 × 100 = 1 last (i.e. 13,200 herrings).

Danish seinenet: known also as the 'Whispering Trawl'. This was a net which enabled the low-powered steam drifters to trawl for whitefish in the slack season for pelagic species. Instead of towing the net through the water to catch the fish the vessel shot a long warp down, as it were, one side of a triangle, then shot the attached net across the base, and then another warp up the other side so as to return to its original point where it retrieved the first warp, which had been attached to a buoy, and then hauled the net through the water with its winch, so trapping the fish in its path. It seems to have not come into widespread use in East Anglia until after 1914.

demersal: the species of fish which are bottom feeders and caught by trawl or hook and line.

drawnet: a shore-operated seinenet.

drifter: used by the fishermen to denote a vessel which used only driftnets and fished for herring and mackerel. In the text they are noted as sail or steam where this is relevant. *See also* driftermen.

driftermen: the fishermen exclusively engaged in catching herring and mackerel by means of the driftnet. Their name and the name of their steam vessels 'drifters' or 'steam drifters' is taken from the net type. It should be noted that their sailing vessels were also referred to as 'drifters' but more commonly as 'luggers' from the type of sails such boats originally used. Note also that inshoremen will also use driftnets on a smaller scale and some of their vessels will be lugger-rigged. *See also* smacks.

driftnet: see pp. 36–7.

Dutch Auction: even contemporary accounts of this system do not explain it very clearly. Basically the auctioneer started at a high price and then gradually reduces it until a buyer accepted the price. The iniquity of the system lay in the fact that auctioneers had private arrangements with buyers (and apparently sellers, although this is less clear) that they would be allowed one or two 'lowers'; that is that they would actually pay two reductions less than their actual public bid. Presumably this was intended to keep up the price to those not in the know. The opportunities for corruption are obvious and the crew could never know what price their fish had actually been sold for because they did not know if the buyer was allowed 'lowers' or not.

English net: see p. 36.

first class fishing vessel: in general a boat of over 15 tons. Second class were those less than 15 tons but having a keel upwards of 18 feet. Those with less than 18 feet keels were third class.

fleeting: see pp. 19–25.

half a crown: two shillings and sixpence. *See under* money.

hooping: a method of catching shellfish by lowering a hoop attached to a handline to the seabed. The centre of the hoop consisted of netting which was baited, when shellfish crawled onto the net it was hauled to the surface. Frequently used at the beginning of the crab or lobster season to test the water to see if they were on the move and so worthwhile laying crab pots.

inshoremen: men who usually worked with small vessels and a variety of fishing gear from their own location. They include the Essex fishermen who worked as crew on the luxury yachts of the period.

last: about 2 tons of fresh herrings.

liner: a fishing vessel so called from its method of fishing. This was the main method of catching whitefish before the spread of trawling. Longlining was a system by which a fishing vessel the size of a sailing trawler would shoot a line up to seven miles long containing thousands of baited hooks. This would then be hauled and the fish removed. This was the method of catching live cod used by the welled-vessels in the late eighteenth and early nineteenth centuries, although as a method lining continued into the twentieth century and even steam vessels went lining in the interwar period. Inshore vessels also used similar methods on a smaller scale to catch whitefish. The deepsea vessel lining also sometimes used handlines, particularly when fishing for cod, that is, having a handline with a few hooks which was lowered over the side of the vessel and hauled in every time a fish took the bait, each member of the crew operating one line. Driftermen used to do this while drifting in Scotland to increase their personal earnings.

longlines: see liner above. Also used by inshoremen fishing from the beach. They would cast lines from the beach at low tide and haul them after high tide had covered them and brought in feeding fish.

longshoremen: interchangeable with inshoremen.

lugger: originally a class of sailing vessel which might be used for any purpose and so called because of its type of sails and rigging. It predominated in drifting, however, and in the sailing period 'lugger' and 'drifter' were almost synonymous. Only a handful were still operating in East Anglia in 1914 and none operated after 1918.

money: the oral extracts refer to pre-decimal currency of 240 pence to the £1.

4 farthings = 1 penny
12 pennies = 1 shilling
20 shillings = 1 pound

offal: most of the whitefish caught, the less expensive whitefish, for example, haddock, ling, skate and whiting.

otter trawl: this replaced the heavy beam trawl. It held the mouth of the net open by means of attachments to the two corners of the mouth of the net which pulled apart when drawn through the water. It needed the continuous pull and speed of steam power to operate successfully. It was not used by sailing trawlers.

paleagic: species of fish which feed near the top of the water and are caught there, notably herring, mackerel and sprats.

penny, pence: see under money.

poundage: a system of payment common in trawl fishing but used in East Anglia during this period only by the 'fleeters'. It supplements a basic wage with a bonus payment of so much in the pound (sterling) fetched by the fish when sold. The amount varied according to crew status.

prime: this refers to the most expensive of the whitefish. For example, Dover sole, halibut and brill. It is in contrast to offal.

principal: the main aim of the fishing voyage, that is, the types of fish which were covered by the agreement on the share system. It is distinguishable from 'stockerbait' which was fish sold entirely on behalf of the crew or on favourable shares.

rooker: a local name for skate.

Scotch net: see p. 36.

seinenet: has many variations. Basically a length of netting with long ropes at either end. If used from the shore a boat will row out at right angles from the beach leaving the end of one rope with helpers on the shore, when it has payed out all that rope it then rows parallel to the beach casting the net and then returns to the beach with the other rope. The ends of the net are then pulled to the shore trapping all the fish in that stretch of water. *See* Danish seinenet for deepsea usage.

shilling: see under money.

ships' husband: a shoreworker who was responsible for ensuring that a boat was properly serviced while in port. He would arrange for supplies to be sent, repairs to be done and generally see to a smooth turnround. Not much used in East Anglia because small owners would fulfil these tasks themselves.

shooting: a term used to describe the casting of nets.

shot: used by the driftermen to describe the results of a complete cycle of shooting and hauling the nets, that is, the catch. Unless qualified it implies a good catch.

smack: this is the term used for the sailing vessels used by the Lowestoft trawlermen. *See* trawler.

smacksmen: see trawlermen.

stockerbait (stocky): species of fish which did not constitute the main purpose of the voyage and which were sold and the money given to the crew; if landed in large quantities the owner would have half the money.

stowboatnetting (stowboating etc.): a method of catching sprats used only in Essex. A large stocking-shaped net was rigged under the vessel, held open at the mouth by two large baulks of timber. The vessel looked for the shoals and the direction they were travelling in, anchored in their path and cast its nets.

sweep: a large oar used on the sailing drifters.

swill: a large basket used for landing herring. 20 swills = 1 last.

trawler: used in this text as interchangeable with (and mainly a substitute for) smack. In general fishermen's usage 'smack' referred to a fishing vessel using trawlnets but propelled by sail, while 'trawler' usually refers to a steam fishing vessel.

trawlermen: the fishermen who were exclusively engaged in catching demersal species by means of a trawlnet. In this period in East Anglia these men worked from sailing vessels called 'smacks' and are frequently called 'smacksmen' to distinguish them from 'trawlermen' who worked on steam vessels. In the text trawlermen has been used as a matter of simplification and consistency.

trip: used by the trawlermen to refer to one fishing expedition from the time of leaving port to the return. In Lowestoft four or five days. Sometimes used by inshore fishermen when they left their home location for a few days. Driftermen refer to 'voyages'.

voyage: the driftermen's term for a complete season's engagement. Most of them worked only two voyages a year. One lasted from May to August which took most of them to the Scottish ports, the other from October to December from their home port. A large number of Lowestoft boats had a third voyage to the West Country mackerel fishing in the first four months of the year.

warp: a term for a long heavy rope used for towing the trawl, or for the driftnets. Also would refer to a tow rope between two vessels.

Notes

Introduction

1   Material is drawn from forty interviews with men and twenty with women. They were collected as part of the Social Science Research Council project HR 2656/1 'The Family and Community Life of the East Anglian Fishermen', directed by Paul Thompson. Janet Parkin transcribed the interviews which were conducted by the author. For fuller details see appendix.
2   Martin Bulmer, 'Sociology and History: Some Recent Trends', *Sociology*, Vol. 8, No. 1 (1974), pp. 146–7.
3   The meaning of these terms will become apparent through usage, but there is a glossary of technical and unfamiliar terms.
4   P. Friedlander, *The Emergence of a U.A.W. Local, 1936–39* (Pittsburgh, University of Pittsburgh, 1975), p. xxxiii. His introduction is an interesting discussion of oral evidence.

Introduction to Part One

1   My own figures have been established from the original registration books referring to first class vessels trawling or drifting. I have taken the number of crew employed on active vessels. The discrepancy between my figures and the Customs' can to some extent be accounted for by frictional unemployment; the growing divergence apparent in 1931 would reflect the reality of structural unemployment not included in my calculations. The figures for inshore are less certain as the registration of inshore boats varied throughout the period and the degree to which boats were active less certain. For a fuller discussion of the difficulties of fishery statistics see my Ph.D. thesis 'The East Anglian Fishermen: 1880–1914' (University of Essex, 1981), Appendix C. Subsequently Lummis 1981a.
2   Compiled from Parliamentary Papers, 1914, Vol. XXX Cd 7373, Appendix XXIV, pp. 42–3.

1. Inshore

1   Essex Oral History Archive, interview number 3001. In future interviews will be identified by number only. The appendix contains brief biographical details.

183

2 Regional wages were extremely low and fishermen's earnings must be considered in this local context. These are discussed in chapter 4.

3 Parliamentary Papers, 1914, Vol. XXX Cd 7373, p. xiii.

2. Trawling

1 In this text trawler and smack are used interchangeably except where qualified. In strict usage a smack is a type of sailing craft which could be used for any form of fishing.

2 In the 1880s Hewett of Barking was the largest owner in the country with 130 smacks operating from Yarmouth. By then some of the fleet's catch was being sent from Yarmouth by rail and in 1884 the Columbia fleet (set up by Baroness Burdett-Coutts) began landing its catches at Yarmouth for dispatch to London. Eventually, the fleets based in East Anglia could not compete against the more prolific grounds further north and the fleets of steam trawlers.

3 For an account of fleeting from the founder and director of the Mission to Deep Sea Fishermen see E.J. Mather, *Nor'ard of the Dogger* (London, James Nisbet and Co., 1889), or for a vivid account of this and fishing more generally J. Dyson, *Business in Great Waters* (London, Angus and Robertson, 1977). Both have illustrations of boarding fish.

4 Capstan and winch appear to have been used interchangeably. Both perform the same function but capstans have a vertical drum while winches have horizontal ones.

5 The table's contents are taken from Parliamentary Papers, 1894, Vol. LXIX C 7576, Appendix I.

6 Public Record Office (henceforth P.R.O.) BT 144/1–5. This series started in 1884. The agreements list the wage rates of all crew members. There are some variations but the figures cited are the norm.

7 P.R.O. BT 144. The table has been constructed from approximately forty signings in each crew position save the seventh hand which occurred only twenty-four times.

8 J. Mitchley, 'The Steam Carriers', *Norfolk Sailor*, No. 12 (Norwich, 1966), states that the fleet grew to ninety-four vessels. But the company, which had been formed by local smack owners, directors of the Ice Company and similar local interests, did not launch its first carrier until 1885 and went into liquidation in 1887.

It is apparent from a report in the *Lowestoft Journal*, 5 April 1884, that the impetus for the Lowestoft initiative came from the higher prices for fish obtained by the Columbia Market Fleet which was then landing its catch at Yarmouth and sending it by rail to London rather than having it seaborne all the way. The Columbia Fleet was no longer in existence by June 1894: see the report of fleeting in P.R.O. MAF 12/13.

9 The *Lowestoft Journal*, 20 and 27 May 1911.

10 Parliamentary Papers, 1911, Vol. XXIV Cd 5874, Annual Report for 1909, Table D. Compares with about 18 cwt daily for steam trawlers in the same waters, i.e. the North Sea.

11 Parliamentary Papers, 1893–4, Vol. XV, p. 69. Evidence of Mr Hame.

12 Crew Agreements, P.R.O. BT 144, and oral evidence.

13 Yarmouth trawling was depressed from the late 1880s. Local press reports (*Yarmouth Mercury*, 28 February 1891) that in the four years since 1887 trawlers had declined from 606 to 348 with a loss of 1,500 jobs. The *Lowestoft Journal*, 1 April and 15 April 1899, reports Hewett laying-up trawlers and 300 men unemployed in Yarmouth, although Lowestoft smacks were 'doing well'. There is no doubt that the expansion of drifting did absorb many of these fishermen but the local press after this period has frequent references to Yarmouth men working out of the Humber ports; Fleetwood and Aberdeen also had a number of Yarmouth families moved there. This distress is evident in the oral evidence where childhood accounts refer to the poverty at that period.

14 Walter Wood, *North Sea Fishers and Fighters* (London, Kegan Paul, 1911), p. 47, claimed that 150 new smacks were fitted out in Yarmouth between 1883 and 1886. The 1901 Grimsby strike was over the same issue also at a time of declining catches. The crisis happened earlier in East Anglia because of the earlier development and exhaustion of local fishing grounds.

15 *Eastern Daily Press*, 10 March 1887.

16 *Ibid.*, 12 March 1887.

17 *Ibid.*, 7 and 14 March 1887.

18 *Yarmouth Mercury*, 10 October 1891, also *The Fisherman*, November 1891, report Hewett discharging prominent skippers and these going to other ports. They claimed 309 union members of which 170 were skippers. The reliability of the local press in reporting these matters is confirmed in that they not only reported the incident but did so in much greater detail than the union journal. See Webb Trade Union Papers, Section B, Vol. 106, Items 52–4.

19 This assertion might be challenged on the grounds that many of the men employed in fleeting at this time came from Barking and did not have 'traditional' East Anglian attitudes. Nevertheless, the earlier strikes by the indigenously manned drifters establish the relations of production as the cause of conflict rather than 'fundamental' attitudes. These are discussed in chapter 4.

20 *The Fisherman*, October 1891: an article signed R.M. (i.e. R. Manton, organising secretary).

21 According to my calculations the difference between the two methods of financing the winch were minimal. One can only assume that this was also apparent to contemporaries and it might be argued that it was a dispute without much substance. Even if this were so it is still of some significance that the employers conceded their preferred system.

22 The *Lowestoft Journal*, 7 July 1890.

23 *Yarmouth Mercury*, 9 January 1891. See also *Fish Trades Gazette*, 17 January 1891.

24 The weak trade unionism of earlier years had disappeared by this time. The *Lowestoft Journal*, 12 January 1895 has a letter instancing harsh treatment of a smack's crew (i.e. forced to sail on Christmas Day) and advocating the formation of a 'federation' for the men as one did not exist.

3. Drifting

1 R.W. Duff, 'The Herring Fisheries of Scotland', *Papers of the International Fisheries Exhibition*, No. 9 (London, 1883).

2 This and the following account of the early period are taken from the Caird Commission (1866) and J.G. Nall, *Great Yarmouth and Lowestoft* (London, Longmans, Green, Reader and Dyer, 1866). Some salting of herrings at sea continued throughout the period, but this was not as profitable to the owners and crew as landing fresh herrings.

3 J.R. Coull, *The Fisheries of Europe: An Economic Geography* (London, Bell, 1972), p. 25.

4 Parliamentary Papers, 1908, Vol. XIII Cd 4304, p. 418.

5 This is too complex an issue to pursue in detail. Traditionally, the main product of the East Anglian region was the highly salted and smoked red herring which was exported. This meant that drifters did not have to return to port each day with their catch as salting them at sea started the curing process and boats would stay at sea for up to a week or so if daily catches were light. This product did not entirely disappear and some of the oral accounts refer to salting the catch at sea. This market was replaced in importance, however, by the Scotch cure, that is the preserving of herring through barrelling them in salt. For this the herring need to be at a particular point in their life-cycle and *fresh*. The great expansion before 1914 was based on the seemingly endless growth of this market: the catch going mainly to the northern European countries especially Germany and the Baltic. Because of the incredible volatility of the daily market it became increasingly important to be able to return to port daily and preferably ahead of other boats. It was this which stimulated the change to steam propulsion. Because of the density and reliability of the herring shoals and the size of the market many steam drifters fished only eight months of the year and laid up (like the earlier large Yarmouth drifters) for the rest of the year.

The growth of the rail network and the use of ice opened up some seasons which had not been possible before, as did the growth in the market for semi-preserved products such as kippers and bloaters. These seasons for the home market were pursued mainly by the small fishermen-owners of Lowestoft. These developments will be expanded where they are relevant to the industrial identity of the fishermen.

6 Norwood Committee, Parliamentary Papers, 1882, Vol. XVII C 3432, p. vi.

7 The agreements are taken from a number of sources. The three for the 1860s are taken from Nall (1866:336) where he accounts for the differences as a result of the growth of the size of fishing vessels. The agreement for 1876 is

an original in the author's possession; 1881, from Parliamentary Papers, 1882, Vol. XVII C 3432, Appendix XXI; 1901, the *Lowestoft Journal*, 8 February 1902, the details are given with reference to a legal report; 1911, P.R.O. Crew Agreements, P.R.O. BT 144; 1930s, Great Yarmouth Maritime Museum, a typescript report from Bloomfields, undated, circa 1929. Because of their availability over a long period and their relevance to the older system the table is limited to Yarmouth share agreements. The Lowestoft system was less favourable to the crew at 134:79 than at Yarmouth with a ratio of 124:79. The proportions going to each crewman were different too with the skipper and mate at Lowestoft having a smaller differential over the rest of the crew. This means that, in effect, the large commercial companies paid their crews more highly than the local fishermen-owners and elevated their skippers more highly.

8 3023: the informant states that her brother-in-law did precisely that in 1913. Her memory is accurate in that the drifter named went on the register in 1913 in the appropriate name (pp. 9 and 26).

9 The *Lowestoft Journal*, 11 May 1907, carries a report of a court action which stated that the skipper had been paid £105 for three voyages. If one adds £15 for cash stockerbait it brings this case well within the predicted range. There is no comment as to whether this represented a good or bad year's earnings. The skipper was suing for payment for work that he did in the slack season chipping the ship's boiler. This shows that skippers may have had the option of maintenance work on the drifters while they were laid up.

10 The *Lowestoft Journal*, 21 April 1894.

11 Circumstantial evidence suggests that it was aimed particularly at the drifter-men. Data taken from the *Lowestoft Journal*, 5 November 1904.

12 The *Lowestoft Journal* of the period gives good coverage of union activities reporting new branches, their demands and their social evenings. The leader of the Builders Labourers Union thanked the editor (letters 1 July 1899) for keeping the newspaper's columns open to the strikers and the union's point of view. Had there been a fishermen's union during this period it could hardly have failed to be mentioned.

13 The *Lowestoft Journal*, 15 November 1913, reports speeches were made by Havelock Wilson and Will Thorne, M.P.s, and their intention to open an office in Lowestoft. Edward Tupper appears to have been involved in this, see his *Seamen's Torch* (London, Hutchinson, 1938), pp. 83–4; it is noticeable, however, that it is recounted in his usual optimistic tone but makes no specific claims for organisational success.

4. Working relationships

1 The population figures are taken from the decennial census figures published in the Parliamentary Papers.

2 *Fish Trade Gazette*, 10 April 1913. Correspondence about 'lazy Cornishmen' wanting government aid and restricted fishing grounds are specifically

contrasted with the East Anglian fishermen who are evidently the epitome of hard work. Certainly the East Anglian men appear to have been the only regional group which habitually worked all week while drifting.

3 This and subsequent examples in this section have been extracted from the *Lowestoft Journal*: 21 January and 7 October 1899, 12 May 1900, 1 June 1901 and 20 September 1902.

4 Interview Spare 5 (untyped).

5 The *Lowestoft Journal*, 12 February 1910.

6 These small differentials between urban and rural wages within the region (as opposed to national rates) give reason for some reconsideration of the position of the agricultural labourer in the wage hierarchy. A. Wilson Fox, 'Agricultural Wages in England and Wales during the Last Half Century' (1903), reprinted in E.W. Minchinton, *Essays in Agrarian History*, Vol. 2 (Newton Abbot, David and Charles, 1968), agrees that agricultural wages were 12s. weekly at this period but states that an extra £9 annually would be earned from various forms of harvest and piecework; a potentially higher gross annual total than local unskilled urban labour. He allows for lost earnings through wet time and under-employment for his final estimate of £33 annually in 1902. Clearly to better themselves to any degree the rural worker had to move outside the region as the labour surplus prevented most local wages rising much above what they could earn on the farm.

7 Figures taken from the careers of the 233 male siblings of the sixty informants. See Lummis 1981a: Appendix B3.

8 3005:15. It is possible that this skipper was also a part-owner, a situation which clearly created a more complex relationship to the main partner.

9 Jeremy Tunstall, *The Fishermen* (London, MacGibbon and Kee, 1962), p. 127, remarks that 'The normal importance of food comes to assume on a trawler a heightened significance ... Normal outlets such as sex and drinking are not available on a trawler and consequently food has to carry an immense burden of emotional freight.'

10 V. Aubert and O. Arner, 'On the Social Structure of the Ship', *Acta Sociologica*, Vol. 3 (1958), pp. 200–19, and K.Weibust, *The Crew as a Social System* (Oslo, Oslo University Press, 1958), are examples of analysing crew separation by status.

11 *Yarmouth Mercury*, 27 December 1913. The incident happened on 15 October and the newspaper account is very similar to the one above which caused the breakdown of the cook and the mate. In this case there were landings of 120, 100, 40 and 113 crans on successive days.

12 It might be thought that this is due to nostalgia and the 'good old days' distortion that many people are prepared to ascribe to oral history. To balance this, however, there is the 'wooden ships and iron men' syndrome which tends to exaggerate the hardships of certain occupations.

13 By my calculations for Lowestoft, and extrapolations from Tunstall's (1962) study of Hull, I estimate that Lowestoft fishermen stayed twice as long with their ships as the Hull men. See Lummis 1981a, pp. 133–4.

5. The concept of community

1 J. Rule, 'Bibliographic Essay: The British Fishermen 1840–1914', *Bulletin of the Society for the Study of Labour History*, No. 27 (Autumn 1973).
2 D.H. Allcorn and C.M. Marsh, 'Occupational Communities – Communities of What?', in Martin Bulmer (ed.), *Working-Class Images of Society* (London, Routledge and Kegan Paul, 1975), p. 208.
3 M. Stacey cited in C. Bell and H. Newby, *Community Studies*, London, Allen and Unwin, 1971. This book reviews the extensive literature on communities and cites one which found ninety-four definitions.
4 For an earlier treatment of this subject see Trevor Lummis, 'The Occupational Community of East Anglian Fishermen: An Historical Dimension through Oral Evidence', *British Journal of Sociology*, Vol. 28, No. 1 (March 1977).
5 S.M. Lipset, *Union Democracy* (Glencoe, Free Press, 1956), p.X.
6 Robert Blauner, 'Work Satisfaction and Industrial Trends in Modern Society' in W. Galenson and S.M. Lipset (eds.), *Labour and Trade Unionism* (New York, John Wiley and Sons, 1960), pp. 351–2.
7 P. Willmott, *The Evolution of a Community: A Study of Dagenham after Forty Years* (London, Routledge and Kegan Paul, 1963), p. 109.

6. The social structure of ownership

1 There may well have been private arrangements. This statement is intended as a contrast to the usual (perhaps only) method of purchasing a trawler or drifter which was through a formal loan. These loans were registered with the Customs Authority. See n. 8.
2 The tables have been constructed from published lists of fishing vessels. The choice of dates was partly restricted by the availability of similar data for both ports. Apart from Lowestoft 1912, the information has been taken from *The Great Yarmouth Printing Company's Annual* (Yarmouth, 1899 and 1913), and the information for 1931 from *Flood's List of Fishing Vessels* (Lowestoft, 1931). These were preferred to O.T. Olsen's *The Fishermen's Nautical Almanac* (London, Hull, 1912), because the others list fuller information on the details of ownership. Details of the age, tonnage and type of gear used, as well as the name and location of the owner(s), has been coded for computer analysis. The entire lists have been coded and where uncertain or missing information exceeds 5 per cent this has been indicated. I am grateful to Phil Holden of the Department of Sociology, University of Essex, for his advice on coding, and for devising the program and putting it through the computer.

One of the defects of published lists of fishing vessels is that they record all the vessels on the port register. As there was no formal mechanism for removing unused or even derelict vessels from the registers this can cause serious distortions. For example, at Lowestoft in 1898 25 per cent of the registered trawlers were not in use. The true figures have been established by reference to the original registers in the P.R.O. (BT 145). There are a number of difficulties with establishing reliable estimates and reference should be made to Lummis 1981a: Appendix C.

3 Other tables not produced here show that fishermen-owned vessels were not inferior to the company-owned ones in regard to their size or age. It should be emphasised that the tables deal only with first class vessels (see glossary) registered at Yarmouth and Lowestoft. These comprise of all the drifters and trawlers engaged in the work and seasons delineated in Part one.

4 Parliamentary Papers, 1908, Vol. XIII Cd 4304. Answer 9940. Evidence of Mr Bloomfield on value of nets and vessels. My figures are an extrapolation.

5 C. Wadel, 'Capitalisation and Ownership: The Persistence of Fisherman-Ownership in the Norwegian Herring Fishery', in R. Anderson and C. Wadel (eds.), *North Atlantic Fishermen* (Newfoundland, Memorial University of Newfoundland, 1972), p. 111.

6 Commonplace reporting in oral evidence. Also documentary evidence from the Great Yarmouth Maritime Museum.

7 Yarmouth salesmen provided the swills which enabled drifters to discharge their herrings before they were sold. In most ports, including Lowestoft, drifters had to wait until a sale was made and the buyer would provide his own containers. The Yarmouth system allowed a quick turn-round in port but it did reduce the quality of the herring through double handling.

8 3027. For a more modest approach to ownership see E.J. March, *Sailing Drifters* (Newton Abbot, David and Charles, 1952), p. 83: the example of Mr Peek who went to sea in 1893, took a quarter share of a new drifter valued at £2,400 without nets. He cleared his quarter share in three years, after a year took up another quarter and cleared that in two years. In 1914 he took sole ownership. Details of mortgages on fishing vessels are held in registers in local Customs Offices. These have not been used systematically but those at Yarmouth and Lowestoft convince me that this experience was not unusual. It is an area, however, which stands in need of further research.

9 Parliamentary Papers, 1914, Vol. XXXI Cd 7221, Appendix XII, gives the numbers of Scottish steam drifters at particular dates: 1902 – 100, 1907 – 508, 1912 – 824. My proportions are calculated from these figures.

10 The *Lowestoft Journal*, 22 June 1895.

11 *Ibid.*, 22 June 1895.

12 *Ibid.*, 12 May 1894.

13 About one third of the owners are identifiable as skippers or ex-skippers, others may well have been skippers earlier in their careers. But one third ties very closely with Parliamentary Papers, 1902, Vol. XV Cd 1063, Appendix I, p. 65, which estimates 'About one third owned by skippers.' The same report states that there were only 10 steam drifters at the time and 230 luggers and that the 'Steamers [are owned] by companies and luggers mostly by skippers or ex-skippers.' I find the information on steamers rather suspect but the data generally confirms the much higher participation of skipper-ownership in drifting.

14 In an article by R.M. [R. Manton], 'Fish Trade Mortgages on Uncaught

Fish', in *The Fisherman* (June 1891), it is argued that mortgages were given by auctioneers to fishermen because once in debt they could not take their custom elsewhere nor could they complain if they suspected that they were being cheated. The ability to foreclose the mortgage gave the auctioneer total power. Some of these bankruptcy cases allow for that interpretation, but the sheer variety of the people involved suggests that it was limited in extent. The article had trawling in mind and I have found no documentary evidence to support this view of the relationship between lender and borrower in drifting and the oral evidence is to the contrary.

15 Parliamentary Papers, 1914, Vol. XXXI Cd 7462. Minutes of Evidence 4825 and 6990 state that landsmen who provide loans dislike providing money where there is more than one owner as fishermen disagree among themselves. It is also claimed that drifters with only one or two owners are more successful than those with more involved ownership because there is more control.

7. Images of social structure

1 In the book edited by Martin Bulmer (1975) various authors raise different problems associated with using 'images of society' and he writes:

> If the main characteristic of the discussion of class imagery is disagreement and contradiction, that of the historical dimension is emptiness, ... It is, however, fraught with methodological difficulties, both in the collection and analysis of data, and the rigours and difficulties facing the historical sociologist of imagery should not be underestimated. (1975:170)

> It would require a different book to enter into these problems: the issue is raised here only because it is felt that the oral evidence on class imagery presents a particular methodological problem even within the context of interview material. Often information can be located because it is age specific, such as schooling, or linked to specific locations or stages of occupational experience, but class imagery usually lacks that specificity and it has to be acknowledged that social attitudes are more detached from timebound incidents than many other areas of recall. I offer no general framework for assessing the authenticity of such retrospective accounts of class imagery, for I am convinced that each cohort and/or group of interviews needs contextual evaluation. The historicity of the recalled images will vary according to changes in the social and geographical mobility and experiences of the informant as well as the wider historical events spanned by the experience. For example, enough of the informants used the First World War as a reference point for changes in their own experience, politics and social perceptions to carry the conviction that, for this group at least, it was something of a watershed and that, in the main, memories placed before or after that point are more reliably situated than would be the social perceptions of a cohort lacking such a dramatic punctuation.

2 Five interviews are excluded because this area was not covered or proved

unclassifiable. This table departs from the thesis original in that six interviews which were categorised as perceiving no classes have been re-evaluated as holding a two class image with a large lower class.

3 A final comment on the material might be on the difficulty of deciding if the social boundary described was a significant (class ?) boundary or merely a stratum within class. I have not even attempted to draw a distinction between status and class. What I am attempting to establish is the informant's significant social boundaries.

4 I have argued elsewhere that there are some advantages in tabulating small numbers of interviews (Trevor Lummis, 'Structure and Validity in Oral Evidence', *International Journal of Oral History*, Vol. 2, No. 2 (June 1981), subsequently Lummis 1981b). The tables are not offered as being statistically valid but as a demonstration of the distribution of data upon which my argument is based. The authenticity of the data comes from its internal consistency and its triangulation with other sources.

5 The trawlermen's perceptions, however, do not fit so well with my estimates of their earnings compared with regional wage levels ashore. My assessment places both trawler mates and skippers at the top of the working-class income levels. Although I may have not allowed sufficiently for slack periods in calculating the income of trawlermen I would maintain the validity of the placement in general. The lower estimate of the informants comes, I am sure, from the fact that most of their working life in sailing trawlers was experienced in the 1920s and 1930s when their earnings suffered a relative decline. It reinforces my point in n. 1 above that class images are particularly difficult to locate in time.

6 Wadel, in Anderson and Wadel 1972:111. See also A.P. Cohen, *The Management of Myths: The Politics of Legitimation in a Newfoundland Community*, Newfoundland Social and Economic Studies No. 4 (Memorial University of Newfoundland, 1975), p. 29.

7 Interview Spare 4 (untyped).

8 *Ibid.*

9 The *Lowestoft Journal*, 10 November 1894. Note that this coincides with the peak of bankruptcy cases for smack owners and one would expect relations between them and the buyers to be most strained at this period.

10 D. Lockwood, 'Sources of Variation in Working-Class Images of Society', *Sociological Review*, Vol. 14, No. 3 (1966). It is reprinted in Bulmer 1975. The reference, p. 17, is to this reprint, as are subsequent references.

11 See Lummis 1981a: Table 19, p. 208.

12 R.S. Moore, 'Religion as a Source of Variation in Working-Class Images of Society', in Bulmer 1975:52.

8. Political attitudes

1 H. Pelling, *The Social Geography of British Elections 1885–1910* (London, Macmillan, 1967), pp. 87–105.

2 The value of tabulating data from such a statistically invalid source is a matte

of judgement, but when so used the interviews not only reveal the political colouring noted by Pelling but also a move to Conservative voting up the status divisions in fishing and show the well-known affinity between religious denomination and party voting. That this small 'accidental' sample conforms so tightly to a number of expected historical and social trends demonstrates an impressive coherence.

3   H. Newby, *The Deferential Worker* (London, Allen Lane, 1977), p. 110.

4   Given Newby's acknowledgement that deference cannot be studied as mere behaviourism, the lack of any data on political attitudes in his empirical evidence is a surprising omission. For since the Secret Ballot Act of 1872 the franchise has been one of the few legal covert acts through which the powerless could oppose the powerful.

5   This trend is apparent from my analysis of interviews held in the Essex University Oral History Archive. See also Newby 1977:137 n. 73 for further references.

6   Because of the central concerns of my research the political history of any one constituency has not been pursued. But my impression of politics in Lowestoft is that local issues and personalities were more important than national issues. There were fierce battles over religious issues (municipal cemetery) and drink (the licensing of public houses). Throughout the 1890s the Liberals were in power although the Conservatives gained a majority in 1899. This, incidentally, shows that the fishing vote could not have been decisive as the expansion of drifting should have reinforced the Liberal vote, or that 'Free Trade' did not influence them as claimed. The first *candidate* in the Labour interest did not appear until 1913.

7   The *Lowestoft Journal*, 6 June 1906.

8   This rather archaic flavour of politics was apparent in other fishing towns and there is an account of treating voters from Harwich. In the smaller places such as Brightlingsea and Mersea elections seem to have been the excuse for some mild public riot.

9   R. McKenzie and A. Silver, *Angels in Marble: Working-Class Conservatives in Urban England* (London, Heinemann, 1968). See also R. Samuel, 'The Deferential Voter', *New Left Review* (January/February 1960).

10   It could also be an indication of the degree of social control although that must have been weakened in the short term by such a demonstration; recall that he supported the formation of a fisherman's union and generally fought for a better deal for the working class. I suspect that most of his unpopularity came from his opposition to the drink trade.

11   The *Lowestoft Journal*, 16 January 1897.

12   The degree to which fishermen were involved in these activities is impossible to state. Press reports, however, confirm the oral evidence that fishermen did not consider themselves as 'unemployed' during the period January to April when many driftermen had no work. In the distress of 1904 'only a few' fishermen attended a meeting of 300 unemployed, in 1908 of a meeting of 500 'only twenty-two of them were sailors and fishermen'. As hundreds must have been without employment at this time it confirms that they accepted the

seasonality of their employment and regarded the income earned in those seasons as their full annual income.

Introduction to Part three

1 This should not be taken as implying belief in a mechanistic process. Oral evidence shows that one is not shaped simply by circumstances but also by reaction to them: there are, for example, accounts from informants who endured severe corporal punishment in their childhood reacting against this by never chastising their own children. Children are often only too painfully aware that their own family's domestic practice may not be 'normal' and determine to emulate examples other than their own parents.

2 The interview material comes most fully from the twenty females plus the account of forty wives from the males and of their sixty mothers. That their experiences were fairly typical is confirmed by the brief occupational histories of some 138 female siblings.

9. Female waged labour

1 T. Cornish, 'Mackerel and Pilchard Fisheries', *Papers of the International Fisheries Exhibition*, No. 6 (London 1883). For an account of the amount of work undertaken by women see Peter Frank, 'Women's Work in the Yorkshire Inshore Fishing Industry', *Oral History*, Vol. 4, No. 1 (1976).

2 Sally Festing, *'Fishermen: A Community Living from the Sea'* (Newton Abbot, David and Charles, 1977).

3 In East Anglia women were involved in launching lifeboats in certain locations where these had to be pushed into the sea from flat beaches.

4 Reported in the *Lowestoft Journal*, 12 December 1910.

5 This extract (circa 1920s) is subsequent to McIver's account and shows that there was a drop in wage rates between the two dates. I have no evidence as to when the reduction took place, but there was a reduction in the wages of women employed in curing herring for kippers in 1904.

6 The details of the strike, see p. 123 and n. 4, reveal that the women also received a fixed wage of 8s. a week in addition to their piecework earnings. This is included in my estimate.

7 The *Lowestoft Journal*, 10 December 1904.

8 Of the 138 female siblings of the sixty informants with known occupations, thirty-one were beatsters before marriage. All except two were the daughters of skippers or owners. This suggests that influential links with the fishing community were a help in securing this employment.

9 The wages reported by informants appeared to be incredibly low, but it is the occasional contemporary documentary confirmation which creates confidence in the oral accounts. The oral evidence reports living-in wages for young domestic servants, usually working in quite modest lower middle-class homes, at around £8 a year in the period 1900 to 1914. It is these wage levels against which the earnings in other occupations need be measured.

10. Domestic life

1 Much of the material used here has previously appeared in an essay the author contributed to *The Father Figure*, edited by Lorna McKee and Margaret O'Brien published by Tavistock Publications Ltd, 1982, and is reprinted here with their permission.

2 A consideration of the long hours worked by many males of this period often in unpleasant and unhealthy circumstances suggests a need to consider the historical depth of the unfair burden of domestic labour and the dual burden. It would appear to have been less unfair (at least in this region) before waged labour contracted to a short five day week while domestic labour still operated over seven days. This comment is not intended to oppose a more radical restructuring of gender roles but to suggest that, comparatively at least, women's share of domestic and waged labour may have grown less favourable in the more recent past.

3 M. Anderson, *Family Structure in Nineteenth Century Lancashire*, Cambridge Studies in Sociology No. 5 (Cambridge, University Press, 1971). This approach is most fully articulated by Anderson although he does allow that a 'more functional and less calculative orientation to kinship' (p. 179) probably developed in the later nineteenth century.

4 M. Kerr, *The People of Ship Street* (London, Routledge and Kegan Paul, 1958), chapter 5 (e). Her section on children's work stands in marked contrast as boys appear to exist as perennial infants to be minded by their older sisters.

5 Helen Bosanquet, *The Family* (London, Macmillan, 1906). Citing Miss Loane.

6 An attempt at rigorous categorisation may have under-recorded the number of men helping in the home. For example, in interview 3011 the informant stated that his father never helped in the home because it was only a two roomed cottage so little housework was necessary, but it had a large garden in which his father worked all his spare hours. He is categorised as 'Never' helping in the home. In fact his father was a horseman who rose at 4.40 a.m. every day to feed his horses at 5 a.m.; he would then light the fire (there was no gas or electricity) in order to cook his breakfast and make tea before calling his wife who would then rise and see to the children while he returned to work. Now it might be argued that rising first, preparing the fire and so on before anyone else is even up constitutes not only regular, but unpleasant domestic duties. In any case his level of help was due to the requirements of both his work and domestic labour not to male chauvinism.

7 P.F. Anson, *Fisher Folk-Lore* (London, Faith Press, 1965), p. 143. See also G.F. Alward, *The Development of the British Fisheries* (Grimsby, The Grimsby News Co., 1911), p. 159, who observed that, at Brixham, all fish was auctioned by women until the arrival of the railway in 1868 replaced them with male buyers on the national market.

11. Leisure

1 In Norfolk and Suffolk lifeboat and salvage services were provided by companies of men who operated in competition with others and organised their own rota of watchmen. For a full account of how these were organised and how they functioned see Robert Malster, *Saved From the Sea* (Lavenham, Terence Dalton, 1974).

2 See A.E. Dingle, 'Drink and Working-Class Living Standards in Britain, 1870–1914', *Economic History Review* (November 1972). This shows a secular decline in the United Kingdom as a whole from the mid-1870s. My concern is not the degree to which the decline among fishermen is part of a national trend but to establish changes within our period and the effect of drinking on domestic leisure patterns and brutality in the home.

3 For an account of the Mission's work see E.J. Mather, *Nor'ard of the Dogger* (London, James Nisbet and Co., 1889); A. Gordon, *What Cheer O* (London, James Nisbet and Co., 1890).

4 The *Lowestoft Journal*, especially 8, 22 and 29 March 1884.

5 This material is very difficult to categorise. The most unsatisfactory category is labelled 'Customary'. This includes the few cases where excessive drinking caused hardship and brutality. But it also includes all those where usage was non-specific, such as 'Dad enjoyed a drink' and those cases where recourse to a pub was regular without consumption being specified. 'Moderate' includes regular drinking but accompanied with a statement of limited consumption, an example of this is the widely reported custom of the father having a drink at lunchtime but never going out in the evening. 'Occasional' is very occasional indeed, usually one who did not drink save at Christmas, pay-off day or similar semi-ritual occasions. 'Never' refers mostly to those who were committed teetotallers.

12. Religion: practice and belief

1 Religious practice was part of the interview with all informants. The high level of Don't Knows is due partly to the open-ended interview technique and partly due to my own coding practice. I suspect that many of the Don't Knows could be categorised as non-attenders, for where religion was an important part of life it is more likely to be mentioned than if it played little or no role. As stated all informants attended some form of service or Sunday school during their schooldays and, although not specifically mentioned in the interviews, I believe that all the informants would have attended baptisms, weddings and funerals.

2 One cannot generalise this point to the dozens of different parishes inhabited by the informants. Their missionary efforts were, however, found in the two main fishing centres of Yarmouth and Lowestoft. The two extracts come from Cromer and Yarmouth respectively.

3 *Whitby Gazette*, 3 February 1899. For the Newlyn Riots see the *Lowestoft Journal*, May and June 1896, see also 5 September for riots at Scarborough as

Lowestoft men attacked West Countrymen. That the issue was a long-standing grievance see 3 February 1894.

4   An earlier and more extended version of this analysis of superstition appeared as chapter 11 in Paul Thompson, with Tony Wailey and Trevor Lummis, *Living the Fishing* (London, Routledge and Kegan Paul, 1983).

5   See G. Jahoda, *The Psychology of Superstition* (Bungay, Pelican Books, 1970).

6   An analysis which comes to the same conclusion is P.B. Mullen, 'The Function of Magic Folk Belief among Texas Coastal Fishermen', *Journal of American Folklore* (July/September 1969).

7   The figures have been constructed by aggregating all the deaths reported in the *Lowestoft Journal* over a twenty year period ending in 1913. This is, perhaps, the only way to construct a reliable figure because official statistics give deaths in the region they occur and deaths to Lowestoft men while fishing in the West Country or Scotland appear in the statistics for those regions. Similarly, one can discount the deaths of other fishermen in East Anglia. The number of deaths has then been calculated against the number of men employed in each section for each year: the figures apply to Suffolk only as this area included all the trawlermen. The figures are for the twenty years; 1 in 1,000 inshore, 1 in 480 in drifting and 1 in 143 in trawling.

8   Parliamentary Papers, 1908, Vol. XIII, p. 420. Answers 10024, 10025, 10028 and 10030. Evidence of Mr Bloomfield.

13. Community and conclusion

1   One of the advantages of formal organisations is that they provide a collective tradition which is wider and longer than individual memory. The only trace of earlier unionisation in all the interviews was one man who remembered an old fisherman who used to sing about a strike. The informant could not remember the words and assumed it referred to Grimsby.

2   3027:42. I have not investigated the truth of his assertion that the small owner survived the 1930s more successfully than the companies. It may well be that companies were moving their capital to more profitable activities.

3   The 808 first class fishing vessels at Lowestoft and Yarmouth in 1912 had no less than 354 distinct owners.

4   This assertion is based on the high proportion of fishermen and ex-fishermen-owners, and the number of small-scale businessmen involved in the wider commercial activities of fishing.

5   The greater emphasis on individuality common in the middle class was possible because of their material circumstances. The use of servants for domestic labour, the ability to purchase sufficient space for separate rooms, to pay for the objects and tuition necessary for family members to pursue their individual interests and so on. This was reinforced by the examination ethic of the Grammar schools thus finally producing a competitive individual. This could, and did, coexist with warm and affectionate family relationships, but the ability to combine individual competitiveness with such relationships

generally require that the demands of one should not deprive another.

6 E. Roberts, 'Working-Class Women in the North West', *Oral History*, Vol. 5, No. 2 (1977), pp. 8–9.

7 As interview material is virtually the only substantial body of evidence for normal family life the authenticity of one dimension which will respond to tabulation is of interest. Table 17 has been constructed from the number of siblings that the informants reported as having died. Often precise details were not available and the reportage will include stillbirths, infant mortality and even deaths up to the age of about thirteen. It cannot be compared, therefore, to official statistics of mortality but there is no reason why the level of reporting should have varied between informants. The table provides a check on the internal consistency of the data and a test of its conformability to known historical trends. Section A gives the figures for the whole sample so providing a baseline. Given the known effect in the period one would expect a valid sample to show a higher mortality rate in urban than in rural areas. Section B shows that the sample conforms to this trend. Section C divides the group into cohorts by decade of birth and again the mortality decline is what one would expect from a valid sample. The increase in family size in the final cohort is against the historical trend, it may be a bias in the sample, although it could represent a local trend as it was a prosperous decade for the fishermen. This rather impressive coherence in a small non-random sample is enhanced by looking at its internal coherence as in section D. High mortality is associated with income and this shows much more clearly when the data is structured than would have been anticipated from the qualitative reading of individual interviews. This gives grounds for confidence that where oral evidence is used in considering domestic relationships and practices it is indicative of their particular social and historical location and not simply a disconnected collection of idiosyncratic accounts.

8 3047 and 3025.

9 I am not arguing that the behaviour of men in general has no effect on the nature of their community. Where industrial conditions give rise to a sense of solidarity, especially if this is accompanied by the formation of the organisations of class struggle, their activity feeds into the community by local politics and pressure groups. What I am seeking to highlight is that the fundamental class experience which occurs regardless of the level of formal or informal male organisation has its terms set by the action of women in their locality.

Table 17 *Reported family size and mortality*

	Average number of siblings per informant		Reported number of sibling deaths		Percentage of sibling mortality	Number of cases
A All respondents	8.0	(482)	1.0	(58)	12	60
B Urban	8.0		1.2		15	32
Rural	8.0		0.7		9	28
C 1889	9.6		1.3		14	18
1890–9	7.0		1.0		14	27
1900–9	8.0		0.5		7	15
Trawlers and drifters only						
D Owners	8.2		0.8		11	9
Skippers	8.3		1.3		16	13
Crew	9.5		2.3		25	6
E Drifting	8.0		1.3		16	16
Trawling	9.4		1.6		17	12
Inshore	6.7		0.5		7	20
Non-fishermen	8.9		0.8		8	12

Bibliography and sources

Bibliography

Allcorn, D.H., and Marsh, C.M. 'Occupational Communities – Communities of What?', in Martin Bulmer (ed.), *Working-Class Images of Society*, London, Routledge and Kegan Paul, 1975, pp. 206–18.

Alward, G.L. *The Development of the British Fisheries*, Grimsby, The Grimsby News Co., 1911.

Anderson, M. *Family Structure in Nineteenth Century Lancashire*, Cambridge Studies in Sociology No. 5, Cambridge, Cambridge University Press, 1971.

Anson, P.F. *Fisher Folk-Lore*, London, Faith Press, 1965.

Aubert, V., and Arner, O. 'On the Social Structure of the Ship', *Acta Sociologica*, Vol. 3, 1958, pp. 200–19.

Bagshawe, Joseph R. *The Wooden Ships of Whitby*, Whitby, Horne and Sons, 1933.

Beechey, Veronica. 'Women and Production: A Critical Analysis of some Sociological Theories of Women's Work', in Annette Kuhn and Ann Marie Wolpe (eds.), *Feminism and Materialism*, London, Routledge and Kegan Paul, 1978, pp. 155–97.

Bell, Colin, and Newby, Howard. *Community Studies*, London, Allen and Unwin, 1971.

Bertaux, Daniel (ed.). *Biography and Society: The Life History Approach in the Social Sciences*, Sage Studies in International Sociology 23, Beverly Hills, 1981.

Blauner, Robert. 'Work Satisfaction and Industrial Trends in Modern Society', in W. Galenson and S.M. Lipset (eds.), *Labour and Trade Unionism*, New York, John Wiley and Sons, 1960, pp. 339–60.

Bosanquet, Helen. *The Family*, London, Macmillan, 1906.

Bulmer, Martin. 'Sociology and History: Some Recent Trends', *Sociology*, Vol. 8, No. 1, 1974, pp. 138–50.

Bulmer, Martin (ed.). *Working-Class Images of Society*, London, Routledge and Kegan Paul, 1975.

Cohen, A.P. *The Management of Myths: The Politics of Legitimation in a Newfoundland Community*, Newfoundland Social and Economic Studies No 4, Memorial University of Newfoundland, 1975.

Cornish, T. 'Mackerel and Pilchard Fisheries', *Papers of the International Fisheries Exhibition*, No. 6, London, 1883.

Coull, J.R. *The Fisheries of Europe: An Economic Geography*, London, Bell, 1972.

Dennis, N., Henriques, F., and Slaughter, C. *Coal is Our Life*, London, Eyre and Spottiswoode, 1956.

Dingle, A.E. 'Drink and Working-Class Living Standards in Britain, 1870–1914', *Economic History Review*, November 1972.

Duff, R.W. 'The Herring Fisheries of Scotland', *Papers of the International Fisheries Exhibition*, No. 9, London, 1883.

Dyson, J. *Business in Great Waters*, London, Angus and Robertson, 1977.

Edinburgh, H.R.H. the Duke. 'Notes on the Sea Fisheries etc.', *Papers of the International Fisheries Exhibition*, No. 10, London, 1883.

Festing, Sally. *Fishermen: A Community Living from the Sea*, Newton Abbot, David and Charles, 1977.

Fox, A. Wilson. 'Agricultural Wages in England and Wales during the Last Half Century' (1903), reprinted in E.W. Minchinton, *Essays in Agrarian History*, Newton Abbot, David and Charles, Vol. 2, 1968, pp. 121–98.

Frank, Peter. 'Women's Work in the Yorkshire Inshore Fishing Industry', *Oral History*, Vol. 4, No. 1, 1976.

Friedlander, P. *The Emergence of a U.A.W. Local, 1936–1939*, Pittsburgh, University of Pittsburgh, 1975.

Gordon, A. *What Cheer O*, London, James Nisbet and Co., 1890.

Gray, M. *The Fishing Industries of Scotland 1790–1914*, Aberdeen University Studies Series No. 155, Oxford, Oxford University Press, 1978.

Hammond, J.L., and B. *The Village Labourer*, London, Guild Books, 1948.

Haswell, G.H. *The Maister: A Century of Tyneside Life*, London, W. Scott, 1894.

Horobin, G.W. 'Community and Occupation in the Hull Fishing Industry', *British Journal of Sociology*, Vol. 8, No. 4, December 1957.

Jahoda, G. *The Psychology of Superstition*, Bungay, Pelican Books, 1970.

Jenkins, James T. *The Sea Fisheries*, London, Constable and Co., 1920.

Jevons, W.S. *Methods of Social Reform*, London, Macmillan, 1883.

Johnstone, James. *British Fisheries: Their Administration and Their Problems*, London, Williams and Norgate, 1905.

Kerr, M. *The People of Ship Street*, London, Routledge and Kegan Paul, 1958.

Lipset, S.M. *Union Democracy*, Glencoe, Free Press, 1956.

Lockwood, D. 'Sources of Variation in Working-Class Images of Society' (1966), reprinted in Martin Bulmer (ed.), *Working-Class Images of Society*, London, Routledge and Kegan Paul, 1975, pp. 16–34.

Ludlow, J.M., and Jones, L. *Progress of the Working-Class 1832–1867*, London, Strahan, 1867.

Lummis, Trevor. 'The Occupational Community of East Anglian Fishermen: An Historical Dimension through Oral Evidence', *British Journal of Sociology*, Vol. 28, No. 1, March 1977, pp. 51–74.

Lummis, Trevor. 'Structure and Validity in Oral Evidence', *International Journal of Oral History*, Vol. 2, No. 2, June 1981 (U.S.A.), pp. 108–20.

Lummis, Trevor. 'The Historical Dimension of Fatherhood: A Case Study 1880–1914', in Lorna McKee and Margaret O'Brien (eds.), *The Father Figure*, London, Tavistock Publications, 1982, pp. 43–56.

MacIver, Daniel. *An Old-Time Fishing Town*, Greenock, James McKelvie and Sons, 1906.

McKenzie, R., and Silver, A. *Angels in Marble: Working-Class Conservatives in Urban England*, London, Heinemann, 1968.

Malster, Robert. *Saved from the Sea*, Lavenham, Terence Dalton, 1974.

March, E.J. *Sailing Drifters*, Newton Abbot, David and Charles, 1952.

Mather, E.J. *Nor'ard of the Dogger*, London, James Nisbet and Co., 1889.

'MEMS About Members: House of Commons 1906–1911', *Pall Mall Gazette*, n.d.

Mitchley, J. 'The Steam Carriers', *Norfolk Sailor*, No. 12, Norwich, 1966.

Moore, R.S. 'Religion as a Source of Variation in Working-Class Images of Society', in Bulmer 1975.

Mullen, P.B. 'The Function of Magic Folk Belief Among Texas Coastal Fishermen', *Journal of American Folklore*, July/September 1969.

Nall, J.G. *Great Yarmouth and Lowestoft*, London, Longmans, Green, Reader and Dyer, 1866.

Newby, H. *The Deferential Worker*, London, Allen Lane, 1977.

Pelling, H. *The Social Geography of British Elections 1885–1910*, London, Macmillan, 1967.

Reynolds, S. *Alongshore*, London, Macmillan, 1910.

R.M. [R. Manton]. 'Fish Trade Mortgages on Uncaught Fish', *The Fisherman*, June 1891.

Roberts, E. 'Working-Class Women in the North West', *Oral History*, Vol. 5, No. 2, 1977, pp. 7–30.

Rule, J. 'Bibliographic Essay: The British Fishermen 1840–1914', *Bulletin of the Society for the Study of Labour History*, No. 27, Autumn 1973, pp. 53–63.

Samuel, R. 'The Deferential Voter', *New Left Review*, Jan/Feb 1960, pp. 9–13.

Sider, G.M. 'Christmas Mumming and the New Year in Outport Newfoundland', *Past and Present*, May 1976, pp. 102–25.

Thompson, Paul. *The Edwardians*, London, Indiana University Press, 1977.

Thompson, Paul, with Tony Wailey and Trevor Lummis. *Living the Fishing*, London, Routledge and Kegan Paul, 1983.

Tressell, R. *The Ragged Trousered Philanthropists*, St Albans, Panther, 1965.

Tunstall, Jeremy. *The Fishermen*, London, MacGibbon and Kee, 1962.

Tupper, E. *Seamen's Torch*, London, Hutchinson, 1938.

Wadel, C. 'Capitalisation and Ownership: The Persistence of Fisherman-Ownership in the Norwegian Herring Fishery', in R. Anderson and C. Wadel (eds.), *North Atlantic Fishermen*, Newfoundland, Memorial University of Newfoundland, 1972.

Weibust, K. *The Crew as a Social System*, Oslo, Oslo University Press, 1958.

Westergaard, J.H. 'Radical Class Consciousness: A Comment', in Martin Bulmer (ed.), *Working-Class Images of Society*, London, Routledge and Kegan Paul, 1975, pp. 251–6.

Willmott, P. *The Evolution of a Community: A Study of Dagenham after Forty Years*, London, Routledge and Kegan Paul, 1963.

Wood, Walter. *North Sea Fishers and Fighters*, London, Kegan Paul, 1911.
Young, M., and Willmott, P. *Family and Kinship in East London*, London, Routledge and Kegan Paul, 1957.

Newspapers and trade journals

Aberdeen Weekly Journal, 1901.
Eastern Daily Press, 1887.
The Fisherman, 1891 (Webb Trade Union Papers, Section B, Vol. 106, Item 52-4).
Fish Trades Gazette, 1884, 1894, 1913, 1911, 1904, 1910.
Lowestoft Weekly Journal, 1879, 1884, 1889, and 1894–1913.
Whitby Gazette, 1899.
Yarmouth Independent, 1859/61, 1881, 1887 and 1912.
Yarmouth Mercury, Gorleston Herald and East Norfolk Advertiser, 1891, 1913.

OFFICIAL PUBLICATIONS

The year and volume numbers refer to the Parliamentary Papers unless otherwise stated.

A. Commissions, Reports, etc.

1866, Vol. XVIII, Minutes of Evidence 1866; Vol. XVIII, Caird Commission on Sea Fisheries, Report of the Commissioners Appointed to Inquire into the Sea Fisheries of the United Kingdom (Chairman: Sir James Caird).
1881, Vol. LXXXII C 2878, Report ... on the Outrages Committed by Foreign upon English Fishermen in the North Sea (etc.).
1882, Vol. XVII C 3432, Norwood Committee on Sea Fishing Trade, Report ... under the Board of Trade ... to Inquire into and Report whether Any and What Legislation is Desirable with a View to Placing the Relations between Owners, Masters, and Crews of Fishing Vessels on a More Satisfactory Basis (Chairman: C.M. Norwood).
1893–4, Vol. XV, Report ... Select Committee on ... (Preservation and Improvement) of Sea Fisheries.
1894, Vol. LXIX C 7576, Investigation of the Fishing Apprenticeship System.
1902, Vol. XV Cd 1063, Report ... Inter-Departmental Committee ... to Inquire into ... Collecting Fishery Statistics in England and Wales.
1908, Vol. XIII Cd 4268 and Cd 4304, Report of Committee ... Scientific and Statistical Investigations ... Fishing Industry.
1914, Vol. XXX Cd 7373 and Cd 7374, Howard Committee, Report of the Departmental Committee on Inshore Fisheries (Chairman: Sir E.S. Howard).
1914, Vol. XXXI Cd 7221 and Cd 7462, Report of the Scottish Committee on the North Sea Fishing Industry.

B. Annual Report(s) of the Inspector of Sea Fisheries

1887, Vol. XXI
1889, Vol. XXII
1892, Vol. XXL C 6653
1901, Vol. LXXIX
1902, Vol. XIV Cd 1185
1908, Vol. XIII Cd 4064
1911, Vol. XXIV Cd 5874
1912–13, Vol. XXVI Cd 6291
1914, Vol. XXX Cd 7449 and Cd 7448

C. Annual Statement(s) of Navigation and Shipping

General Tables. Boats Registered under the Sea Fisheries Act, 1868 (and subsequent legislation).
1872, Vol. LVI
1882, Vol. LXVIII
1892, Vol. LXXVII
1902, Vol. C
1912–13, Vol. LXXXV
Annual Statement of Navigation and Shipping in the U.K 1921–4, H.M.S.O., London.
Annual Statement of Navigation and Shipping in the U.K 1929–32, H.M.S.O., London.

D. Census of England and Wales: 1851–1931

Public Record Office.
Agreements and Crew Lists: Series IV: Fishing Agreements, BT 144.
Statistical Register of Fishing Vessels, BT 145.
The Port Registers for East Anglian Registration Districts for: 1894, 1898, 1903, 1908, 1911, 1913 and 1931.
List of Trawling Fleets in Existence June 1894, MAF 12/13.
Share Fishermen and Unemployment Insurance, MAF 29/7/SFC 88.
Transcripts and Transactions: Series IV: Closed Registries, BT 110.

OTHER SOURCES

Lummis, Trevor. 'The East Anglian Fishermen: 1880–1914', Ph.D. thesis, University of Essex, 1981.
Thompson, Paul (Director). 'Family Life and Work Experience before 1918', Essex University Oral History Archive.
Thompson, Paul (Director). *The Family and Community Life of East Anglian Fishermen*, T. Lummis (Senior Research Officer), J. Parkin (transcriber), Social Science Research Council, project HR 2656/1, 1974–6.

Woolner, A.H. *The Economic Geography of the Development and Present Position of Lowestoft as a Port and Holiday Resort*, Ph.D. thesis, University of London, 1956.

Great Yarmouth Maritime Museum: various documents, particularly crew share system for circa 1930 and information on share holdings in the large drifter companies.

Lists of fishing vessels: the computer data on ownership was taken from *The Great Yarmouth Printing Company's Annual*, Yarmouth, 1899 and 1913; *The East Norfolk Annual*, 1894; *Flood's List of Fishing Vessels*, Lowestoft, 1931; O.T. Olsen's *The Fishermen's Nautical Almanac*, London, Hull, 1912; these were corrected from P.R.O. BT 145. *Olsen's* was also consulted for the East Anglian areas not covered by the computer analysis.

Index

Lowestoft and Yarmouth do not appear as separate entries in this index because they are the locations for the greater part of the evidence and argument. As such they appear throughout the text.